the series on school reform

Patricia A. Wasley
Coalition of
Essential Schools

Ann Lieberman
NCREST

SERIES EDITORS

Joseph P. McDonald
Annenberg Institute
for School Reform

This series also incorporates earlier titles in the
Professional Development and Practice Series

SUSAN FOLLETT LUSI
FOREWORD BY RICHARD F. ELMORE

THE ROLE OF STATE DEPARTMENTS OF EDUCATION IN COMPLEX SCHOOL REFORM

Teachers College
Columbia University
New York and London

This research was supported by a generous grant from the Innovations in State and Local Government program of the Ford Foundation and the Kennedy School of Government. The conclusions reached are the author's alone and do not necessarily reflect the beliefs of the above sponsors.

Published by Teachers College Press, 1234 Amsterdam Avenue, New York, NY 10027

Library of Congress Cataloging-in-Publication Data

Lusi, Susan Follett.
  The role of state departments of education in complex school reform / Susan Follett Lusi.
      p.   cm. — (The series on school reform)
  Includes bibliographical references and index.
  ISBN 0-8077-3629-5 (cloth : alk. paper). — ISBN 0-80773628-7 (pbk. : alk. paper)
      1. State departments of education—United States—Case studies.
  2. Educational change—United States—Case Studies.   3. Education and state—United States—Case Studies.   I. Title.   II. Series.
  LB2809.A2L875   1997
  379.73—dc21   97-9743

ISBN 0-8077-3628-7 (paper)
ISBN 0-8077-3629-5 (cloth)

Printed on acid-free paper
Manufactured in the United States of America

04 03 02 01 00 99 98 97   8 7 6 5 4 3 2 1

To Bobby and Christina, who bring tremendous joy to my life and help me keep my life and work in perspective.

To Steve, whose unshakable and good-humored love and support give me great happiness and saw me through this process.

And to my parents and parents-in-law, whose pinch-hitting and support helped me to meet my final deadlines.

This work reflects the contributions of us all.

Contents

Foreword

State departments of education have, throughout the history of education policy and governance in the United States, been among our most intriguing and problematic governmental institutions. By formal constitutional doctrine, states have primary responsibility for setting the purposes, providing for the financing, and administering the regulations that govern schools. Yet virtually from the beginning, states have relied heavily on local school boards and administrators to implement these responsibilities. Hence, ours is a system of *de jure* state control and *de facto* local control of schooling. The traditional model of state governance and administration that has grown up under these conditions, as Susan Lusi argues in *The Role of State Departments of Education in Complex School Reform*, stresses regulatory oversight geared to minimum standards, with minimum state capacity to guide schools and school systems in the difficult problems of improving their organizational performance. With the advent of systemic education reform, this traditional state role is shifting away from regulatory oversight and compliance and toward constructive support and assistance to schools and school systems, introducing new forms of organization and new instructional practices to meet the growing demand for improved student performance. Lusi's book provides the first comprehensive and systematic analysis of how state departments of education are grappling with this new vision of their role. This study will be a model for future research on this subject, in both its depth of analysis and its overarching perspective on the strategic problems posed for states by systemic reform. It will stimulate broad discussion of a particularly constructive kind about the practical problems of shifting the mission and organization of state departments of education. It also sets a standard for clarity and detail in research on state agencies, and provides a picture of state agencies in transition, working on the specific problems of organization and practice that will determine the success or failure of systemic reform in the United States.

This book also addresses another persistent theme of the state role in education—the politics surrounding broad-scale education reform. Since the early 1980s, state legislatures, governors, and chief state school officers have been drawn into an increasingly visible and active role in setting policy for local schools and school systems. State officials have sometimes been reluctant, and sometimes entrepreneurial, participants in this new period of education reform, but they have, with few exceptions, been forced to become more active and visible political actors. The press for a more active and visible state role in education reform has, in some instances, come from the courts, as in the case of Kentucky. More often, it has come from a more general dissatisfaction with schools and the academic performance of students, against public expectations and international comparisons. Hence, the movement to reform state departments of education occurs in an increasingly active, and sometimes hostile, political environment. Legislators and governors, driven by two- and four-year electoral cycles, are typically impatient for results. State and local administrators are stuck with orchestrating these political demands while they are attempting to solve organizational problems that require time and resources. These tensions are an inevitable by-product of our democratic system. Susan Lusi does a masterful job of putting the detailed problems of organizational reform of state departments of education in their political context. She shows the importance of attending to the political environment of school reform, while at the same time attending to the details of organizational improvement. In this sense, *The Role of State Departments of Education in Complex School Reform* is a *tour de force* of political analysis as well as of organizational analysis.

Because they are driven by the immediate demands of politics and organizational change, policy makers and high-level administrators seldom have the luxury of reflecting on the basic principles that govern their actions. In this regard, Lusi's analysis does a profound service to education research and reform. Her argument advances from the first premises of systemic reform by asking what specific state functions and activities are implied by systemic educational reform, and by using these premises as a basis for building a new model of the role of state educational agencies. She then analyzes state departments of education in two leading reform states, Kentucky and Vermont, to show how these new expectations and functions play out in the actual implementation of reform. This type of analysis is a new and important contribution to the scholarly literature on policy implementation. It also provides a more practical focus for analysis than past research. Lusi has used her skills as a researcher well, both to create a new model for research on policy implementation and to provide practical guidance for reformers.

On a personal note, working with Susan Lusi on this project has been a singularly rewarding professional experience for me. Watching an important new idea for research take shape in the mind of a promising apprentice scholar, watching this idea unfold into a demanding program of research, watching the research take shape into an analysis of stunning detail and sophistication, and then watching the analysis become a book that will change the field in important ways—these are the things that make academic life rewarding. During this period, I have also been privileged to see Sue advance from a graduate student of enormous potential into a full-fledged colleague, who is now in a position to be more of a teacher to me than a student. Her work carries her into a role as a leading expert and analyst of public policy. I am pleased to have been along for the ride, and even more pleased to see, in the final analysis, that the role of teacher and student have been reversed. I have learned many things from this enterprise, and now others will have the benefit of this learning.

This book should be read by anyone intending to do research on broad-scale educational reform or engaging in such reform. Its main message is that researchers and reformers alike should focus first on the basic premises of reform and evaluate their work by how well it guides policy makers and practitioners to act consistently with these premises. Its perspective is clear-headed, even though its subject matter is complex. It holds researchers and reformers to a high standard, and in doing so, contributes enormously to our understanding of what educational reform is all about.

Richard F. Elmore
Graduate School of Education
Harvard University

Acknowledgments

This research and writing span five years, first to produce a dissertation and ultimately to create this book. I have accrued countless debts to numerous individuals and institutions during this period.

I am extraordinarily grateful to all the practitioners of both policy and schooling who allowed me to interview them. I particularly want to thank the staff and commissioners of the Kentucky and Vermont departments of education, with whom I spent the bulk of my time in the field. All of the people I interviewed were under great pressure to implement reform and had no time to spare. They exhibited tremendous grace under this pressure, and I thank them for their forbearance and their interest in my work.

I owe my biggest debt of gratitude to my advisors, and particularly to Mary Jo Bane and Richard Elmore. I thank Mary Jo for her insight, honesty, and ongoing support. She was always able to read what I had written, ask insightful questions, and give focused feedback, even after she went on leave from the Kennedy School. Mary Jo remained my advisor even after moving to the Cuomo and then the Clinton administrations. A person with lesser dedication to her students would have told me to find a new advisor early on in the process. I am thankful for the continued interest she demonstrated in my work.

Dick Elmore gave me a tremendous amount of time, advice, and support, for which I will be eternally grateful. He has read more drafts of this work and related pieces than anyone would ever care to and was able to give me helpful feedback every time. He pushed my thinking, enabling me to move beyond description to analysis. Above all, I thank Dick for getting me through the crisis point in this research. He told me that it would ultimately be good work—something I desperately needed to hear at the time.

Donald Warwick joined my dissertation committee with little prior knowledge of me or my work. In spite of this, he became a dedicated and valued advisor. He always gave me thoughtful feedback with very fast turn-around time. I profited from his insights, gained from having done similar work over a number of years.

Tom Loveless and Michael Barzelay also gave me valuable assistance. Tom joined my committee late in the game. I am thankful for his willingness and ability to get rapidly up to speed and to give me useful feedback. Michael gave me helpful advice in the early stages of my work. He approached my work from the perspective of public management, and I benefited from this perspective.

I owe an enormous debt of gratitude to Thomas James at Brown University. Tom has been a valued friend and colleague for some time. He studied Kentucky education reform during the time that I did and beyond. Tom has been astonishingly generous with his time, insights, and materials on Kentucky. He provided me with detailed commentary on my Kentucky chapter, which helped me to refine it both conceptually and factually. I really cannot thank him sufficiently.

Bob McNamara at the Vermont Department of Education has helped me in many ways. He was interviewed a number of times during the course of this research and has kept me apprised of the progress of the Vermont reforms since that time. In addition, Bob contributed the title of this book, without which no copies would have sold. Thank you, Bob!

Jill Rosenblum, formerly of the Vermont Department of Education, gave me valuable and detailed comments on my Vermont chapter. These comments were invaluable for ensuring the accuracy of my report. I appreciate Jill's willingness to give of her limited time.

Friends and colleagues at the Annenberg Institute for School Reform have provided me with both moral and intellectual support. Patricia Wasley has assisted in the publication of this book. Pat has also given substantive feedback and useful advice to a novice author—thank you! Theodore Sizer has given me an intellectual push for many years. Even as I chose to study and write about states, I had what Ted taught me about schools ringing in my ears—a ringing that helped me to see how the work of state departments of education and schools connects.

Joanne Thompson has provided me with research and administrative support and so much more. Over the past year and a half, Joanne has become more than my right arm. The numerous updates that have been made throughout these two case studies were made possible by Joanne's tenacious search for additional facts. In addition, Joanne has edited this manuscript down to comma placement, and has helped to do everything else I've left undone at the Policy Unit of the Annenberg Institute. I cannot thank her enough.

I also received valued secretarial, research, and moral support from Wendy Angus at Harvard and Sara Nathanson at Brown. Wendy transcribed hours upon hours of interview tapes with speed, accuracy, and good humor. Sara found sources, put my bibliography together, and helped in any way needed. Without Joanne, Wendy, and Sara, this book still would not be complete.

This work would not have been possible without the generous support of the Innovations in State and Local Government program of the Ford

Foundation and the Kennedy School of Government. I am particularly grateful to Marc Zegans, Associate Director for Research for the Innovations program, for his ongoing interest and support. Marc became a valued colleague as well as a funder.

Last but not least, I want to thank my family. I wouldn't be where I am today without their love and support. I hope I can return it many times over.

THE ROLE
OF STATE
DEPARTMENTS
OF EDUCATION
IN COMPLEX
SCHOOL
REFORM

CHAPTER 1

Introduction and Statement of Problem

When I started this research in late 1991, state departments of education (SDEs) had operated in relative obscurity for over 20 years. While there were management studies of some individual departments and reports on departmental statistics—for example, number of staff and percentage of federal funding—there were no recent empirical studies of what SDEs actually *did* and, more particularly, of how they influenced school and classroom practice.

At about this same time, we were entering a period in which interest in "systemic school reform," as defined by Smith and O'Day (1990), was at what may well prove to be an all-time high. A number of states were working to develop aligned systems of curriculum frameworks, assessments, and teacher training designed to reinforce the teaching and learning of an identified set of knowledge and skills. These reform efforts were intended to promote and support school-site redesign of teaching and learning with the goal that all students would learn ambitious content knowledge and higher-order skills (Smith & O'Day, 1990).

It seemed to me that the answers to the questions of whether or not coherent policy contexts could be created and, once created, whether or not they could promote school-based change, depended largely on how specific complex reform proposals were implemented. Similar complex reform designs could achieve quite different results depending on the implementation approach chosen.

It is because of the importance of implementation decisions that I chose to focus on SDEs engaged in complex reform. Even though SDEs were generally not the initiators of state-level reform efforts in the 1980s and 1990s (Fuhrman, Clune, & Elmore, 1988), they are responsible for the implementation of the reforms, and they are the arm of the state that works most closely with schools and districts. It is through the policy implementation work of SDEs that changes in teaching practice will be brought about, if at all.

Since the inception of my research, interest in SDEs and their restructuring has grown substantially (see, for example, David, 1994; Madsen, 1994). According to a recent report by the Council of Chief State School Officers (1995), the SDEs of 41 states have reorganized to support local district reform efforts. There are calls for the activities of SDEs to change from regulating and monitoring to leading and facilitating, with a smaller but still essential regulatory role (LeMahieu & Lesley, 1994). It is acknowledged that this type of role shift will necessitate not only putting different emphases on what SDEs currently do, but also fundamentally redefining what they do and how they do it. There is to be a new emphasis on building local capacity for reform, and this capacity-building work will necessitate "facilitating learning, sharing and collaboration" (David, 1994, p. 11).

Still, there has been little empirical study of what SDEs do and of the context in which these institutions operate. It is important to understand what exactly we mean when we ask SDEs to shift from regulating and monitoring to assisting and serving, and it is vital to understand the changes and difficulties that such shifts entail.

The case studies of Kentucky and Vermont presented here begin to build these kinds of understanding. Such understanding is partial both because these are only two cases and because the studies were done early in each state's systemic reform history. Still, these case studies are important because they examine what these SDEs do and how what they do influences local ability to reform. In addition, the cases present the contexts—educational, institutional, and political—within which these SDEs are trying to accomplish their new undertakings. These contexts are vital to understand because of their influence on both how SDEs can and cannot change and also on if and for how long SDEs can sustain a particular reform agenda.

We have also recently entered a period in which the role of state departments (and states more generally) in education has become increasingly contentious. While discussions of standards-based, systemic reform à la Smith and O'Day persist, they are accompanied by discussions of choice, contracts, and charter schools—proposals that might well weaken the role of the state if broadly implemented. In addition, SDEs have increasingly become the target of the current trend of reducing government and increasing local control (see for example Harp, 1995, pp. 1, 13, and Lindsay, 1995, p. 12). These debates are far from resolved.

The case studies that follow are important regardless of the outcome of the national debate on systemic reform, for it will remain the case that schools need to change fundamentally and that, given the structure of our current education system, the actions of state departments can either facilitate or impede that change. For better or worse, and probably for some of each, schools interact with state departments, and that interaction influences what schools can and cannot do, as well as the relative ease with which they can do it.

OUTLINE OF THE BOOK

This book examines the role of state departments of education (SDEs) in implementing "complex" school reform, focusing on the cases of Kentucky and Vermont. I generally refer to the reform efforts I study as "complex" rather than "systemic," in recognition of the fact that whether or not states can achieve the degree of alignment envisioned by the proponents of systemic reform is still an empirical question. While I believe this distinction to be important, however, I do at times use the term "systemic" because that is how this type of reform is labeled in the literature.

I chose the cases of Kentucky and Vermont because both states are engaged in ambitious complex reform—attempting to change curriculum, assessment, and governance, among other things—and both have been engaged in these reform efforts for a longer time (albeit still not long) than most other states. (See the Appendix for a detailed discussion of methodology and sample selection.) The reform efforts of both states began in 1990.[1]

This study addresses the following questions:

1. Given the existing literatures on systemic reform, bureaucracies, and innovative organizations, what changes would we expect to see in SDEs successfully implementing complex reform?
2. How do these expected changes compare to what is actually occurring in the cases of Kentucky and Vermont, and how can the differences between what is occurring and what was expected be explained?
3. How do the SDEs' actions seem to be affecting local implementation of complex reform?
4. What broader lessons can be drawn from the analysis of these two cases for SDEs engaged in complex school reform?

Chapter 2 addresses the first question. I use the literature on systemic reform, bureaucracies, and innovative organizations to design a framework of changes I would expect to see in SDEs successfully implementing complex school reform.

This framework is applied to the cases of Kentucky and Vermont in Chapters 3 and 4, respectively. Research questions two and three are addressed in these chapters. The framework is used as a lens through which to examine the activity in each state and to judge the consequences of that activity for the implementation of complex reform. Each case contains a brief description and analysis of the state's version of complex reform, a detailed description of changes that have and have not occurred in the state department of education, and a formative analysis of the effects of SDE activity on local reform implementation. The analysis of the effects on local reform is formative, first because of the relative newness of the reforms, and second because I was only able to visit a small number of schools and districts in each state. Each case ends with an analysis of what is occurring, focusing first on explanations based on conditions within the agency and second on explanations based on conditions in the external environment in which the agency is situated.

It is important to keep the following context in mind while reading these cases. First, the information in these cases is already historical. The bulk of my data collection took place between March 1992 and February 1993. Much has changed in each of these states since then. Some of these changes are discussed in the notes, and others have been outlined in the Epilogue. Second, these data were collected in the second and third years of what are designed to be long-term reforms. These cases present an early picture and analysis of the reforms taking place. Third, change always brings pain and confusion, even if it is ultimately beneficial. Readers should realize that SDE staff and practitioners' understandings of and reactions to these reforms will very likely change over time.

Chapter 5 presents my cross-case analysis and conclusions. I use the two specific cases of Kentucky and Vermont to give greater definition to the general problem facing SDEs engaged in complex school reform and address my fourth research question by proposing seven broader lessons for SDEs engaged in such reform.

The remainder of this chapter is devoted to further explication of complex reform and how it came to be on the education reform agenda, a critique of the claims of systemic reformers, and a description of the education system SDEs are trying to change.

MOVING TO THE SYSTEMIC SCHOOL REFORM AGENDA

Moving to a systemic reform agenda was proposed as a result of an analysis of the shortcomings of the 1980s education reform efforts. These efforts were focused around two streams or, as they are more frequently described, "waves" of school reform.

The first wave of education reform in the 1980s began with the publication of *A Nation at Risk* (National Commission on Excellence in Education,

1983) and consisted of state efforts to raise standards through mechanisms such as teacher and student testing and increased graduation requirements. These state reforms have been broadly characterized as "more of the same" (Firestone, Fuhrman, & Kirst, 1989; Fuhrman et al., 1988). States focused on easily manageable reforms and used well-understood technologies. They avoided reforms that were

> complex, requiring new administrative arrangements, new technologies or inventions, or new behaviors from teachers and administrators; and/or redistributive, moving money, status, or authority from those in more advantaged positions to those in more disadvantaged positions. (Firestone et al., 1989, p. 11)

Wave one has been criticized as a disconnected, piecemeal approach to education reform (Cohen & Spillane, 1992; Smith & O'Day, 1990). Existing policies in one area of education (what I call component policies) have frequently undermined improvement attempts in other areas. For example, when numerous states increased graduation requirements with the goal of increasing student achievement, no attention was paid either to the fact that a suitable curriculum did not exist to be taught in these new courses, or to the fact that many teachers lacked the prerequisite skills and knowledge to teach such a curriculum if it did exist (Clune, White, & Patterson, 1989).

In addition, there was no careful examination of the additive effects of these policies on schools (Cohen & Spillane, 1992). For example, states frequently ranked schools based on student test scores, giving schools no incentives to move to the teaching of higher-order thinking skills and ambitious content knowledge, since this was not what tests measured. Nor did teacher testing, also geared to the measurement of basic skills, give teachers incentives to rethink and redesign their teaching. The additive effects of the policy regime did not support or encourage schools to strive for the teaching and learning of ambitious content knowledge, even though the need for this kind of teaching and learning was commonly espoused.

Overall, the wave one reforms left the nature of teaching and learning unchanged and did not bring about the sought-after dramatic improvements in student achievement (Cohen, 1988; Cuban, 1990; Firestone et al., 1989).

The second wave of reform in the 1980s came in the form of school restructuring. School restructuring calls for "fundamental changes in expectations for student learning, in the practice of teaching, and in the organization and management of public schools" (Elmore, 1990, p. 1). The restructuring literature, along with the implementation literature, calls for school-by-school, locally adapted change that is respectful of local education practice and context (Berman & McLaughlin, 1978; Elmore & McLaughlin, 1988; Sizer, 1984). Good schools differ, the restructuralists argue, and education reform must come from the "bottom up," as opposed to from the "top down," as occurred in wave one.

The restructuring movement has produced examples of successfully restructured schools in which teaching and learning are qualitatively different from traditional practice, but these examples are not widespread and are often short-lived:

> Their very existence represents tremendous commitment, expertise, and effort on the part of school and perhaps district personnel. Moreover, even with all that effort, the stability and future of such schools are at base quite fragile. Changes in principal, staff, school population or district policy may serve to undermine a hard-built but nonetheless tenuous foundation. (Smith & O'Day, 1990, p. 236)

In addition, it is difficult to generalize school-by-school restructuring strategies to the reform of the over 100,000 educational institutions in the nation (Smith & O'Day, 1990). When a restructured school often has no effect on the practice of other schools in its own district, it is difficult to argue that the presence of a handful of restructured schools will lead to the reform of all the schools in a state. The state's concern is to foster high-quality education in all schools, not a select few.

This analysis of the 1980s reform efforts has persuaded some researchers that a new policy approach is needed to bring about the level of student achievement desired (Smith & O'Day, 1990). Systemic school reform differs from the reform attempts of the 1980s in at least two important ways. First, systemic school reform strives to reform the education system *as a system;* it works for coherence across the system's component policies, something that the piecemeal reforms of the past did not achieve. For example, if a state chooses to promote the teaching and learning of ambitious content knowledge and higher-order skills through the development of curriculum frameworks, state assessments must also be redesigned to measure achievement on the knowledge and skills outlined in the frameworks, and teachers must receive the preparation necessary to teach the skills and knowledge in ways that will enable students to learn them.

Second, systemic school reform explicitly strives to support school-site efforts at redesigning teaching and learning with the goal that all students will learn ambitious content knowledge and higher-order skills (Smith & O'Day, 1990). It is insufficient to promulgate mandates such as increased graduation requirements from the "top" of the education system (the state). The "bottom" of the system (schools and districts) must be supported and activated to transform teaching and learning. This means that the additive effects of policy on schools will have to be carefully examined. Policies that do not support and push schools to fundamentally redesign practice are counterproductive to the goals of systemic reform.

Systemic reformers claim that a coherent and supportive policy context can be established at the top of the system and that such a context will leverage and support the bottom–up redesign of schools. It is important to evaluate the strengths and weaknesses of these claims.

A CRITIQUE OF THE SYSTEMIC REFORM PROPOSAL

The promise, or potential strength, of systemic reform is that reform at the top of the system can bring about reform at the bottom, that

> a coherent *systemic* strategy . . . can combine the energy and professional involvement of the second wave reforms with a new and challenging state structure to generalize the reforms to all schools within the state. (Smith & O'Day, 1990, pp. 234–235, emphasis in original)

Systemic reformers argue that significantly higher levels of student achievement can be brought about for *all* students in *all* schools using this approach.

The two fundamental challenges raised to these claims are: 1) coherence cannot be achieved at the state level; and 2) centralization, even if achievable, is the wrong mechanism to promote school improvement.[2] I will discuss each of these challenges in turn.

Cohen and Spillane (1992) argue that achieving policy coherence may be impossible given U.S. governance structures that were made incoherent by design:

> The U.S. political system was specifically designed to frustrate central power. Authority in education was divided among state, local, and federal governments by an elaborate federal system, and it was divided within governments by the separation of powers. These divisions were carefully calculated to inhibit the coordinated action of government, and they gained force from the country's great size and diversity. (p. 5)

They further argue that past attempts at strengthening the linkages between policy and practice through increased central control have met with only limited success and have only worked to increase the political fragmentation of the education system. Political fragmentation has increased because, in the absence of centralized authority, each new program had to develop its own administrative and authority systems to coordinate activity across many levels of government (Cohen & Spillane, 1992, pp. 9–10).

Fuhrman (1993), however, argues that there is reason to believe that coherence can be achieved within the existing political system. She points to the increasing influence of powerful ideas on the policymaking process, the increasing willingness of policymaker associations to forward these ideas, and existing examples of coordinated policymaking in education as reasons for optimism on the viability of systemic reform. In addition, Fuhrman cites three other factors that enhance the political chances of these reforms:

> First, larger developments in the culture [such as pressure for more ambitious student outcomes] surround and support coherent policy, improving the destiny of policy efforts. Second, systemic reform efforts are prompting policymakers to experiment with new structures, which in turn offer an avenue for the maintenance of coherent reform over time. Third, systemic reform strategies speak to the strategic interests of educators and education policymakers, in enlarging support for education and in finding a way to promote common ground. (Fuhrman, 1993, p. 20)

Other researchers, however, argue that centralization is not the way to encourage and promote school reform—that a coherent policy context, even if achievable, will not create energy and capacity for reform at the bottom of the system. Darling-Hammond (August 1994) argues that "federal and state policies should aim to create a system in which improved teacher knowledge and school capacity are the starting points for systemic change" (p. 481). She further proposes three key elements as the basis for state and national policy agendas: 1) making a well-prepared teaching force available to all students; 2) assuring that the resources and conditions for learning are available to all; and 3) creating "ongoing supports for school-based inquiry and change that create a press for continual improvement" (Darling-Hammond, August 1994, p. 498).

Clune (1993), while agreeing with systemic reformers that instructional change requires higher standards and coherent policy, argues that

> A common curriculum is difficult, if not impossible, to apply considering the immense diversity of American schooling, and a tolerable link between policy at the top and change at the bottom is all but unattainable. (p. 250)

He proposes a decentralized system using state-sponsored, curriculum development networks, with which schools would voluntarily affiliate, as the primary change agents. This system would use "diverse curricula approved as ambitious and chosen by local schools and [would] emphasiz[e] issues of capacity-building, such as teacher training and school finance" (Clune, 1993, p. 250). Fullan (1994) also proposes a "coordinated decentralized" approach to achieving systemic reform (pp. 199–200).

Cohen and Spillane (1992) also argue that there is very thin evidence to support systemic reformers' assertion that improved instructional guidance—in the form of state curriculum frameworks and assessments—can bring greater consistency to teaching and learning. They further argue that lack of capacity presents enormous barriers to the changes in teaching and learning expected by this type of reform. They describe these capacity barriers as follows:

> One concerns teachers' knowledge. The recent reforms demand a depth and sophistication in teachers' grasp of academic subjects that is far beyond most public school teachers. . . . More important, teachers would have to shed established modes of understanding and adopt more modern, constructivist versions of knowledge. Such change is not just a matter of learning more—it could fairly be termed a revolution. Scholarship in several fields has shown that intellectual revolutions are very difficult to foment.
>
> Another obstacle lies in teaching. Even if teachers knew all that they needed, the reforms propose that students become active, engaged, and collaborative. If so, classroom roles would have to change radically. . . . Teachers would have to become coaches or conductors and abandon more familiar and didactic roles in which they "tell knowledge" to students. Researchers have studied only a few efforts at such change, but they report unusual difficulty, for teachers must manage very complex interactions about very complex ideas in rapid-fire fashion. The uncertainties of teaching multiply phenomenally, as does teachers' vulnerability. (pp. 30–31)

Finally, Sizer, McDonald, and Rogers (1992–93) argue that standards are context-specific and that standard-setting should not become removed from the local school and community:

> To know where and how to seek standards, we think one must come to terms with the fact that good standards are not things which are clear, discrete, and fit for checklists. Much in the fashion of Aristotle, who claimed that essence is necessarily intertwined with experience, we believe that standards cannot exist apart from experience. To answer the question, "What is good enough here?" one must refer to images of good enough: the way people look, talk, act, or feel while being good enough in whatever performance they attempt. (p. 30)

They propose an accountability system composed of school-based, public exhibitions of mastery and student portfolios, supplemented by basic general testing and state audits of student portfolios. In addition, the authors advocate developing "accountability capacity within . . . school[s]":

> By this, we mean the dedication of time, space and institutional priority to building and designing standards, collaborating on assessment across classrooms, communicating with stakeholders, and ensuring that individual students do not fall through the cracks in the system. . . . This last objective will involve the invention of mechanisms of "continual collegial inquiry in which hard questions are posed." (Sizer et al., 1992–93, p. 34)

There is substantial disagreement over whether creating a coherent policy context is possible and/or desirable. There is also disagreement over the power of that policy context, if and when created, to promote school-based change. These debates can only be settled empirically as systemic reform efforts evolve over time.

THE PROBLEM FOR SDEs ENGAGED IN COMPLEX REFORM

SDEs engaged in complex reform face an implementation task that is fraught with difficulty. It is important to understand the magnitude of the task these SDEs are undertaking when examining the case studies that follow.

States are engaged in complex school reform in order to improve the academic achievement of all students in all schools. Improving student achievement, however, requires changing the core processes of teaching and learning, which in turn requires changing the behavior of teachers. The problem presented by complex school reform, then, is the problem of how the SDE can bring about specified changes in the practice of a large number of practitioners over whom it has little, if any, direct control and to whom it has no proximity.

The implementation and public management literatures provide more clarity to the problem faced by SDEs attempting complex reform. The teachers, whose behavior the SDE needs to change, are classic examples of "street-level bureaucrats" (Lipsky, 1980). They exercise broad autonomy in their work with students, and the sum of the choices they make in their work comprises the *de facto* policy of the school. It is because teachers work directly with students and because their decisions make policy that it is imperative for the state to influence their behavior.

The broad autonomy that teachers exercise is the result of the nature of their work, the nature of the organizations in which they work, and the nature of the system in which these organizations are embedded. Good teacher practice cannot be clearly specified:

> At root effective teaching is a problem-solving activity that relies heavily on teacher judgment and discretion in developing a situationally effective response. . . . Teacher effectiveness is highly contextual and conditional. (Elmore & McLaughlin, 1988, p. 39)

The organizations in which teachers work—schools—are what Wilson (1989) terms "coping organizations" (p. 168). Coping organizations are those in which neither the outputs nor the outcomes of key operators can be observed. Teachers cannot be constantly monitored in the current structure of schools, and even if they could be, it would be difficult to determine what students were learning as a direct result of teacher practice. Further, these organizations are part of a "loosely coupled system," making it difficult to predict how change in one part of the system will influence the activity in other parts of the system (Weick, 1976).

Predicting how changes in policy will affect practice is complicated by the fact that policy is filtered through existing practice and beliefs. Cohen and Ball (1990), for example, found that some teachers who viewed mathematics as a string of topics to be covered responded to California's mathematics framework by simply adding estimation and problem-solving to their curriculum as discrete topics, rather than infusing these techniques throughout the math curriculum as intended by the policy. California's policy did change practice to a degree, but not to the full extent desired.

A further twist to the problem facing SDEs is that there is significant evidence that local characteristics and implementation choices matter more than policy strategies and choice of educational methods to the ultimate success of an innovation:

> We found that federal change agent policies had a major effect in stimulating local education agencies to undertake projects that were generally consistent with federal categorical guidelines . . .

> But the adoption of projects did not ensure successful implementation; moreover, successful implementation did not guarantee long-run continuation. Neither those policies unique to each federal program nor those policies common to them strongly influenced the fate of adopted innovations. . . . The difference between success and failure depended primarily on how school districts implemented their projects. (Berman & McLaughlin, 1978, p. vi)

McLaughlin (1991) reviewed the Rand Change Agent study, of which this finding was a part, ten years later in light of subsequent implementation research. She found that this conclusion still held—"implementation dominates outcome" (p. 147).

The state's problem, then (and the SDE's problem as the agent of the state), is complicated. Not only is the state trying to change the practice of a large number of practitioners over whom it has little control and no proximity; in addition, it is trying to make this change in a profession where good practice is nearly impossible to clearly specify and in an environment in which it is difficult to predict the effect of its actions. Even if good teaching practice can be more clearly specified, it is not clear that the SDE will be able to bring that kind of practice about.

Complex school reform adds the further complication of trying to change the whole education system in ways about which there exist little knowledge and expertise. The work of SDEs will change dramatically as they engage in this uncertain, developmental work.

One challenge for the implementation of complex reform is whether or not SDEs can change in ways that will better enable them to do this new work. How they might be expected to change in response to their new responsibilities is the subject of the next chapter.

CHAPTER 2

Framework

Engaging in complex school reform requires state departments of education (SDEs) to engage in very different work than they have before, work for which a traditionally bureaucratic state agency seems ill-suited.[1] An examination of the literature on systemic school reform and bureaucratic and innovative organizations led me to expect to see numerous changes in the work, the conditions of work, and the working relationships of SDEs as they undertook this type of reform.

EXPECTED CHANGES IN SDEs

These expected changes, outlined below, form the lens or framework I will use to examine the two cases of Kentucky and Vermont in subsequent chapters. It should be acknowledged at the outset that this lens was constructed from the literature and from my early observations of complex reform activity. It was not constructed from the stated goals of the two states, although there is a good deal of similarity in some instances. Consequently, this framework should not be used as an evaluative tool; it is a set of criteria developed externally to the individual state efforts.

The lens will instead be used to carefully explicate what is happening in the two state departments and some of the schools with which they work. The consequences of that activity for achieving complex reform will then be examined.

The changes I expected to find in my study of SDEs engaged in complex school reform fall along five broad parameters, each with a number of dimensions:

1. Changing Substantive Work
2. Building Organizational Capacity
3. Increasing Organizational Flexibility
4. Building Local Capacity
5. Developing Collaborative, External Connections

Changing Substantive Work

SDEs have traditionally engaged in work that is largely well understood, predictable, and routine. These agencies have well-established mechanisms for licensing teachers and accrediting schools, for example, and the staff are well familiarized with this work.

SDEs engaged in complex school reform are taking on a very different charge. They are faced with leading and managing complex, knowledge-intensive, uncertain change. This change is complex because it impacts every part of the education system. It is knowledge-intensive because the goals of complex school reform are that all students learn ambitious content knowledge and, by implication, that all teachers have the ability to teach such knowledge. It is uncertain because this kind of far-reaching change has never before been attempted in the history of education reform. It is not clear how, or indeed if, this kind of reform can be brought about. This new work is more akin to innovation—uncertain, knowledge-intensive, and with a steep learning curve (Kanter, 1988).

Little is known, by SDE staff or anyone else, about how to establish a coherent policy system that promotes and supports the redesign of teaching and learning in schools, enabling all students to learn ambitious content knowledge. Designing reliable performance-based assessments and curriculum frameworks, which will prompt the redesign and reorientation of local curricula, is also an area where relatively little work has been done and many questions and design issues remain. How to best assist schools in using these assessments and frameworks, once designed, is also ill-defined, although it is clear that much help will be needed. Staff of SDEs engaged in complex reform are being asked to work on the frontier of knowledge about schooling and its reform.

Consequently, I expected to see changes in the work of SDEs along the following dimensions:

- *Development.* SDEs would be increasingly involved in product development as well as implementation, especially in the early stages of the reform. Products to be developed might include performance-based assessments and curriculum frameworks.
- *Assistance and Training.* The successful implementation of these newly developed products and processes would require increased attention to technical assistance and training. The focus of this assistance and training would also change in the ways described below.
- *Rapid Change.* SDEs' work would change rapidly as new information was acquired and desired products and processes were modified in light of this information.

Building Organizational Capacity

Engaging in innovative work aimed at bringing about complex reform requires people with the skills and resources to do the work. Staff in traditional SDEs are accustomed to working in fairly narrowly defined areas and to performing predefined tasks. They tend to focus on the regulatory criteria to be followed in doing their work, as opposed to the objectives to be achieved (Sroufe, 1967, p. 20).

Staff of SDEs engaged in complex school reform, conversely, need to focus on outcomes: Is the reform being successfully implemented? Is student achievement increasing? They need to work on broad areas of the reform, performing ill-defined tasks that will require ongoing learning. They will need new skills, as well as new training and learning opportunities in order to gain them.

Finally, SDE staff will be trying to bring about reform in the whole education system and thus will need easily accessible information about that system.

I consequently expected to see the organizational capacity of SDEs increase along the following dimensions:

- *People.* The people with the necessary skills to perform innovative work would have to be present, hired, or created through training.
- *Training.* Structures would be put in place for ongoing learning/training from people both inside and outside the organization.
- *Infrastructure.* The necessary infrastructure, including computers and easy access to information on the state educational system, would be put in place so that SDE staff had a knowledge base to draw on.

Increasing Organizational Flexibility

Performing work of an uncertain nature requires continual, collaborative learning. SDE staff will need to learn from each other's expertise and experience as well as from knowledgeable outsiders in order to push complex reform forward. SDE staff will be striving to build what Senge terms a "learning organization"—an organization in which generative learning occurs, learning that goes beyond what individuals by themselves can create (Senge, 1990).

In order for this ongoing learning to occur, the internal working relationships of SDEs will have to change along three dimensions. The structure that organizes the working relationships will change; the mechanisms that shape the relationships will change; and the norms that govern the relationships will change.

Since there is no recent literature (and little past literature) on the internal working relationships of SDEs, much of this discussion draws inferences about SDEs from the traditional literature on bureaucracy. These inferences largely seem to ring true from my own work in SDEs, but may or may not accurately characterize individual departments. In the discussion that follows, I sharply contrast the internal working relationships of traditional SDEs with those engaged in complex reform in order to make the distinctions clear. In reality, the internal working relationships of individual SDEs probably lie along a continuum from traditional to complex.

The "well understood, predictable, routine, and repetitive" work of traditional SDEs is well suited to bureaucratic structures and mechanisms (Perrow, 1986, p. 142). The traditional SDE structure is hierarchical, headed by the Chief State School Officer and generally including some combination of deputy commissioners, associate commissioners who head offices, directors who head divisions, professional staff who work in each division, and support staff. The number of layers in the hierarchy varies by the size of the given SDE, but generally follows this or a similar pattern (Council of Chief State School Officers, 1983, Appendix B).

The working relationships of SDEs are further shaped by the mechanisms of clear divisions of labor, rules that govern employee actions, and movement of information up and down, as opposed to across the hierarchy. Roles and responsibilities are clearly assigned to divisions, offices, and individuals in SDEs. For example, the Division of Instruction is responsible for all instruction-related programs and activities; the Office of Curriculum Services, within the Division of Instruction, is responsible for providing curriculum-related services; and curriculum specialists, who work in the Office of Curriculum Services, are responsible for visiting and assisting teachers in schools.

Rules govern the actions of SDE employees. The Director of Chapter I knows the reporting requirements of the federal government and is obliged to follow them. An employee in Certification knows that all forms must be properly completed, required exams must be taken and passed, and all course requirements must be fulfilled before a teaching license can be awarded. Managers manage the work of employees by seeing to it that the appropriate rules and procedures are followed, rather than by judging employee performance by the outcomes achieved.[2]

Information in SDEs moves up and down, as opposed to across the hierarchy. The bureaucratic structure of traditional SDEs does not encourage or require communication across the various offices. Each office has its specified domain and the authority to act within that domain. Superiors in the hierarchy must be kept informed and condone the activities of an office, but there is no parallel responsibility or need to inform other offices in the organization.

Traditional SDEs are "segmented" organizations:

> [There are] a large number of compartments walled off from one another . . . [and] only the minimum number of exchanges takes place at the boundaries of [the] segments. . . . Segmentalism assumes that problems can be solved when they are carved into pieces and the pieces assigned to specialists who work in isolation. (Kanter, 1983, p. 28)

Traditional SDE structure and mechanisms do not encourage cross-office initiatives. The work of each office is largely self-contained. This type of structure tends to stifle innovation and creativity, according to Kanter.

Implementing complex school reform will require work and learning that span the boundaries of SDEs. Consequently, the structure and mechanisms of SDEs will need to change in ways that make them more closely resemble organizations that encourage and support innovative work.

Innovative work is best supported by structures—either formal or informal—that differ substantially from those of a typical bureaucracy:

> Integrative thinking that actively embraces change is more likely in companies whose cultures and structures are also integrative, encouraging the treatment of problems as "wholes," considering the wider implications of actions. Such organizations reduce rancorous conflict and isolation between organizational units; create mechanisms for exchange of information and new ideas across organizational boundaries; ensure that multiple perspectives will be taken into account in decisions; and provide coherence and direction to the whole organization. In these team-oriented cooperative environments, innovation flourishes. (Kanter, 1983, p. 28)

SDEs engaged in complex school reform will consequently need to develop structures that are more team-oriented and less hierarchical. Working in teams facilitates the free exchange of information and brings the expertise of numerous individuals to bear on given problems (Kanter, 1983).

Flattening the hierarchy, either formally or informally, will facilitate doing the uncertain work that SDEs engaged in complex school reform are asked to accomplish:

> The greater the degree of uncertainty regarding the bureau's activities, the flatter its hierarchy is likely to be. When uncertainty prevails, potential relationships among the possible components of a task cannot be foreseen accurately. Hence the task cannot be divided into many parts assigned to specialists unless the

specialists are in constant communication with each other and can continually redefine their relationships as they gain more knowledge. This requirement is best served by a flat hierarchy, since it provides greater authority to each official and allows greater emphasis upon direct horizontal relationships. These factors are essential because:

1. Each official must be free to coordinate directly with a great many others in unpredictable ways, so formal channels cannot be set up in advance.

2. The need for dialogues among officials and for constant redefining of tasks makes working through intermediaries inefficient.

3. Communications among officials who have about the same status are less likely to be inhibited than those among officials on different levels.

4. Coping with highly uncertain tasks requires very talented specialists who can be retained in the organization only if they are given relatively high status and responsible positions incompatible with a many-level hierarchy.

5. Talented specialists working under novel conditions often know much more than their supervisors about how to coordinate their activities. (Downs, 1967, pp. 57–58, used by permission of the RAND corporation)

The mechanisms that guide the internal work of SDEs will also change. Since it is uncertain exactly what SDEs need to do to bring about complex school reform, a high premium will be placed on idea generation and learning.

> Idea generation is . . . aided when jobs are defined broadly rather than narrowly, when people have a range of skills to use and tasks to perform to give them a view of the whole organization, and when assignments focus on results to be achieved rather than rules or procedures to be followed. (Kanter, 1988, p. 179)

Implementation of complex school reform will have to be done through thoughtful "groping along"—making intelligent adjustments along the way as desired actions become clearer (Behn, 1988).

These approaches to work and implementation imply that the actions of SDE staff will have to be governed by a shared set of beliefs, values, and purpose. Whether this set of shared understandings is called vision (Senge, 1990), mission (Wilson, 1989), or culture (Burns & Stalker, 1961), it is clear that it is important in guiding people's actions in situations where these actions cannot be carefully prescribed. "Shared vision fosters risk taking and experimentation," as well as commitment to the long term (Senge, 1990, p. 209). A sense of mission "permits the head of the agency to be more confident that operators will act in particular cases in ways that the head would have acted had he or she been in their shoes" (Wilson, 1989, p. 109). And,

> [innovative firms in which non-routine decision making is the norm] have to rely on the development of a "common culture", of a dependably constant system of shared beliefs about the common interests of the working community and about the standards and criteria used in it to judge achievement, individual contributions, expertise, and other matters by which a person or a combination of people are evaluated. (Burns & Stalker, 1961, p. 119)

Shared understandings enable employees to work in concert and to pull and push in the same direction, even if their roles and tasks are ambiguous.

If people's roles and tasks are ambiguous and they are expected to act on a set of shared beliefs, values, and purposes that permeate the organization, it seems sensible that they must also be given the power to act. Giving everyone in the organization the power to act implies that information and resources must be widely shared, as opposed to located only in the upper levels of the hierarchy. SDE employees will need to be able to respond flexibly to needs as they arise. Flexible response is enabled by the wide availability of what Kanter terms "power tools"—information, resources, and support (Kanter, 1983). According to Kanter (1983), "The degree to which the opportunity to use power effectively is granted to or withheld from individuals is one operative difference between those companies which stagnate and those which innovate" (p. 18, emphasis deleted).

The norms that determine acceptable work practices in SDEs will also change. The norms of bureaucracy, and by extension of traditional SDEs, promote caution in employees.

> This very emphasis leads to a transference of the sentiments from the *aims* of the organization onto the particular details of behavior required by the rules. Adherence to the rules, originally conceived as a means, becomes transformed into an end-in-itself; there occurs the familiar process of *displacement of goals* whereby "an instrumental value becomes a terminal value." (Merton, 1980, p. 231)

That this type of goal displacement has occurred in SDEs is evidenced by Sroufe:

> A central problem confronting SDE's in fulfilling regulatory activities appears to be that the criteria established to determine acceptable performance become too easily and too frequently as important as the actual performance. For a while we asked respondents to indicate what they were trying to accomplish in their particular job, expecting to receive objectives expressed in terms of school sys-

tem, classroom, or pupil performance. We were disappointed to find that few respondents saw their role in this fashion; most responded in terms of the regulatory criteria which had been set up to monitor performance. (Sroufe, 1967, p. 20)

The norms of the new SDEs will need to support the required risk-taking—employees exercising informed judgment and initiative.[3] Employees must become committed to the SDE and its goals as a whole, as opposed to only following the rules in their narrow area. Burns and Stalker found that "organic" organizations—those appropriate to changing conditions—were characterized in part by "the shedding of 'responsibility' as a limited field of rights, obligations and methods. . . . [and] the spread of commitment to the concern beyond any technical definition" (Burns & Stalker, 1961, p. 121).

Finally, there must be the norm of respect for individuals and their abilities to act in uncertainty in the new SDEs (Kanter, 1983). Exercising control over employees through rules springs at least partially from distrust (Gouldner, 1980). Unless the norms of SDEs promote trust in individuals, the kind of flexible working environment that has been described above will not exist.

Because SDEs engaged in complex school reform need to become more like innovative organizations, I expected to see their organizational flexibility and responsiveness increase along the following dimensions:

- *Hierarchy.* The hierarchy would be flattened in practice if not in formal structure, allowing for direct communication between different groups that might violate the formal chain of command.
- *Organizational Boundaries.* Organizational boundaries would be permeable, allowing information, knowledge, and communication to flow freely between different areas of the organization.
- *Vision/Mission.* The organization would be driven by its vision and mission rather than by rules and oversight. People in the organization would have the flexibility to act in a variety of ways that meet the vision and mission, as opposed to in ways predefined by organizational rules and protocols.
- *Decision-Making and Planning.* Decisions would be made at the lowest possible level, and people at those levels would have the power—information, authority, and resources—to act (Kanter, 1983). Planning would occur, but would be flexible, allowing for intelligent adjustments to be made fairly easily through a collaborative process (Fullan, 1991, pp. 94–113).
- *Norms and Culture.* The norms of the organization would promote trust, risk-taking, and excellence. The culture would be collegial and supportive. People would be rewarded for taking initiative and responsibility. Generative learning would be prized.

Building Local Capacity

The goal of complex school reform is to promote and support school-site efforts at redesigning teaching and learning so that all students learn ambitious content knowledge and higher-order skills (Smith & O'Day, 1990). The proponents of complex reform also argue that schools should be given maximum flexibility to meet the goals established by the state; they should be held accountable for the student outcomes they achieve, rather than the inputs and processes they use to achieve those outcomes (Smith & O'Day, 1990).

This goal and this approach differ markedly from those of the traditional SDE, which are to establish the conditions that should be present in all schools and to enforce the meeting of those conditions by regulating the inputs and processes of education (Friedman, 1971). Traditionally, SDEs have tried to establish and enforce a minimum standard of inputs; under complex school reform, SDEs are trying to push and help schools attain a common high level of output—student achievement.

In addition, SDEs engaged in complex reform are trying to ensure that *all* schools reach this high level of student achievement. This might seem to imply that SDE staff would increasingly provide technical assistance to individual schools. However, there are many more schools in a state then there are SDE staff, and SDE staff have been criticized since at least 1967 for the ineffectiveness of using school visitations as their primary strategy:

> It makes little sense for professional personnel to define their role primarily in terms of visitation to the schools, as did most of those we interviewed. There are simply too many schools, too many teachers, and too few qualified person-nel. How effective can a two-hour visit once a year by a subject matter consul-tant be? (Campbell & Sroufe, 1967, p. 85)

In the absence of hiring many more SDE staff members, a step that seems unlikely, SDE staff will need to change not only the focus but also the methods of their work. They will need to focus on building the capacity for reform in local schools and districts so that practitioners will eventually have the skills and knowledge needed to advance their own reform efforts. Capacity-building strategies might include: 1) working with whole schools, rather than individual teachers; 2) working with larger groups of schools and teachers; and 3) training staff within schools and districts so that they can in turn train their colleagues.

Other strategies for building local capacity could center around the de-velopment of the state reforms themselves and the products—such as assess-ments and curriculum frameworks—that the reforms will require. First, these products should be flexible and should evolve over time so that they do not become impediments to future school change efforts. They should be frameworks that enable school change rather than bound it. As we learn still more about the nature of teaching and learning, assessments and curriculum frameworks developed today, no matter how future-oriented, will no longer be cutting-edge. Second, practitioner involvement in the development of the reforms and reform products can, in itself, be a powerful professional development exercise by promoting thinking, learning, and consensus around the issues of reform. In addition, this involvement can provide practitioner knowledge and expertise to the reform efforts.

In summary, I expected SDEs' focus and methods to change along the following dimensions:

- *Attention to Outcomes.* SDEs would focus on performance outcomes achieved by schools rather than on regulating the process through which school performance was brought about.
- *Assistance Aimed at Building Capacity.* SDE staff (and others) would help schools and districts increase performance by bringing knowledge, expertise, and assistance to bear on the problem and by equipping local educators with the skills and knowledge needed to address immediate and future problems.
- *Creation of Flexible Products.* Products created for use in schools, e.g., curriculum frameworks and assessments, would be flexible, preventing them from becoming constraints to schools' improvement of instruction in the future. What is cutting-edge today will not be tomorrow; state systems need to be adaptable to the changing needs of local sites.
- *Practitioner Involvement.* Practitioners would be involved in the creation of SDE products such as assessments and curriculum frameworks. This involvement would result in increased knowledge and understanding of both the goals of the product and the product itself for both practitioners and SDE staff. This involvement would also increase the likelihood that the products developed would be useful to and used by practitioners.

Developing Collaborative, External Connections

SDEs will be unable to reform the entire educational system by themselves and will consequently need to develop numerous partnerships with other groups and policy players. Such partnerships could help SDEs with their work along the following dimensions:

- *Design and Maintain a Coherent Policy System.* Strong working relationships with the legislature, state board, and other policy players would aid in the design and maintenance of a coherent policy system.

- *Increase Capacity for Providing Information and Training.* Working with teachers, academics, and other professional development providers would increase SDEs' capacity for providing information and training to local educators.
- *Build Capacity Within the SDE.* Working with these outside groups would also increase the base of knowledge and expertise available to SDE staff members to facilitate their own learning.

CONCLUSIONS

The above framework of expected changes in SDEs engaged in complex school reform gives us a starting point for examining the changes that are occurring in actual SDEs engaged in this work. Applying this framework to actual cases should help us to systematically examine and better understand the changes that are occurring. This examination and understanding should in turn help us to raise questions as to why what is happening is occurring and what implications this seems to have for the implementation of complex reform.

My analyses of the Kentucky and Vermont departments of education that follow adhere to the above framework fairly closely. There is some variation between the two cases, however, and not all portions of the framework are addressed in each. I have used the parameters and dimensions of the framework that are most salient for each case.

CHAPTER 3

Kentucky

Kentucky has a population of about 3.8 million people. While the state has traditionally been viewed as rural, about 52% of its population lived in urban areas as of 1992. The state's public school system is made up of 176 districts, 1400 schools, and approximately 40,000 instructional staff. The system serves just over 639,000 students, 89.7% of whom were white in 1993.

Kentucky is not a wealthy state. In 1990, per capita personal income was $15,000, ranking the state 45th in the nation. Per pupil expenditure for 1991–92 was estimated to be $4,616, 39th in the nation. The state's estimated average teacher salary was $31,915 for 1992–93, ranking it 28th in the nation. The state paid an estimated 69.4% of the cost of public education in 1991–92, ranking it fourth in the nation.[1]

THE HISTORY OF KERA

Kentucky has historically had a strong state presence in education. In the 1980s, following the publication of *A Nation at Risk* (National Commission on Excellence in Education, 1983), the General Assembly passed legislation that required testing of new teachers and basic skills testing of students, specified the percentage of time in schools to be spent on the development of basic skills, and provided for state takeover of educationally deficient districts (Legislative Research Commission, 1984).

The Court Ruling

The genesis of the Kentucky Education Reform Act (KERA) began with the 1989 ruling of the Supreme Court of Kentucky in *Rose v. The Council for Better Education, Inc.* The plaintiffs in the case were the Council for Better Education, a nonprofit corporation of 66 Kentucky school districts, 7 local school boards, and 22 public school students (Dove, 1991).

The plaintiffs alleged that Kentucky's "statutory structure for funding public schools" was inadequate and inequitable in violation of the state constitutional provision requiring "an efficient system of common schools throughout the State." (Dove, 1991, pp. 12–13)[2]

They sought a ruling from the court requiring the General Assembly to increase the funding for public schools and provide an equitable and adequate funding program for all students (Dove, 1991).

The state of the Kentucky school system at the time of the Supreme Court ruling, in the opinion of the court, was:

> Kentucky's system of common schools is underfunded and inadequate; is fraught with inequalities and inequities throughout the 168 local school districts; is ranked nationally in the lower 20–25% in virtually every category that is used to evaluate educational performance; and is not uniform among the districts in educational opportunities. . . . [Further,] the achievement test scores in the poorer districts are lower than those in the richer districts and expert opinion clearly established that there is a correlation between those scores and the wealth of the district. (*Rose v. Council, Ky.,*1989, p. 197)

In response to this evidence, the Supreme Court of Kentucky ruled that "the General Assembly of the Commonwealth ha[d] failed to establish an efficient system of common schools" as required under the Kentucky Constitution (*Rose v. Council, Ky.,* 1989, p. 215). The court went to some lengths to be clear that it was ruling the *entire* school system unconstitutional:

> Lest there be any doubt, the result of our decision is that Kentucky's *entire system* of common schools is unconstitutional. There is no allegation that only part of the common school system is invalid, and we find no such circumstance. This decision applies to the entire sweep of the system—all its parts and parcels. This decision applies to the statutes creating, implementing and financing the *system* and to all regulations, etc., pertaining thereto. This decision covers the creation of local school districts, school boards, and the Kentucky Department of Education to the Minimum Foundation Program and Power Equalization Program. It covers school construction and maintenance, teacher certification—the whole gamut of the common school system in Kentucky. (*Rose v. Council, Ky.,* 1989, p. 215, emphasis in original)

The court further declared that it was the sole responsibility of the General Assembly to create a new school system and that this new system must be efficient as defined by the following criteria: The establishment, maintenance, and funding of the system is the sole responsibility of the General Assembly; the schools in the system are free and available to all Kentucky children; the schools are substantially uniform and "provide equal educational opportunities to all Kentucky children, regardless of place of residence or economic circumstances"; the schools are "monitored by the General

Assembly to assure that they are operated with no waste, no duplication, no mismanagement, and with no political influence"; the schools exist based on the premise that all Kentucky children "have a constitutional right to an education"; the system is sufficiently funded to provide each child an adequate education; the goal of an adequate education is the development of seven capacities (*Rose v. Council, Ky.*, 1989, pp. 212–213):

1. sufficient oral and written communication skills to enable students to function in a complex and rapidly changing civilization;
2. sufficient knowledge of economic, social, and political systems to enable the student to make informed choices;
3. sufficient understanding of governmental processes to enable the student to understand the issues that affect his or her community, state, and nation;
4. sufficient self-knowledge and knowledge of his or her mental and physical wellness;
5. sufficient grounding in the arts to enable each student to appreciate his or her cultural and historical heritage;
6. sufficient training or preparation for advanced training in either academic or vocational fields so as to enable each child to choose and pursue life work intelligently; and
7. sufficient levels of academic or vocational skills to enable public school students to compete favorably with their counterparts in surrounding states, in academics or in the job market. (*Rose v. Council, Ky.*, 1989, p. 59)

The reasons for this ruling, which went beyond the plaintiffs' request for more equitable funding, are open to interpretation. In the view of one researcher, however, the ruling was "the result of legal, social, and political forces coming together at the right time in history" (Dove, 1991, p. 3). These forces included, in addition to the lawsuit, "publicity and support from the media and citizens' groups," the "political courage, connections and stature" of key players involved, and "the widespread belief that the legal remedy need not involve a redistribution of wealth from rich districts to poor districts" (Dove, 1991, pp. 28, 32, 34).

The General Assembly's Response

In July 1989, the General Assembly responded to this ruling by appointing the Task Force on Education Reform, composed of House and Senate leadership and appointees of the governor (Legislative Research Commission, 1991, September, p. 7). The Task Force divided into three subcommittees—Curriculum, Governance, and Finance—that worked with nationally known consultants David Hornbeck, John Augenblick, and Lavern Cunningham, among others, to develop its reform proposal.

The work of the Task Force was an educational process for Kentucky legislators, according to one outside observer. By the end of this process, members of the Task Force understood the key issues being discussed in education reform nationwide, and the ultimate reform package reflected this understanding.[3]

The Kentucky Education Reform Act (KERA) became law on July 13, 1990. It is a multifaceted reform package, designed to change all of Kentucky's educational system, as required by the court ruling. Although KERA is not called "systemic reform" (Smith & O'Day, 1990) per se in the legislation, it does have the key ingredients of this type of reform, including curriculum frameworks, assessments aligned with those frameworks, and additional decision-making authority at the school site. The legislation required that a statewide curriculum framework be adopted and disseminated to schools by July 1993 and that a new statewide assessment system aligned with this framework be in place by the 1995–96 school year. This assessment system is to use performance-based student testing to measure the success of each school, and rewards and sanctions will be awarded to schools based on student performance. An interim testing program was administered to students during the 1991–92 school year to provide baseline data for determining school success in the 1993–94 school year, and schools received rewards or sanctions based on their 1993–94 performance.[4] Schools, with some exceptions, must have school-based decision-making (SBDM) by July 1996;[5] and each district was required to have at least one SBDM school by the 1991–92 school year.

Some additional provisions of KERA in the area of curriculum are: All schools were required to have ungraded primary programs fully implemented as of the 1993–94 school year; Family Resource and Youth Services Centers would be established over five years in areas where at least 20% of the students qualified for free school meals; schools were to provide extended school services to students needing additional time to meet learning outcomes; and a five-year technology plan for the state was to be developed and implemented.

In addition, KERA also contains provisions for reforms in governance and finance. The elected Superintendent of Public Instruction was replaced by a Commissioner of Education serving at the pleasure of the State Board of Education; the first Commissioner started on January 1, 1991. All positions in the Kentucky Department of Education (KDE) were abolished as of June 30, 1991, and a reorganized department opened on July 1, 1991. As of July 1990, local school board members were required to have at least a high school education and were made ineligible for election if they had a relative employed by the school district. In addition, school board members were prohibited from attempting to influence the hiring of any district employee except the superintendent. The Office of Education Accountability (OEA) was established under the Legislative Research Commission to monitor the education system and implementation of the Reform Act, review the state's system of school finance, verify the accuracy of school district and state performance, investigate unresolved allegations of wrongdoing at the state, regional, or district level, and report to the Legislative Research Commission. A biannual tax increase of nearly $1.3 billion was passed to finance all of these reforms, and the Support Education Excellence in Kentucky (SEEK) formula was established to better equalize education funding throughout the state. All factors and components of SEEK were fully funded for the first time in January 1995.[6]

KERA: An Analysis of the Policy

Before studying the implementation of any policy, one should determine the likelihood of the policy, as written, accomplishing its goals. In this particular case, it is important to ask whether KERA, as constituted, has the potential for transforming Kentucky's school system with the goal of dramatically increasing student achievement.

As already discussed, the history of education reform is predominantly one of failure, particularly failure to change the core processes of teaching and learning. Given this history, then, a prudent person probably would predict that KERA would also fail to transform these core processes.

On the other hand, the KERA reforms do have some strengths that may make this reform effort more successful than those of the past in changing teaching and learning. First, the reforms attempt to be systemic—to change all pieces of the system in coordinated ways so that the system works as a coherent whole. As discussed in Chapter 1, the proponents of systemic reform predict that such coherent policy will succeed in changing teaching and learning where other policies have failed because the various component policies, for example, curriculum and assessment, will align with one another, sending clear messages and incentives that will prod and assist teachers in changing practice in the desired ways. In addition to this alignment, there are strong accountability mechanisms in the policy in the form of the rewards and sanctions given to schools based on student performance. The consequences of success or failure in implementation are real.

A second strength of the KERA reforms is that the legislation and the court ruling leading up to it were bold, attention-getting steps that required a powerful political consensus to accomplish. The governor and legislative leadership stood solidly behind both KERA and the tax increase necessary for its implementation. In addition, they were supported by citizens' groups, businesspeople, and the popular media, as well as state education associations.

This powerful political consensus should make the reforms more salable and difficult to ignore at the local level, especially given the fact that local citizens are shouldering the added tax burden.

The above strengths of KERA also harbor the policy's potential weaknesses, however. First, while the component policies are aligned, or "systemic," in many respects and while the major reforms do seem to be based on current notions of best practice held by the field, there are aspects of the reform that are not systemic:

> The law had little to do with higher education as one piece of educational reform, it was not designed to have much [effect] on teacher education, it offered almost nothing to the workplace professional development of teachers, [and] it said nothing about the restructuring of high schools (Thomas James, personal communication, October 26, 1994).

Second, the coherence, or internal consistency, of the overall policy falls short. The philosophy that lies behind the KERA legislation calls for freeing schools from regulation and oversight so that practitioners may develop the programs and practices that will best help their students meet the state-mandated outcomes. It is these outcomes for which schools are to be held accountable. This philosophy of holding schools accountable for outcomes instead of process is clearly articulated in principles III, IV, and VIII of the *Statement of Principles* of the Curriculum Committee of the Task Force on Education Reform:

> *III.   Curriculum content must reflect high expectations and instructional strategies must be successful ones. What* children learn should be commonly challenging. . . . *How* we teach; *where* teaching and learning occur; *when* teaching and learning take place; and *who* teaches should be different for different students, classrooms and schools. The variability should be governed by what works . . .
> *IV.   Ours must be a performance-based system.* . . . What students actually know and can do is what counts . . .
> *VIII.   Non-essential regulations must be reduced significantly.* The rhetoric of school based management is empty if at the same time we bureaucratically impede or frustrate those decisions with layers of process. (Curriculum Committee Task Force on Education Reform, n.d., pp. 2–4, emphasis in original)

This statement of philosophy very much reflects the emerging philosophy of systemic reform (Smith & O'Day, 1990): The state establishes achievement standards that schools are accountable for meeting while at the same time freeing schools from regulation and oversight so that practitioners may develop the programs and practices that will best help their students meet the state-mandated outcomes. While making provisions for holding schools accountable for outcome standards, however, KERA also dictates many aspects of the programs and practices of schools. For example, all schools *must* have school-based decision-making (SBDM), and all SBDM councils *must* be composed of three teachers, two parents, and the principal.[7] All elementary schools *must* become ungraded primaries. The legislation contradicts the philosophy on which it is supposed to be based. A portion of the systemic reform paradigm is present—high standards of achievement will be set, and schools will be held accountable for meeting them. But a portion of the inputs paradigm also remains—the legislation dictates a number of the processes that schools must follow. This contradiction, created by mixing the new paradigm with the old, may weaken the strengths of systemic reform and make the success of the KERA reforms less likely.

The third potential weakness of the reform is that the powerful political consensus that brought it about may not be sustainable for the length of time required for successful implementation. The six-year time line in the legislation, while probably too short given the ambitious nature of the reforms required, is a long time politically. In addition, the added tax burden that comes with the reform legislation could lead to anti-tax sentiment that could weaken political support for the reform package as a whole. Whether or not the political support required to protect the reform from its enemies and to maintain the financial commitment it requires can be maintained for even the minimal six years is questionable.

Even initially, KERA must overcome a number of challenges in order to change teaching and learning. It must overcome its internal inconsistencies and maintain a fragile and costly political consensus in order to make implementation possible. In addition, successful implementation will require that numerous changes take place in the KDE and, ultimately, in schools and districts.

THE KENTUCKY DEPARTMENT OF EDUCATION[8]

The Kentucky Department of Education (KDE) has a staff of 520 people located in a 20-plus-story office tower in Frankfort, Kentucky, as well as an additional 49 staff members in 8 Regional Service Centers (Boysen, 1992, December).

The KDE has undergone a number of changes as a result of the passage of the 1990 Kentucky Education Reform Act (KERA). First, there was the change in leadership. The first Commissioner, Thomas Boysen, came into office as of January 1, 1991 and served through June 30, 1995. Boysen was succeeded by Dr. Wilmer S. Cody.

Second, as was mentioned before, the new Commissioner was expected to reorganize and staff the department as he saw fit. Most of the staff turnover occurred at the top levels of the organization, with only 18.5% of deputies, associates, and division directors from the old department remaining in top-level management positions (Boysen, 1992, December). Much less turnover occurred at the lower levels; just over 80% of the department's merit employees were kept on in the new department (Boysen, 1992, December). Many of the rehired employees did not retain their previous positions; 80 were demoted, and a few were promoted (Boysen, 1992, December; Steffy, 1992).

Third, the KDE was charged with implementing the massive reform effort now under way in Kentucky. KERA was intended to redesign Kentucky's entire education system, and the legislation established the time frame in which the department was to accomplish this redesign and its implementation.

The KDE is a department of education engaged in complex school reform. How, then, does what is taking place in this department compare to the framework of expected changes outlined in Chapter 2?

Changes in the KDE's Work[9]

The substantive work of the KDE has changed to a large degree. The department no longer accredits schools, something that was one of the former department's main thrusts. The KDE does still certify teachers, but the Kentucky Education Professional Standards Board is working to redesign "program approval, teacher assessment, and licensure based on valued educator outcomes which state in performance terms what teachers in Kentucky must know and be able to do" (KDE & Kentucky Education Professional Standards Board, 1992, p. 3). The attainment of these valued outcomes will be judged through the use of performance-based assessment tasks (KDE & Kentucky Education Professional Standards Board, 1992).

The priority work of the KDE has become implementing KERA, and consequently the department has been heavily involved in development since the passage of the reform act. Examples of this development activity are: A three-part performance-based assessment system has been designed and is administered in the fourth, eighth, and twelfth grades.[10] A formula for combining student performance on these assessments, as well as other school performance indicators such as absenteeism and dropout rates, has been constructed, allowing the KDE to generate baseline and threshold performance standards for each school.[11] State-level curriculum frameworks have also been developed.

Assistance and training are being provided in a number of areas of the KERA reforms, including assessment, school-based decision-making, ungraded primary schools, and, to a certain extent, curriculum. (The Curriculum Division has been primarily involved in developing the state's curriculum frameworks up to this point.) The goal of this assistance is shifting to one of building capacity in local schools and districts, as will be discussed in detail in the schools section of this case study.

The work of the KDE does change and develop rapidly. A number of people mentioned the challenge of all the work being brand-new. The work changes and evolves so quickly that establishing clear priorities is difficult. Said one commissioner: "With the way that KERA is moving . . . I can give you some priorities of the day, and they can change tomorrow. . . . That's how difficult this piece is."

Organizational Capacity

Skilled People. As the KDE was reorganized to better align with the KERA reforms, tremendous emphasis was put on hiring the "best and the brightest" to fill leadership positions. A majority of the new leadership came from outside the department and many from outside the state. Of the 65 people in leadership positions, 12 came from the old department, 30 came from other positions in Kentucky, and 23 came from out of state (Boysen, 1992, December).

The KDE was allowed to go outside the regular state personnel system and salary structure in order to attract new people from both within and outside the state with competitive salaries. These flexible hiring arrangements in effect have given the KDE three hiring mechanisms. The first is the traditional state personnel hiring procedure, through which people are tested and ranked according to their qualifications for placement on the state register. When the department hires from the state register, it is required to hire one of the top five individuals listed. The problem with hiring from the state register, in addition to that of low salaries, is that the state scoring system heavily weights education and experience and does not allow for unique skills—experience with school-based decision-making, for example—that might make an individual more uniquely qualified for a particular job. Therefore, individuals with the specific skills and experience sought by the department may not be listed in the top five positions on the registry.

The second and third hiring mechanisms involve using Memoranda of Agreement (MOAs), which are a method of contracting with eligible nonprofit agencies. The first type of MOA is a contract with a school system. These MOAs in effect allow the KDE to "borrow" employees from school districts for two to three years. The KDE pays the district for the borrowed employee, and the district continues to pay the individual's salary. This system allows the department to pay employees their district salaries rather than those dictated by the state salary schedule. The second type of MOA allows for the hiring of people who are not presently employed by a Kentucky district. These MOAs are through the Ohio Valley Education Cooperative (OVEC) and have been used primarily to hire department leadership. Again, department money is paid to OVEC, which then pays the employees.

Other state agencies are also allowed to hire employees using MOAs, but the KDE is allowed to hire a greater number of employees through this process. The legislature passed language in its 1992 biennial budget package that allows the KDE to hire up to 50% of its positions below the level of division director using MOAs. The OVEC option is limited by the total amount of the contract. As of November 1992, there were approximately 50 people paid through OVEC.[12]

This tripartite personnel system has advantages and disadvantages for the KDE. The primary advantage, according to staff, is that the department is able to attract good-quality educators and to pay them accordingly. The disadvantages are that this system is difficult, controversial, and may not be sustainable. One commissioner, when asked if it was easy to hire the people the KDE wanted, responded:

> No. It's terribly difficult. . . . Through the state personnel system there are so many limitations that it's almost impossible to hire the best person to do the job. . . . The MOA system . . . requires approval [from outside] agencies. . . . So . . . there are limitations and that slows it down, and we lose people because they can't afford to wait . . . [the] two weeks to six months [it may take] to get approved. . . . OVEC . . . seems to be the most functional of them all because you don't already have to be an employee of an existing agency in the state in order to qualify for that. . . . I spent the first year 25 to 30% unstaffed in [my area]. And that didn't affect time lines or expectations at all. And then at the end of the year we reduced positions to staff the regional service centers from an already incomplete [staff]. . . . I think everybody in the department is frustrated by the personnel system.

The system is also controversial. First, it creates salary inequities among KDE staff. Staff retained from the old department remained under the state salary scale so that, for example, directors coming from the old department are making $47–$50,000 per year while directors coming from the outside are making $65,000. Similar inequities exist at the associate commissioner and program consultant levels. There is some evidence that these inequities have caused capable Kentuckians to leave their positions in the KDE. Second, employees in other state agencies view the flexibility that the KDE has been granted as a threat to the entire personnel system, raising questions about this flexibility's long-term viability.[13]

Whether or not the system is politically sustainable is a question of debate. One director feels that it is sustainable:

> I think you need to realize that the controversy, as it relates to personnel, is primarily limited to this local [newspaper]. . . . [For] other newspapers . . . I really don't think it's news because they've investigated and found out that there's nothing illegal about what we're doing. And it is, in fact, to the betterment of KERA that we do this because we're able to attract the outstanding educators in this state and through[out] this nation.[14]

A commissioner, however, wasn't so sure:

> I don't know [if the system is sustainable]. . . . It sustains until the next biennium . . . because the budget language will hold until the '94 session which gives us this authority. My suspicion would be that there will be an attempt by either the personnel board or personnel department in state government to put more restrictions upon us, simply because they don't like us having a separate system. [But] the Commissioner has not given up on a separate personnel system.

Ongoing Learning and Training for KDE Staff.   Staff reports vary on the amount and adequacy of training available for KDE staff, particularly from the perspective of the department's program consultants. One consultant reported that training was lacking and that the only way to gain new knowledge was by doing your own research. Another consultant in the same division said that while there was no organized effort to ensure that everyone received training, training was available if you took the initiative to find it. This person said that while there was limited opportunity to go around the country and hear from primary theorists, there was almost unlimited opportunity to go out and learn from the experiences of schools. Consultants in other divisions, however, have received more formal training in their substantive areas. For example, staff in curriculum development received training in multiple intelligences, integrated curriculum, and collaborative strategies, and some staff have received training in project management.

It does seem, however, that there is more training in programmatic substance—curriculum design techniques, for example—than in the skills needed to apply that substance in new ways, both in working with schools and in working within the KDE. One commissioner commented that too little training had been done on how to provide staff development. Another commissioner said:

> When you move from . . . a monitoring and supervisional . . . role to a technical assistance role, it's a big change. And we did not provide the necessary staff development for our people to make that change. . . . People are assuming they know what technical assistance should be and how it should be delivered. . . . And that's why you're getting the mixed messages out there when people go and speak. Some people are talking in terms of "This is a mandate to you. I'm in charge." And some people are talking in terms of technical assistance.

A director commented that in addition, people had to make the shift from providing direct technical assistance to capacity-building:

> My background is more in actually providing technical assistance and doing professional development. . . . But when . . . we switched to developing the capacity of a state to do those kinds of things, that's different. And we don't have a lot of models around.

He said that the department could do a better job of training staff than it does, and that part of that training should be in how to build capacity as opposed to how to provide direct service.

Another director, when asked if there were ways for KDE staff to develop their own skills and capacities, said:

> In a content sense? Yes. In a context sense? No. In the content sense, the people who are developing the new assessment system or who are trying to get school councils established around the state . . . have access to . . . whatever they need really, to learn how to do that. But the way in which they do the work, the context, we are neglecting that. And I know Vermont is pursuing TQM [Total Quality Management] as the context, and we are not.

Some members of the leadership team did mention training sessions on TQM, leadership, and team-building skills, but this training has not been in-depth. Said one commissioner: "We've gone to a variety of . . . these quick and dirty training sessions, inspirational, awareness level and what have you, but not a lot of in-depth training."

Finally, there is not much emphasis on ongoing learning in the department. As one director put it, "We are . . . not a learning organization." Another director said that there was never any time to stop and actually think about what you were doing.

Necessary Infrastructure.   The KDE will eventually have state-of-the-art technology, and, through it, wide access to information on Kentucky's educational system, with the implementation of the Kentucky Educational Technology System (KETS). At this point, however, staff report that the department has a mixture of technology of varying degrees of usefulness and limited access to information on the educational system. Offices have different kinds of computers, which hampers collaborative work on joint products such as proposals. There is also no real database available. One commissioner said that they could not even do a teacher supply-and-demand study—a study commonly done in other states.

Organizational Flexibility and Responsiveness

Hierarchy and Organizational Boundaries.   The formal structure of the KDE remains hierarchical, with professional positions ranging from the Commissioner to deputy commissioners, associate commissioners, division directors, branch managers, and consultants. As can be seen from Figures 3.1 and 3.2, the reorganization of 1991 did redesign and rename most bureaus, offices, and divisions to reflect the strands and priorities of the KERA reforms, but it did not fundamentally alter the department's hierarchical structure. There have been modifications to the organizational chart since the initial reorganization, but these modifications have consisted of moving certain divisions to different offices—again not altering the hierarchical structure.

According to KDE staff involved in the planning for the reorganization, this structure was largely driven by the requirements of the state personnel office, which demanded boxes and lines to make authority relationships clear, as opposed to circles showing the interactions within a service relationship. These staff members also said, however, that the KDE was intended to operate as a more flexible, matrix-like organization in practice, despite its bureaucratic, hierarchical formal structure. One staff member said:

> There's also a lot inherent in that design . . . that's not on paper. . . .
> [Within the formal structure,] we . . . wanted to have a pretty dy-
> namic, almost a matrix type of organization [with] what we call cross-
> over goals teams and task teams . . . that would really cross areas when
> the dialogue and decision-making and even the program development
> itself warrants it. For example, we understand that assessment and in-
> struction and curriculum cannot be separated. And even though they
> are in different components of the organization, it is an expectation
> that those people dialogue on a continuing basis, . . . and that they . . .
> do some of [the] development together as a team. So . . . you may be

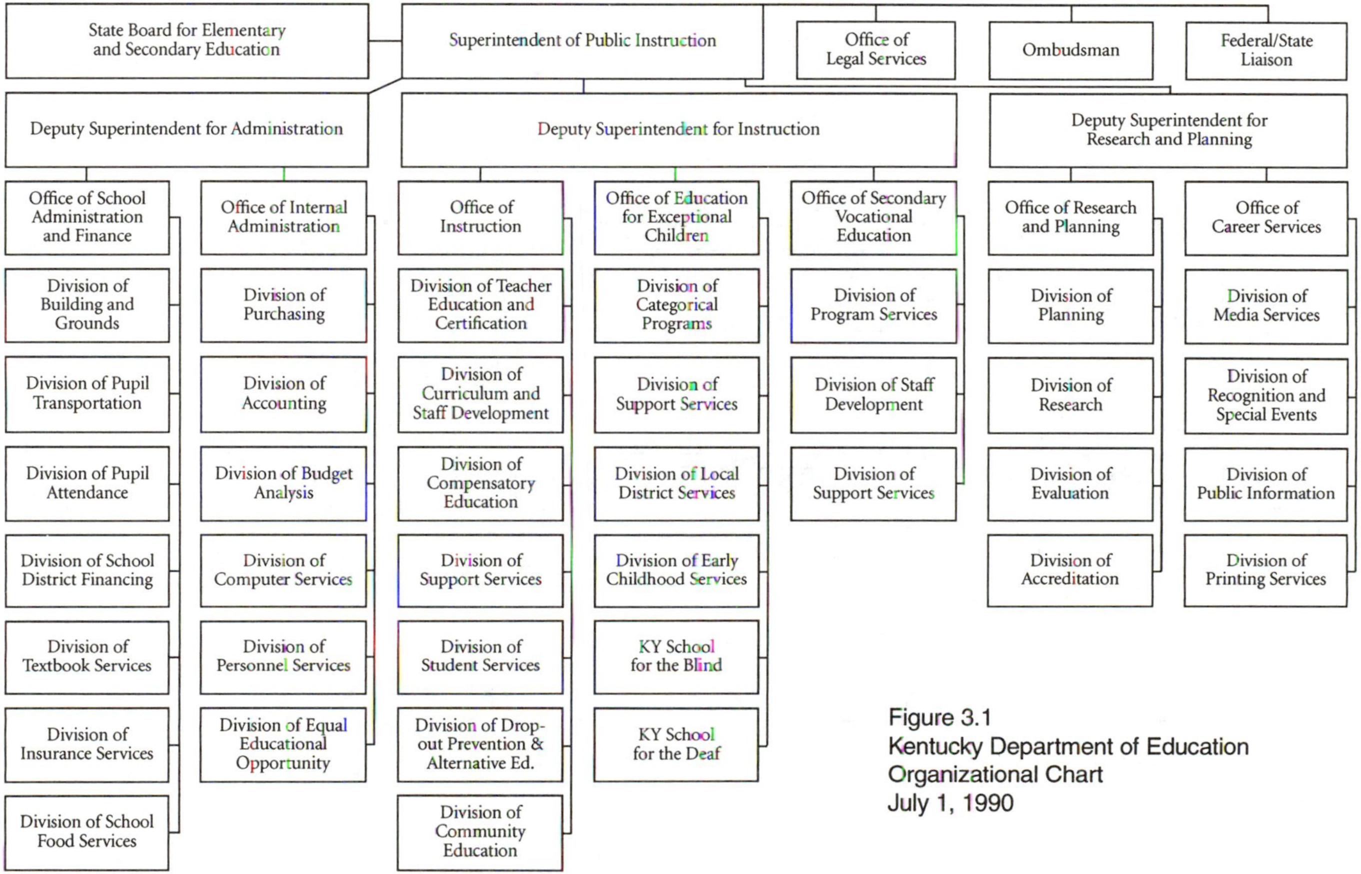

Figure 3.1
Kentucky Department of Education
Organizational Chart
July 1, 1990

State Board for Elementary and Secondary Education

Superintendent of Public Instruction

Office of Legal Services

Ombudsman

Federal/State Liaison

Deputy Superintendent for Administration

Office of School Administration and Finance
- Division of Building and Grounds
- Division of Pupil Transportation
- Division of Pupil Attendance
- Division of School District Financing
- Division of Textbook Services
- Division of Insurance Services
- Division of School Food Services

Office of Internal Administration
- Division of Purchasing
- Division of Accounting
- Division of Budget Analysis
- Division of Computer Services
- Division of Personnel Services
- Division of Equal Educational Opportunity

Deputy Superintendent for Instruction

Office of Instruction
- Division of Teacher Education and Certification
- Division of Curriculum and Staff Development
- Division of Compensatory Education
- Division of Support Services
- Division of Student Services
- Division of Drop-out Prevention & Alternative Ed.
- Division of Community Education

Office of Education for Exceptional Children
- Division of Categorical Programs
- Division of Support Services
- Division of Local District Services
- Division of Early Childhood Services
- KY School for the Blind
- KY School for the Deaf

Office of Secondary Vocational Education
- Division of Program Services
- Division of Staff Development
- Division of Support Services

Deputy Superintendent for Research and Planning

Office of Research and Planning
- Division of Planning
- Division of Research
- Division of Evaluation
- Division of Accreditation

Office of Career Services
- Division of Media Services
- Division of Recognition and Special Events
- Division of Public Information
- Division of Printing Services

Figure 3.2
Kentucky Department of Education
Organizational Chart
July 1, 1991

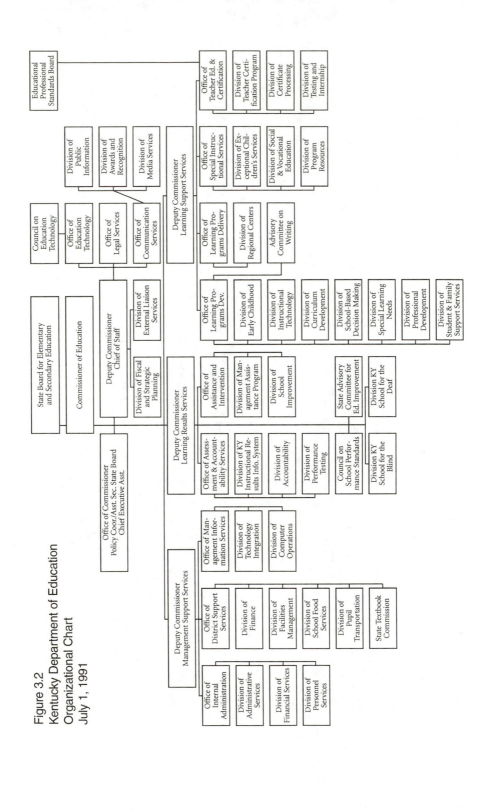

responsible for a division but also working on three other teams related to other areas that you impact.[15]

There is evidence that the KDE has tried to establish formal mechanisms
that promote the kind of boundary-spanning communication described
above and that individual divisions are trying to work together at the inter-
sections of their work. The management meeting structure is one of the
formal mechanisms for promoting communication across boundaries. This
structure includes Leadership Team meetings, Cabinet meetings, and Agenda
Committee meetings. The Leadership Team is composed of directors and
associate and deputy commissioners and meets at least once a month. According to staff, meetings are generally scheduled around a meal to give
people time to talk. The meetings consist of either an update on one of the
department's programs or a presentation by an outside speaker.

Cabinet and Agenda Committee meetings are for higher-level management, and there is an additional meeting structure that surrounds these management meetings. A commissioner explained that the Cabinet—consisting
of the associate and deputy commissioners—meets with the Commissioner
every Tuesday for an hour. Cabinet meetings are a "decision thinking process," used to keep all decision-makers "in the loop." The Agenda Committee—consisting of the four deputies and the Commissioner—meets for
three hours following the Cabinet meeting. The Agenda Committee is the
decision-making group, according to the commissioner. "And at that meeting . . . a lot of the division directors bring program issues [before that group]
so that . . . again, people are in the loop." Deputy commissioners then meet
with their associate commissioners at 4:00 to talk about the issues discussed
by the Agenda Committee and to raise new issues for the same series of
meetings the following week. The same commissioner went on to say:

> [Associate commissioners], in turn, . . . meet with their division direc-
> tors and do the same thing. It's a problem-solving, "Here's something
> that's coming up." And then the division directors, in turn, meet with
> their folks down through the consultants. Now that's the structure
> that's been put in place . . . It's a communication structure but it's also
> a problem-solving, problem initiation [structure]. . . . So it's a two-
> way communication flow.

The KDE also has some matrix teams within the department, established both on a formal and an ad hoc basis. There are three formal "KERA
Teams," one each for the elementary, middle, and high school levels. These
teams meet once a month and have representatives from all areas of the
department, who are supposed to bring information back to their respective

divisions. These meetings center around presentations about various department programs, followed by a discussion of implications not only for the grade levels around which the team is centered but also for the department as a whole. Members of the teams reported that these meetings did leave them better informed. Informal matrix teams also come together periodically to work on specific projects, such as writing grant proposals that entail overlapping responsibilities.

The use of matrix teams actually started during the transition period prior to the closing of the old department and the opening of the new one. Matrix teams during this period took the form of "temporary task forces, groups, or committees [used] to spearhead various aspects of the reform mandate" (Steffy, 1990–91, p. 8).

There is also evidence that divisions are trying to work together in areas where their work intersects. Examples cited by staff include: Curriculum and assessment people have worked together on designing curriculum frameworks and assessments. School-based decision-making (SBDM) staff have worked with staff of other reform areas, for example, ungraded primary and technology, to clarify the role of local SBDM councils in these areas. The staff of the Primary Division has worked closely with the staff of the Curriculum Division in developing both primary-level curriculum frameworks and a process for giving funds to primary schools for instructional materials. In some instances, divisions also work together to provide professional development.

There is still considerable evidence, however, of insufficient communication across the different divisions of the KDE. Virtually everyone interviewed punctuated their explanations of how internal communication took place with comments such as this one made by a commissioner: "Now does it work 100%? No, it doesn't. . . . There is a tendency in a bureaucracy, especially, I think, one that has a vertical building structure, for people not to think beyond their floor."

One program consultant commented that he thought internal communication had been better in the old department:

> I'm less likely to know what other divisions in this agency do today
> than five years ago. I think perhaps whoever is in charge of the agency
> really hasn't made inter divisional communication a priority. I think
> [five years ago] someone . . . at or near the top of the agency required
> that associate commissioners . . . require their consultants and branch
> managers to communicate with each other. And I saw a lot more pa-
> per then that informed me about what other divisions were doing
> than I do now.

This consultant said that he still knew quite a bit about what other divisions were doing as a result of his own initiative and of feeling that it was important for doing his job. He also said that because he had been in the department for some time, he knew people in almost every division and could use these informal contacts to get information.

The most telling evidence of the need for better internal communication, however, is the consistent complaint from local schools, districts, and the people who work with them about receiving mixed messages from the department. According to one person in another area of state government:

> [Internal communication is a problem] when [the department's] giving assistance to local districts. They'll get a question on the primary program . . . and the answer doesn't fit with how decisions should be made if the school is in a school-based decision-making mode. They just need to have a better feel for . . . how all the pieces fit together.

Staff in the KDE, ranging from a consultant to the Commissioner, also recognized that mixed messages were a problem. According to a consultant:

> [It's critical] that this agency . . . represents the appropriate image out in school districts. . . . [The Commissioner] or someone under his authority needs to make sure that that happens. . . . We as an agency need to speak with one voice . . . on major issues. And we need to resolve what that message is before it's ever presented. . . . We should be [allowed differences of opinion,] but we need to come to some consensus on the department position on the major issues. [That's not happening] to a degree that I'm comfortable with.

And according to the Commissioner:

> I think [people] probably . . . are getting mixed messages. . . . With an evolving program, the issues haven't been experienced before so they might get one answer from one program consultant and another from another one. And we haven't done as much [as we could] to . . . codify the answers. Now we have what we call a rolling Q & A in each area so when the primary consultants get a question they log it, and they're all in the loop on what answers are given. And if the supervisor doesn't feel that's the appropriate answer they can fix it right there instead of having it repeated. . . . Ultimately, I can imagine a computer bulletin board [that people could consult]. . . . [But at this point,] I would say that . . . we have mixed messages . . . [because] it's a dynamic situation and we're encountering a lot of new questions.

There is evidence that the pressure within the KDE and the culture of the organization may prevent attempts at internal communication from being successful, and specifically may hamper the development of informal methods of communication that might be more effective. There is strong pressure to meet the timelines for the KERA reforms set forth in the legislation. One commissioner said staff members are incredibly focused on their own piece of work because of the strong emphasis on meeting deadlines and getting things done. Consequently, this commissioner thought that people did not think about the benefits of bringing other people in on their decisions. Numerous staff mentioned that finding the time to communicate was a problem. Another commissioner said:

> No, it doesn't happen as it's supposed to everywhere. And it takes diligent effort because our schedules get so [full]. . . . We spread people out in all sorts of directions [around the state]. And again, communication is so critical both internally here and out in the field that it's just absolutely essential that we do that. So . . . I'd love to say it's working wonderfully well but it's something that we're [working on].

A director summarized the conflict between the need to communicate and the demands of the department:

> I think almost everyone would say that . . . [internal communication] could always be better, it should be better. But on the other hand, I guess I see people running as fast as they can in the areas they're in. . . . There is little time, if at all, to deal with anything else. And . . . I personally think that needs to be addressed better than it's been addressed. But on the other hand, I know they have a variety of opportunities here. Vehicles have been put in place to try to convey information. It's just a matter of if you can fit them into your schedule with everything else that you're dealing with.

Vision, Mission, Decision-Making, and Planning.   After interviewing numerous staff members of the KDE, the picture that emerges is that of an organization primarily driven by centralized control and top-down decision-making, as opposed to that of an organization driven by vision and mission with decision-making authority broadly dispersed.

The KDE does have an inspirational mission statement:

> The mission of the Kentucky Department of Education, as the national catalyst for educational transformation, is to ensure for each child an internationally

superior education and a love of learning through visionary leadership, vigorous stewardship, and exemplary services in alliance with schools, school districts, and other partners. (Boysen, 1991)

And some staff members refer to this mission, or a related vision statement such as "all kids can learn," as a motivating force behind their work. New staff members, however, were not in the department when the mission statement was written, and some, when asked about the KDE's vision and/or priorities, say that they are simply to implement the law. "The vision that guides the department is basically . . . to get this reform implemented," said one director. Another commissioner said, "We have a mission statement. We are in need of going back and revisiting that."

The organization is driven from the top by detailed decision-making and oversight. When asked for examples of the kinds of decisions made by the Commissioner, one director said, "You may find this hard to believe, but all the decisions are made at the top, even minute, detail decisions." Virtually everyone interviewed described the Commissioner as being a very "hands-on," detail-oriented CEO. And even the staff member who gave a decision-making vignette described as "informal and collaborative" still made it clear that everything went back to the Commissioner.

The Commissioner reviews all issues of *Kentucky Teacher,* a KDE newspaper sent to practitioners throughout the state, as well as major news releases and brochures on major areas of KERA. He also oversees the development of all *Program Reviews* (formerly called *Program Advisories*)—publications sent to superintendents outlining programmatic regulations and recommending courses of action to districts and schools.

A KDE staff member described the process of generating *Program Reviews* as follows: The Commissioner meets with the program staff writing the particular *Review* and outlines what he wants to see included. The program staff then draft the piece and return the draft to the Commissioner for approval. The program staff then rewrite the *Review* and eventually it goes to the communications office to have the writing refined and to the legal office to be sure that it is in keeping with all existing laws and regulations. The *Review* then goes back to the Commissioner, who may again change the focus and direction of the publication. If this happens, the *Review* is cycled back to the program people.[16]

Program Reviews are also normally reviewed by the Cabinet—associate commissioners and up—and the Agenda Committee—deputies and the Commissioner. The Commissioner has the option to fast-track any *Review,* however, bypassing the Cabinet and Agenda Committee and, according to staff, has frequently done so. The result of this fast-tracking is that program people, whose work is affected by the policies articulated in the *Review,* sometimes have not been consulted, and the published KDE positions take them by surprise.[17]

Consultants who remain from the old department report that decision-making is more centralized than it was in the past and that this centralized process is time-consuming. For example, one of them said:

> Everything I do has to be passed upward. . . . Everything. . . . I started working on a . . . plan for . . . two years of [my] program in July [the interview took place in February of the following year] . . . I still have as yet to get all of that approved and in place. [It has to be approved by] the division director . . . [the associate commissioner, the deputy commissioner and the Commissioner.] . . . And we've done lots of revisions and things, but . . . because we have all had so much to do, . . . frequently the people who need to give me input are not available to do it for a couple of weeks.
>
>   So I sit for a couple of weeks and then I find out, well that's not quite the direction they wanted it to go. . . . I left here at 8:00 o'clock last night ready to quit. . . . I am at the point, "Just tell me what you want. I'll do anything you want me to do." . . . The mechanism for getting that kind of feedback . . . needs to operate more quickly than it does. . . . Really, everything that you do is signed off on all the way up.
>
>   . . . [In the old department] it might go all the way to the deputy commissioner to be made aware of. But there was an element of . . . the deputy commissioner told the associate commissioner, "This is what I expect you to do. We want to see these things occur." It comes down to the division directors who each were given their charge. . . . And in my instance, she came and she said, "Okay, you've got [X] dollars. I want to see your overview plan. I want a programmatic budget to go with it. I don't want lots of detail. . . ." Then as each piece under that was developed, she and I would discuss it and she'd say, "Okay, go with it." . . . And then it became her responsibility . . . to justify the rest of the way up, however far. . . . But . . . [in most cases,] I did not have to wait.

The KDE's strategic planning process is another way of centralizing organizational control at the top. The department has a formal strategic planning procedure: Each of the divisions writes annual action plans centering around two to four major objectives. The plans identify activities to reach these objectives, individuals responsible for the activities, and timelines for activity completion. These plans are then signed off on by the supervising associate commissioner and deputy commissioner and sent to the Commissioner.[18] According to one director:

> [The Commissioner] is a very hands-on, very involved in detail, kind
> of CEO. And we take a two-week period and he spends an hour on
> each action plan reviewing it in considerable detail. And out of those
> discussions, come changes and amendments and new things that
> people hadn't thought of [that he] thinks need to be included. And
> so he's really shaping the direction of the department through that
> process.

Action plans are then rewritten in accordance with the Commissioner's
wishes.

Plans can be changed, and staff interviewed indicated that making
changes was not difficult if they were programmatically justifiable. Changes
do have to go through a clearance process, however, with major changes
being approved by the Agenda Committee.

KDE staff do not have the authority to make many decisions on their
own. A director said, "Every decision I make, I run it by [my associate commissioner] as a recommendation to [the Commissioner]. And I encourage
my staff to come to me first before making any major decisions."

Staff do make decisions that fall within the outlines of their action plans.
Directors are responsible for implementing these plans and generally can
make internal decisions such as the staffing of different projects. Consultants
talked about having discretion over their day-to-day schedules—scheduling
trainings that they would be giving and developing their own work agendas,
again in keeping with the division's action plan.

In addition, there is a small amount of evidence of "slippage" in the
higher-level control over decisions. This evidence came from one director
who said:

> There'[ve] been so many interpretive issues we in our little group here
> have decided about the law, and we've offered that advice in written
> correspondence and phone calls for a year and a half. I think if the
> leadership people above me knew about some of our decisions they
> might have agreed with some and disagreed with others. But we've
> been given that sort of license, I suppose. When a specific issue comes
> to their attention that they disagree with then they pull back and say,
> "uh-uh, that's not the way it's going to be."

He added, however, that he did not have the prerogative to send out any
widespread mailings to principals and superintendents without approval of
the Commissioner.

The chain of command also can be violated in an upward direction when division directors go directly to the Commissioner if there is a pressing problem. According to one commissioner:

> Key decisions are made at the division level. From the division level they go to an office level. From the office they go to a bureau. From a bureau they come to . . . the Agenda Committee—the Commissioner and his four deputies who take a look at it. That's the normal track. But the emergencies . . . can go from director to Commissioner. . . . [If] the site-based decision-making director is having some serious problems with his plans, [for example,] he . . . goes right to the Commissioner.

No staff member, with the exception of the director cited above, however, gave examples of key decisions being made by staff at lower levels without first receiving clearance from the Commissioner.

Staff reactions to these planning and decision-making processes are mixed. Some said that they found the planning process helpful. Others said they found it overly time-consuming and unrelated to their work.

A number of staff members said that detailed planning was difficult when they were working in uncharted territory in which design and implementation were happening simultaneously. One director stated this view while at the same time saying that the planning might become more useful over time:

> I can remember [in] the first two years [of my previous job, planning] was less helpful than it was ultimately because I . . . felt like I was writing a plan in the beginning . . . to accommodate people above me, rather than work for me. And that's what I feel like I'm doing now. I'm writing these strategies to show people, . . . rather than to really make sense for us. And . . . that is . . . because we're so close to the battle and we're only an inch ahead of the business basically. So sometimes it's hard to do long-range planning when you're in that kind of . . . arena. I think over time the long-range planning model that's in place here would be much more beneficial to this group.

Reactions to decision-making processes were decidedly more negative, although some support was voiced for these, too. One consultant said: "We're still a lot of top-down, and I don't fault the commissioner for that. You know I can understand that . . . Somebody in my level could mess up big time and really cause a lot of problems and so . . . he's trying to keep his hand in it." And another said:

I think [the review process is] good for several reasons. Number one, it apprises everybody of what's going out; and secondly, we try to have quality control on what we're doing . . . [Without the review,] I would do something and another division would be doing something and we wouldn't have that kind of connection. We may end up, for some reason, being in conflict with what we're saying. And I think this is a good way to avoid some of that.

Most staff interviewed, however, particularly those at higher levels of the organization, found that the decision-making process destroyed initiative and creativity. This viewpoint will be described below in the "Summary" section.

Norms and Culture. The norms of the KDE do not promote trust and risk-taking, but they do promote hard work and excellence. The organizational push for hard work and excellence comes from top-down, centralized control, as opposed to from a collegial and supportive environment.

The organizational norm of caution comes in part from the lack of empowerment to make decisions as described above, but also from the fear of job loss if something goes wrong. Part of this fear springs from the fact that all employees rehired into the new department were put on a year's, rather than the usual six months', probation in order to give their new supervisors a chance to adequately evaluate their performance. This made employees feel insecure in their positions, and this insecurity was buttressed by some terminations. According to a consultant: "We had one employee who was standing in a training environment providing training and said something she shouldn't have said and then by that afternoon her boss showed up and fired her on the spot. Word got back to him." A commissioner told of two directors who had been fired. After the firings, the leadership told the Commissioner that some kind of an explanation should be given to department employees. None was forthcoming. In fact, people in director positions and above can be fired at any time. Most of these people are hired through OVEC, and are not a part of the state personnel system. They serve on year-long contracts at the discretion of their supervisors and can be released without cause with 30 days notice.

A member of the Commissioner's staff explained that the department is intended to become more of a risk-taking organization:

I think . . . it's going to evolve into more of a question asking and risk taking organization. . . . A lot of people's roles and functions have dramatically changed and they're engaged in very, very different types of processes and procedures . . . There has been a tendency [for the professional consultant level] of the organization in this first year . . . to continue to be very cautious . . . because [they were put on] . . . a year's probation . . . as opposed to 6 months. . . . That just ended June 30th [1992]. . . . So they have just now reached . . . I think, a sense of security where they can really begin to believe that this is a different organization and . . . that what we're looking for is for in many cases, the old practices to be totally set aside.

Caution still seems to be the norm, however, even now that the probationary period has ended. When asked what the norms of the organization were, one commissioner replied:

I think we're to the point now that everybody's in a CYA [Cover Your Ass] mode. . . . Because people in the department have the same fear as those [in] districts, that "if you mess up you're gone." And that's the kind of culture we have created here. . . . We're so busy wanting to look good at anybody's expense in a lot of cases and that's what I see happening . . . I mean you get memoed to death . . . If I tell you to do something, to cover myself, I'm going to send you a memo. That's the name of the game.

A consultant, when asked how the new department differed from the old, said, "[There's] less toleration for messing up."

Others spoke of the norms of hard work done at a continually driving pace, held to a high standard of excellence. One commissioner said, "The expectations are incredibly high for almost perfection in the work. And the time line expectations are unreasonable." A number of people spoke of the importance of providing high quality, professional service to school districts in a timely fashion—24-hour turnaround when possible. There is a sense that if you cannot keep up with the pace, you should consider leaving the department. Said one commissioner:

Everybody here has a responsibility for the success of the reform. . . . I think that is a value. . . . I think . . . [in] this bureau they've . . . clearly [gotten] the message . . . that service means 24-hour turnaround time. . . . It means . . . that your job is more than maybe you bargained for in terms of hours and time and commitment. And if it is, it may mean that there's a decision you have to make about doing something differently if that's too hard for you.

According to a director:

There's almost a sense of, well, if you can't work ten hours a day . . . and work at the top of your game endlessly, well then you can't cut it

here. And I think there's a sense of an expectation of that kind of performance. . . . You feel like you just can't keep up with it, you can't do
the job. And I sense that a lot from people throughout the department. And so there's just a sense of push, push, push, go, go, go. I
mean faster, faster, faster, faster.

Building a supportive culture is not attended to in the department. Said
one commissioner, "You're expected to bring your own support system with
you. There's not a lot of time and value spent on creating a culture." Another
commissioner said, "There's been a constant hammer on [people here] all
the time. There's never been enough celebration. We don't celebrate here."
He added that the culture and morale problems in the department would be
addressed when the Commissioner decided they were a priority. A director
said:

> [Tom's] such a genuinely good guy and a caring person. He doesn't ap-
> pear that way to people. He appears kind of cutthroat. I think he'd
> like to do something about that, but I think the pace is such here that
> it's difficult and [I think he believes] there's other priorities. . . . I don't
> think there's anything more important right now than the morale of
> the people that are rolling this thing out and I think it's being ig-
> nored. . . . And I think Tom's view is that . . . the morale of people in
> the organization is not the responsibility of the organization, and I dis-
> agree a little bit with that.

Commissioners also said that discussions of the need to improve the culture
of the department had been squelched.

Summary

In 1990, the Kentucky General Assembly charged the KDE with implementing complex school reform as defined in the Kentucky Education Reform Act. Through KERA, the General Assembly equipped the department
with new leadership, in the form of Kentucky's first appointed Commissioner, and gave the new Commissioner the mandate to restructure the
agency so that it would be better equipped to implement the reforms.

As a result of KERA, the substantive work of the KDE has changed
considerably. The department is now charged not only with uncertain, rapidly changing, developmental work of a kind that traditional SDEs have
never undertaken, but also with making the pieces of that work coherent so
that clear reform messages will be sent to schools.

This type of work puts new demands on the KDE, and there is some evidence that the agency is working to transform itself to better meet those demands. Efforts have been and are being made to put the organizational capacity necessary to do the new work in place, although there is evidence that while staff are being prepared in their new substantive areas, little attention is paid to preparing them to work together in new ways. There is also evidence that staff are trying to cross organizational boundaries so that reform efforts can be coordinated and coherent, although there seem to be more formal than informal structures to encourage this, and there is substantial evidence that the degree of boundary crossing is insufficient.

More interesting, however, are the places where the "new" KDE does not appear to differ much from the "old" KDE, despite being charged with very different work. The lack of difference between the two versions of the department is strongest in the area I have characterized as "organizational flexibility and responsiveness." To date, the organization appears hierarchical in both formal and informal structure. While some boundary crossing is occurring, which is a stated objective of the organization, the culture of the organization does not encourage it, and there is evidence that more is needed. The organization is primarily driven by centralized decision-making and control as opposed to vision and mission, and there is evidence that decision-making is more centralized than it was in the past. The culture and norms of the new department do not encourage either risk-taking or collegial support.

It is important to examine the costs inherent in the new KDE's method of operation because if the costs are not great, then perhaps the agency does not have to change even though charged with radically different work. There do appear to be internal costs incurred by the KDE's method of operation.

The first internal cost is that individual creativity and initiative are stifled. Said one commissioner:

> It's a check and balance system for everything. And people['s] . . . creativity has been stifled. . . . If you know it's not going to be right the first time don't even send it in . . . "let's check and see what so and so wants before we even start the process." . . . [Why] get out there and plan all of this stuff all the way through, and go and bring it through the committee [only] to . . . get shot down . . . and have to redo it. Before you go through that, just check with the head and say, ". . . Now just tell me what you want." And then after . . . the person tells you, . . . you bring it up through the system.

A director commented that this kind of behavior by a CEO becomes a self-fulfilling prophecy: People stop doing creative work when they know that it will be wrong and that the Commissioner will do it his way anyway: "A number of us keep charging up that hill trying to get it right, but, after you've been burned a few times, you eventually start saying, 'How can I do this with the least pain to me'?" Another director said:

> I think Tom . . . has so much ability and skill and his expectations are so high but in a way, I think what's happened here is people have been paralyzed a little bit into working in a way that they're not really going on their instincts and what they think is right but they're working at guessing what Tom Boysen wants and that's not a good situation I don't think.

A second internal cost of the way the KDE operates is organizational flux. One director commented that too many people were being "killed" by the organizational culture. A number of the top leadership have left, or are leaving, after less than two years. A memo was sent from the Commissioner to KDE staff explaining that many department leaders were leaving, others were likely to follow, and this was a natural part of the change process. Many people with expert skills were brought in for program development, and now that the development phase had ended, the department was reexamining staffing needs. In addition, some members of the leadership had been reexamining their own career goals. The memo further said that a dynamic organization was needed in the face of constant change and that the only constant in the department was change.

This memo "landed very heavily in the department," according to one director. The State Board of Elementary and Secondary Education extended Boysen's contract for two additional years in January 1993, thereby ensuring that Boysen would remain Commissioner through 1996—the final year of KERA implementation. KDE staff had hoped that the department would enter a period of stability as a result of the contract extension. A second director said that people laughed at the memo. It was seen as an effort to gloss over and stop rumors when three or four people announced they were leaving in one week: "Thirty percent of the top [leadership] is leaving, and Tom tries to pass it off as a natural part of the change process. But people know you don't sell your house and uproot yourself for only a two-year commitment." The second director went on to say that this turmoil and the uncertainty it creates demoralize everyone and undermine the department. The first director said, "Organizationally, it's really hard to keep going with all this turnover. There will probably be five to six key vacancies for three to five months over the summer."

A third internal cost is that KDE morale is generally described as low.

One director commented that the management style in the KDE was out of sync with the KERA reforms, which were about empowering and valuing people. He said that this upset a lot of people in the department.

An even more important question is how the divergence between the framework and the KDE's activities affects the department's work performance, specifically the implementation of the KERA reforms. Here, the costs, at least initially, appear less clear-cut, because it seems that by and large the work is getting done—the law is being implemented. When you ask legislators and other knowledgeable outsiders whether KERA is on track, they qualify their answers somewhat according to different areas of the reform, but for the most part they say that it is. KDE staff, however, while acknowledging that the work is proceeding, wonder if it is sustainable over time. A director said: "The reform will go forward . . . because it's in the law. But if we were simply relying on the strength of the organization here, the reform wouldn't happen because the department is so undermined by all the uncertainty."

This last statement begs the questions of what "the reform going forward" really means and what kind of "going forward" is truly desired. From the perspective of KDE staff and others, work accomplishment is most easily measured by whether or not timelines are being met—whether products such as the curriculum frameworks are developed on schedule, whether X number of schools have school-based decision-making councils by a given date, and whether the assessment system is up and running on time.

The kind of "going forward" truly desired, however, is that the changes envisioned by the policy occur in schools and districts and, ultimately, student achievement improves.

THE KDE's EFFECT ON LOCAL IMPLEMENTATION

The KDE restructuring is interesting to school reformers because it is intended to be instrumental in implementing KERA. But we must look to the local level in order to make even preliminary judgments about whether and how the reform is progressing and particularly to examine the effects of the KDE's actions on local reform implementation.

The findings from schools and districts reported here should be treated as preliminary because of both the timing and scope of the study. I visited the districts in February 1993, only three years into what is envisioned as a 6- to 10-year reform. I visited 3 districts—a small number of the total 176.

I did, however, choose three districts that represent something of the range of districts that the state is trying to change: 1) an "early adopter" district that was engaged in reforms similar to the current state-level reforms prior to the state's involvement; 2) a "status quo" district that delivered a more or less average traditional education to its students for years; and 3) a "low-performing" district that the state had been concerned about for some time due to its below-average delivery of educational services.

In each district, I visited the schools that district personnel felt were furthest along in their reform efforts and interviewed the teachers most involved in the reforms.[19] I chose schools and personnel with the greatest involvement in the state's reform efforts due to the relative newness of the reform. I reasoned that because the reforms were so new, I would need to look at the best-case scenario in order to see many signs of change. Even using this selection strategy, however, there was still wide variation in levels of involvement and change. (See the Appendix for a more detailed discussion of sampling and methods.)

I visited schools and districts to answer four questions:

1. Is there evidence of reform-related activity taking place in schools and districts?
2. Is the KDE allowing schools and districts maximum flexibility to achieve the desired outcomes by holding them accountable for outcomes as opposed to process?
3. Are the actions of the KDE helping schools and districts to build the capacity needed to institute the KERA reforms in the envisioned manner?
4. What do local practitioners identify as ways the department could help them to better implement the reforms, that is, what advice do they have for the KDE?

Reform in Kentucky Schools and Districts[20]

All practitioners interviewed reported that change was occurring in their schools and districts as a result of KERA, and the vast majority were supportive of the changes taking place. Attitudes ranged from an enthusiastic embracing of all KERA concepts to a concerned or grudging acceptance.[21] Some practitioners said that they had colleagues who still thought these reforms would fade in time, and they would not have to change.

The KERA reforms cited for promoting the greatest amount of change were the ungraded primary program, the KIRIS (Kentucky Instructional Results Information System) assessment system, and school-based decision-making. All of the elementary schools visited are implementing the ungraded primary program as mandated. Implementation of the ungraded primary program requires radical change in elementary classrooms. Teachers are now teaching multi-age groups of students and are increasingly using teaching

techniques that prompt active and interdisciplinary learning, including cooperative learning, learning centers, whole language, math manipulatives,
thematic units, and performance activities. Primary teachers also report that
these changes in instruction make a positive difference for students. One
teacher, who described herself as strictly traditional prior to the KERA reforms, when asked if she would like to add anything else at the end of the
interview, said:

> Just that I think that if you see the children and see them in action do-
> ing the things that we have exposed them to this year, that you will
> see a completely different group than . . . you've seen in the past.
> They're really interested and motivated. . . . They want to know what
> we're doing next. And every time we start a new unit they say, "Now
> what are we going to do here?" . . . It's . . . very exciting to me. . . .
> When I talk to the parents they say, "Well we can tell you're really in-
> volved in this." . . . When . . . a child that could barely read . . .
> come[s] up . . . and tell[s] me that they can read a book . . . that's very
> exciting. . . . That's very rewarding . . . I think it's going to work, I
> really do.

All schools visited with grades 4, 8, and 12, are also participating in the
KERA-mandated assessment system consisting of a transitional test, performance assessments, and portfolios. There is evidence that assessment is driving changes in curriculum and instruction, at least to some degree, in all
sites. Staff and administrators of all three schools in the early adopter district
said that *all* teachers are responsible for student performance in their schools,
as opposed to only the teachers in the 4th, 8th, and 12th grades, in which
students are assessed. Staff at the elementary and middle schools reported
having practice sessions for students to prepare them for assessments, and at
the middle and high schools, students in all grades keep portfolios. Teachers
in the middle and high schools also reported taking the student assessments
themselves, as a faculty, in order to better understand how students needed
to be prepared.

Practitioners in the status quo district's elementary school reported that
performance activities are being used throughout the school. Middle school
practitioners said that application and understanding are being stressed
throughout the school and that techniques such as cooperative and activity-
based learning are increasingly being used. Practitioners at the high school
reported less schoolwide change as a result of the assessments, saying that
they are only now turning to curricular changes that need to be addressed.[22]

In the troubled district, all students keep portfolios in the elementary
and K–8 schools visited, and elementary teachers reported giving students

problems from the 4th grade assessments. In the high school, teachers reported that more group work is being done and that portfolios are being used where required.[23]

Staff reports on changes in instruction varied from school to school and teacher to teacher. A number of staff in the early adopter district reported that they already had been teaching in the ways envisioned by KERA, as did a few staff members in the other two districts. Other staff in all three districts reported that their teaching is changing in response to the move to ungraded primary and performance-based assessments. Some of these teachers talked about entirely redesigning their teaching and curriculum in response to KERA, while others talked about adding portfolio work to their traditional curriculum.[24]

Five of the 10 schools visited have adopted school-based decision-making: the high school in the early adopter district, the elementary and high schools in the status quo district, and the elementary and one of the K–8 schools in the troubled district. Staff in nonparticipating schools in the early adopter and status quo districts reported that they are well satisfied with the shared decision-making structures they already have in place. Staff in the troubled district reported that the negative experiences of one SBDM school in the district had scared some faculty into voting against its adoption.[25]

In addition to pushing non–reform-minded schools, there is evidence that KERA has pushed early adopter schools to deepen their reform efforts and has given other schools direction for their reform activities. For example, one early adopter teacher who said that her team in many ways exemplified the type of teaching envisioned by KERA said:

> The English portfolio is something that we had worked on. We had never been able to nail down what it was we wanted to have in it. And it was going to take us perhaps another 10 years at the rate we were moving to make decisions, come back, pretend we were at ground zero again and remake the decisions, and . . . never quite get it really happening so that it mattered and it was a requirement for graduation. And what happened with KERA was bingo. It was there. We had to do it. We didn't know what we were doing exactly but we had to do it. We knew we had to make the kids do it. . . . That's superb.

And a principal at a school in the status quo district said:

> Over the years we have tried lots of different things. . . . [But] . . . prior to [KERA], I don't know that we had a handle on anything, and we were going in some different directions. . . . And . . . it would have taken longer on our own to really get to the point where we needed

to be. So KERA came along and kind of put it together for us and helped us. And so we have embraced the model.

Although they felt affirmed in their efforts to change and pushed to change further, practitioners in the early adopter schools expressed some frustration at having to change some things that were working well simply because KERA had different requirements, as is exemplified by the comments of one teacher:

> I feel very strongly that prior to KERA we were already on the KERA road. We were already well along the road and we have had to make some adjustments, some of which were very reasonable and needed to happen, and some of which . . . one way of doing it was as good as another way of doing it, so why couldn't we just continue. . . . We were doing it well and it didn't seem to make sense to have to change but state departments are state departments. [For example,] I think that . . . our governing board [was very well organized]. . . . I think the KERA method is fine but it seems senseless to change from something that was working.

Giving Schools Maximum Flexibility

Achieving the kind of far-reaching reforms envisioned by KERA requires going beyond simple compliance with the law to a commitment to achieving a new vision of education.[26] It is not enough simply to have the structures of ungraded primary, school-based decision-making, and performance assessment in place or simply to have gone through the motions of planning for them. Full implementation of KERA requires that teaching, learning, and the way schools operate be fundamentally changed.

As was described earlier in this chapter, the philosophy that lies behind the KERA legislation calls for freeing schools from regulation and oversight so that practitioners may develop the programs and practices that will best help their students meet the state-mandated outcomes. It is these outcomes for which schools are to be held accountable (Curriculum Committee Task Force on Education Reform, n.d.). The question then becomes, "Is deregulation with attention to outcomes actually taking place?"

The KDE unquestionably is holding schools accountable for outcomes through KIRIS, the state's new assessment system. KIRIS includes transitional tests, comprised of multiple-choice and open-ended questions; performance events, tasks students must perform either on their own or in groups; and portfolios, compilations of different exemplars of a student's work. Students are assessed in the areas of reading, writing, mathematics, science, and social studies, and noncognitive data on attendance, retention, dropout, and transition to school or work are also factored in for each school (KDE, 1993, February, p. 14). All schools must participate in the assessment system for grades 4, 8, and 12, and schools will ultimately be given rewards and sanctions in accordance with their performance. Schools that exceed their threshold improvement goals will receive monetary rewards from the state, while those that do not meet their goals will be given assistance, become eligible for school improvement funds, and may be declared "schools in crisis" if their performance has declined by 5% or more (KDE, 1993, February, p. 14).[27] The "school in crisis" designation allows students to transfer to more successful schools (Legislative Research Commission, 1991, September, p. 9).

The KDE is also deregulating process to an extent. Some deregulation has occurred at the classroom level through the removal of time-on-task and specific subject area requirements, and a number of teachers expressed gratitude for this. For example, one teacher said she appreciated having more input into her curriculum:

> [Before,] we were handed . . . our books and this was the sequence. And this is how it was whether you really thought that that's the way it should be or not. And now we as a school . . . and that goes along with being site-based too, have more say on what exactly, or when we think this should be taught. . . . All the children will be expected to do these things before they leave the primary program. . . . But [we're allowed more freedom] as far as the way in which we teach it. . . . [We can] look at the needs of our students . . . [and] say, "This group is not ready. I'm going to stay with this a little while longer." Where I think before you know they had it set up, "Now the first six weeks you're going to do this and you're not going to touch on that again." You know, that kind of thing.

This newfound flexibility probably reflects deregulation at the district as well as the state level. Other teachers in this district reported having to have to-the-minute lesson plans prior to KERA, including a five-minute bathroom break. Another teacher said that he had been told by a district administrator that he expected to be able to walk into any kindergarten classroom in the county at a given time and see them doing the same activity.

Deregulation of curriculum and instruction has its limits, however. Schools still must seek individual waivers from the State Board for Elementary and Secondary Education for practices such as team teaching of interdisciplinary classes, adopting textbooks that are not on the state-approved list, teaching courses not listed in the state's Program of Studies, and not meeting course time requirements in the Program of Studies (KDE, 1993, October 14, pp. 4–5). "There is no provision for blanket waivers," and "after January 1995, a school must exceed its [accountability] threshold to be granted a waiver from all regulations" (KDE, 1993, October 14, pp. cover–1).[28] KDE staff said that waivers for such practices were easy to obtain from the State Board. When asked why waivers were required if they were nearly always granted, one staff member said that the waiver process was a way of collecting data on the changes schools were making in order to understand what kinds of changes in regulation needed to be made in the future and that it also ensured that schools did not do anything too drastic.

Nearly half the practitioners interviewed (21 of 47) said that the KDE is overregulating the implementation of KERA and that too much time is spent on reporting on process and filling out paperwork. While virtually all practitioners interviewed expressed strong support for the goals of the reform, they described an implementation process hampered by excessive rules and oversight. Some practitioners felt that the department was even more regulatory than it had been in the past. Said one principal:

> I think that the department of education, in some ways, is more regula-
> tory than they were prior to KERA even though I'm not sure that's
> the intent. . . . Prior to KERA, we had certain mandates from the
> state of things we had to do and how many minutes you had to spend
> teaching language arts . . . and so on. . . . And every 5 years the state
> department would come in and conduct a study and monitor that. . . .
> What I interpreted the Kentucky Education Reform Act to be when
> it was initiated was an opportunity for schools to make some decisions
> about their own destinies, and to be rewarded for those decisions that
> were good and successful, and to be sanctioned for the ones that were
> not. But I also see the amount of information that comes in that says,
> "but you need to do this" or "you must do that" or "this is what we
> mean by this." So in some ways, I feel like there's some conflict there.

Practitioners' examples of the department's overregulation point out several costs that it exacts on the implementation process. First, the process requirements of the department slow the implementation of the reform by giving detailed accounting of dollars precedence over meeting the needs of teachers trying to implement the reforms, as is shown by this example from a superintendent:

> I'll give you a prime example. The state allocated . . . $17.00 per child
> in the primary. . . . We should have had the money in July so we
> could have bought stuff. [But] we had to develop individual plans for

each building. I could not submit it from the central office until they were all in here. And then I had to send them to the regional service center and they reviewed them and they . . . I think they came up with like $250.00 out of $20,000 that they didn't think met the criteria, etc. It then had to go to the state department. So we didn't get our money until October. The teachers were upset because in Kentucky if you don't get prior approval, you can't be reimbursed [for expenditures] . . .

[And I reviewed] that $250.00 worth of things . . . and my opinion is that those primary teachers thought that they were a real important item. . . . If I get caught, then fine, I'll reimburse the $250.00. But I'm not going to question and nickel and dime the teachers, [because] it's an insignificant part of the whole plan.[29]

Second, the detailed process requirements sometimes create confusion rather than assist with planning as intended, as exemplified in this account given by a district administrator:

We get a state board reg. changing evaluation. . . . [The reg.] makes perfect sense. You have a school improvement plan that's like the umbrella—sets up the goals and objectives. You . . . then [have] . . . each certified person in the building, creating a professional growth plan as to how they're going to help that school meet those goals. And then you set up your professional development plan so that the teachers can be trained in the things they need to help the school reach the goals and objectives . . .

The time line is totally screwed. The professional development plan is due in the state the 15th of April. . . . There's no deadlines on the other two [plans]. We're sitting here frantically trying to do professional development plans. . . . But schools don't have to have their school improvement plans done until July and obviously, the professional growth plan can't be done until after that's done.

. . . I just spent time, last week on the phone, with the director of [professional development] saying, "The time line's messed up." "Oh, how's that?" And I explained, and he said, "I hear you. I understand what you're saying." I said, "Then do something about it." "Oh, we're not supposed to do it" [whispered] . . .

It's almost like [the department's] in the way. . . . The time line is messed up. The department could fix that. Pretty easily, it seems to me.

Third, detailed process regulations make those schools that are complying with the spirit but not the form of the law automatically out of compli-

ance. The clearest example of this is the school-based decision-making requirement. The KERA legislation says that school-based councils must have
a 3-2-1 composition—three teachers, two parents, and the principal, who
chairs the council. While the legislation does allow for alternative structures
with the approval of the State Board of Education, the Board has been reluctant to approve alternate structures, and only 11 have been approved in
the state. A number of schools in the state that have been practicing shared
decision-making for some time have opted not to join the state's SBDM
program until required in 1996 due to the strict 3-2-1 requirement. For
example, one district with over 100 shared-decision-making schools has only
3 schools in SBDM. Said the superintendent:

> When the new Kentucky Education Reform Act was being devel-
> oped, we worked hard to frame these regulations in a manner where
> we could work within them without totally changing current reform
> efforts. We had developed 131 [shared-decision-making] schools on a
> voluntary basis. . . . Our shared-decision-making model did not fit the
> legislated 3-2-1 model. In all probability, ours needed more unifor-
> mity and guidelines. Our schools individually decided how they . . .
> wanted to govern themselves. Because of this, the schools really had
> ownership and were very committed to the school decision-making
> model. However, parents and classified personnel did not have the
> same representation or involvement that teachers did and, in this
> sense, the state mode helped our schools and districts rethink their
> model.
>   The legislation that was developed and passed into law basically
> created site based councils made up of three teachers, two parents, and
> one principal. If a school wished an exception to this model, they
> could petition the State Board of Education. One of our schools was
> allowed to be an exception to the 3-2-1 model. The rest all had to
> conform.
>   As [KERA was] . . . implement[ed], a tug of war ensued. I think
> a little more flexibility on the part of the state could have avoided
> some ill feelings. . . . Legislators had built our staff's morale and expec-
> tations by coming to visit the schools in our district to see first hand if
> shared decision-making really did work and how it worked. Then,
> when the legislators' confidence was high from seeing reform work-
> ing, they developed the governance regulations, and these very regula-
> tions forced those who were leading the reform effort to change in a
> drastic way. This seeming arbitrary action lowered morale and delayed
> implementation of a very good reform movement.

The reason that the State Board for Elementary and Secondary Education has been reluctant to approve alternate SBDM models is because it is afraid that alternative models will be used to limit parent influence in the SBDM process. While this is a valid concern, I still question whether making these schools automatically "out of compliance" is the best way to encourage the implementation of SBDM.

Finally, detailed process regulations punish the schools and districts trying hardest to implement the law, as was well articulated by a school principal:

> I think [the department is] overregulating. And I think if they would just concentrate on the accountability piece, then if the schools aren't doing it then deal with that. . . . But what happens when they create so many rules, . . . [is that] the districts who do well keep the rules and it causes more work on them. And the districts . . . who have . . . traditionally been a problem, they don't keep the rules anyway so it just . . . it ends up creating more and more work and difficulty for those who try to do the job right. . . . If you're producing what [you're asked] for then [you] shouldn't have to [be] regulate[d] as closely.

Practitioners paint this picture of KDE overregulation with many qualifications and nuances. This is not a simple story of department staff wearing black hats. Even the department's most vociferous critics acknowledged that department staff were working hard to implement the KERA reforms, although some did think that they could work "smarter."

A number of practitioners said that they thought KDE staff listened to them, although some said that they were not sure what happened to their advice once it was given. Some who thought the department listened were the same practitioners who said the department was overregulating. Teachers and administrators who sat on state-level advisory committees felt that department staff listened to the committees' advice, and teachers said that the department did solicit input into how to improve the assessment process at regional training sessions. One district administrator said that she thought the department's willingness to listen would improve over time:

> Yes, [I do think the state listens to their advisory committees.] Very much so. And . . . I think they may be opening up a little bit more. I mean it may . . . be a phenomenon of they feel like KERA's been up and running long enough that they have some baseline data. . . . And so I think that they may be soliciting more input now and may continue in that pattern. I think it may be a little too early to tell how

much input they're going to solicit from now on . . . In the beginning, . . . I don't think it was solicited because they simply were not
willing to change or tamper, which was the word, "tamper" with anything. [They were] afraid that the whole thing would come unraveled.

Some practitioners said that they were beginning to see the KDE as
more of a support agency and that there was more of a team, as opposed to
an "us versus them," feeling when they worked with department staff. According to one teacher:

[Our interaction with the state department has changed.] . . . When
we raise issues or questions they're very honest in saying they don't
know or they hadn't thought about that . . . I've been to three meetings since June and I've heard: "We hadn't considered that. We didn't
realize this was going on." Or "we didn't know this was happening.
What do you suggest? What has been your experience?" So we're
finding a lot of honesty and openness and admitting that . . . they
don't have all the answers. Where before, I think a lot of teachers
looked at the state department as this guru that had all the answers. . . .
And that's not true any more. We realize they're trying to work out
the kinks and they know that those decisions they've made are not
fool-proof.

Some practitioners also understood that KDE staff were probably having
as much difficulty changing their role as the teachers themselves. One district
administrator explained that the department had not become the service center that she envisioned with the passage of KERA but that she thought there
were reasons for this. First, she felt that the KDE's own internal change
process had created conflict about the proper role of the department. Second,
she felt that department staff received mixed messages from the legislature
and perhaps from the Commissioner's office about what their role should be.
The department's internal change process combined some new staff with
some old staff, creating competing internal conceptions of the agency's role.
In addition, the KDE is charged by the legislature with both service and
monitoring, two tasks that this administrator saw as mutually exclusive. She
concluded:

And so consequently, I don't think there's a lot of clarity about what
their role is supposed to be and how they are supposed to function.
And for that reason, we get a lot of uneven relationship. . . . There's
no consistency in quality of . . . [service] delivery . . . from the state department yet.

A superintendent pointed out that while it was easy to point fingers at the department, practitioners have to change their ways, too, if their interactions with the KDE are to be helpful. He said that the Commissioner was frustrated by the fact that practitioners often do not avail themselves of the department's process created to address the problem of practitioners receiving either no or conflicting answers. This superintendent tried to clarify the KDE's process with his staff:

> Last Thursday I sent out . . . [a memo saying] "If this happens to you, call so-and-so, or Fax so-and-so, and give them an overview. And it will be followed up on immediately." Well what I find is that two things are happening. In some instances they're not getting the answer that they wanted, so then they try again. The other is, in fact, what they say is true but they're afraid that if they tell someone that they're getting the runaround or whatever, that that person's job may be in jeopardy. And my comment to that is "well, if that person isn't doing their job, then maybe their job should be in jeopardy." So . . . I see this as part of the growing up process. . . . Sooner or later people have to start using the system as it was designed.

Finally, some practitioners pointed to outside forces that they felt, in part, caused the KDE to overregulate. One outside force mentioned was the time lines established by the legislature and the State Board, as was articulated by a district administrator:

> In the meetings that I've been in when unreasonable timelines have been discussed, it's been more or less a case of this is a deadline that's been established by the State Board or by the legislature. We have no other choice. . . . So that's why I said in many cases, [the department is] caught between a rock and a hard place as well. . . . It's a case of the whole thing coming all the way down from the top and saying that this is going to take place in a short period of time.

The second outside force mentioned was Kentucky's larger culture of over-regulation. Said one district administrator who was not a Kentucky native:

> Kentucky is, in my opinion, the most overregulat[ed], legislated educational system I've ever seen in my life. They regulate to the nth degree. And the iron[y] is that the reform act was to give considerabl[y] more local control. And I heard . . . a presenter [who] said, "Now that we've gone from the most regulated to the least regulated system in the country . . ." and I almost fell out of my chair laughing! . . . And

to me, it's a sign of mistrust within the state, and it's not just in education. They regulate to the nth degree . . . in every facet of Kentucky
government.

The picture of the KDE painted by practitioners was mixed. Practitioners did strongly express the view that the department was overregulating and that this overregulation did not match the purpose or spirit of the
KERA reforms. They did not, however, depict the department as an evil
ogre, and indeed, many practitioners empathized with KDE staff.

The department, however, was also not depicted as an agency fully designed and functioning in support of KERA. While it does seem that the
KDE listens to individuals and tries to respond in individual areas such as
adjusting assessments, it is quite clear that the paradigm shift away from rules
and oversight to accountability for outcomes envisioned by complex reform
has not occurred.

From the department's perspective, there are reasons why this paradigm
shift has not fully occurred. A director explained that while the KDE wants
to give schools and districts some freedom, it also is concerned that many
districts do not have the capacity to use that freedom wisely. Large dollar
amounts are attached to programs such as ungraded primary and professional
development, and the KDE wants that money to be wisely spent on high-
quality efforts. Requiring districts and schools to plan is one way of trying
to ensure that these expenditures are carefully considered. According to
the director:

> I don't mean to say all the districts have low capacity, but there's
> enough of them where we do have to pay attention to how they're
> spending the money. [So,] . . . we're saying, "we want you to be more
> accountable. We want you to take charge. But at the same time, you
> don't have the capacity to do it. . . . So this needs to be carefully
> thought through. And in the past, things haven't always been carefully
> thought through. . . . So . . . we're going to give you some freedom
> here, but you've got to do the good thinking about it and then you
> get the money."

Building Local Capacity

Building local capacity to implement the KERA reforms is a daunting
task that the KDE is working hard to accomplish. Kentucky is a large state
with low capacity in a number of areas. A practitioner who has worked with
the KDE on professional development commented that the issue of scale
raised enormous challenges. One of these challenges is simply the geographic

distance that needs to be covered. Another is the difficulty of marshaling the necessary resources for professional development on this scale, including finding the needed number of quality people in each area.

A director in the KDE further elaborated on the capacity problem, saying that basic organizational processes—such as having established agendas and recording minutes of meetings—were lacking in many districts. He continued:

> Most of the state, I think, is at a very low level to help themselves. . . . For most of the districts in the state, [for example,] the textbooks have been the curriculum at best. . . . There have not been standing curriculum development committees. I mean there's nothing to develop. You just buy the book and then you do it. . . . And then when you start moving into notions like collaboration . . . in a state that is very top-down, very authoritarian in terms of male/female relationships, all of that. . . . Things that some of us have taken for granted as just the way you do business—you bring people together and you have decent organizational structures that predict what's going to happen . . . —is new information for a lot of these people. So some of the developing capacity is even at that level of just how do you organize yourself to do some work? You don't even get to talk about the work you do yet, but just how do you organize it?

That the KDE is working hard to emphasize building local capacity is reflected in the comments of its staff. As the same director said:

> The department is shifting from the role of providing technical assistance . . . and doing staff development, to that of building capacity in the state. . . . For example, we have one program . . . [in which a] consultant . . . here [used to do] the training, . . . the setting up of the orientations, [and] was very instrumental in coordinating the leadership team. . . . We now have an expanded advisory committee that we're turning over more and more decisions to. . . . We . . . [hope that] in the next 6 or 8 months we will be either completely out of it, or only in a modest advisory capacity so that that [project] is actually running itself. [We're] setting structures up that build capacity for the state to take care of its own needs, instead of having the department do that.

Other examples of KDE capacity-building are that another division is running trainers' summits in which trainers from consortia and other professional groups are brought together to learn how the KDE is doing training on certain issues, and still other divisions are using clusters of trained practitioners to do training in local areas.

The KDE is taking a number of steps toward the goal of building capacity in addition to those cited above. The first of these steps was to establish eight Regional Service Centers around the state that are charged with capacity-building, as explained by the director of one of the centers:

> We can do professional development but if we do . . . we prefer to do a train the trainer type of approach. . . . If we know there's a school district that's interested, for example in cooperative learning, then we try to find others that . . . have that same interest and help build your capacity as a local district. So that we would want to come in and train someone within your district that could serve from this point on as your trainer, your cooperative learning expert. We seek to . . . help build the capacity that way.

The KDE is also attempting to help schools learn how to gather data and make plans to further their change process. An example of this kind of help is the "School Transformation Plan Guidebook" (KDE, 1992, Draft) provided to all schools and districts to assist in the development of school improvement plans. While some might find the "Guidebook" somewhat mechanistic and overly detailed, for example, there are suggestions for what the cover page and the table of contents should include, it is a serious effort to encourage schools to engage in data-based, strategic planning.

In addition, the General Assembly has provided time to schools for additional professional development through the enactment of House Bill Number 596. This bill allows school districts to use up to 5 instructional days or 30 hours during instructional days for additional professional development for teachers for the 1992–93 and 1993–94 school years (Boysen, Thompson, & Matthews, n.d.). Schools must develop a plan for the additional days, and the additional training must be selected from a list approved by the KDE (Boysen et al., n.d.).[30]

Not all districts have taken advantage of this opportunity. Practitioners in one district visited did not feel that they could tell taxpayers that students would have five fewer instructional days when they were paying more than ever before to support education.

Finally, the KDE has provided numerous professional development opportunities for practitioners, taught either by KDE staff themselves or by district and school personnel trained by the KDE. This training was regarded as adequate or better by the majority of practitioners interviewed, with a higher number of teachers in the early adopter district reporting that they had been sufficiently trained, probably due to greater amounts of district-initiated training in that locale. Teachers especially appreciated the fact that many of the state trainings were done by currently practicing classroom teachers.

The majority of professional development offered, however, is within, rather than across, KERA strands, leaving integration to be done by practitioners at the local level. Offering professional development structured in this way can create confusion, as described by one district administrator, who suggested restructuring the KDE as one way of achieving better integration:

> What the state has done so far is . . . these one-shot deals. "Send us five people and we're going to talk to them about the curriculum frameworks or the thresholds," or something like that. . . . That piecemeal [training] . . . is confusing and convoluted . . .
>
> My professional development piece would have begun with reorganizing the department differently. So that instead of being in . . . these corridor teams, SBDM, primary school, . . . you would have been in . . . an integrated team. . . . And then your job would have been to provide the integrated professional development that a district needs. Now there comes a point in time that just the integration alone is not enough. . . . At some point [a] teacher has to develop specific expertise [in certain areas. So the professional development would also have to allow for that] . . .
>
> [But] what I see happening is [that the KDE is] taking discrete specific kinds of things and doing them piecemeal. And nobody quite understands . . . how . . . that all fit[s] [together] in the whole.[31]

A historical example of the confusion created by this piecemeal approach to professional development was given by this administrator: At one point, the Division of School-Based Decision Making was telling practitioners that school-based councils could decide whether or not to include kindergarten in their primary school, while at the same time the primary school team was saying that kindergarten inclusion was mandated by law. This discrepancy created considerable confusion at the local level.

The need for capacity-building in Kentucky is enormous, and the KDE is working in many ways to meet the need. These efforts, however, are not yet as integrated as the reform efforts envisioned for local schools.

Practitioners' Advice to the KDE

Practitioners most frequently offered four pieces of advice to the KDE: 1) reduce regulations and paperwork; 2) be clear; 3) slow the time line; and 4) know the schools and districts you're working with. Advising the KDE to reduce regulations and paperwork is an extension of practitioners' views that they are being overregulated. These views have been amply discussed above.

Asking the KDE to be clear reflects practitioners' feelings that they receive mixed messages from the department—something that one-third of practitioners interviewed cited as a problem in implementation. One principal, when asked what advice he would give the KDE, said:

> The department needs to communicate [internally]. . . . If I call down to Frankfort [the state capitol] and ask a question, I should either be told, "I don't know but I'll find out," or if I get an answer it should be the same answer that I get from other people, especially within that same office. And that's definitely not happening.

And an administrator from another district said:

> Frankfort . . . tell[s] us . . . what's afoot in terms of the new policy or the new regulation, and it changes on a monthly basis. . . . And [we] ha[ve] to be very flexible! And . . . very cautious then about how we . . . interpret that for the school district because what was true today, may not be true in two weeks. And so we may tell a school, "you need to get started doing it this way," and then come to find out in two weeks they didn't need to do that at all. So we have gotten very cautious about how we interpret it and how we explain it to schools and how fast we act on any of it.

Asking for a slowed time line is an extension of practitioners' feelings that they are being asked to do too much too fast and cannot adequately focus on any one piece of the reforms. These feelings stem, in part, from the KDE's numerous reporting requirements, which bring us back to practitioners' initial advice to deregulate. A principal said that this was his best of 14 years as principal because he saw so many good things happening in his school, but that this was also his worst year because of the ungodly amount of paperwork to be done in addition to attending workshops and all the other work required to get reform started. He continued:

> We had to write a primary plan. . . . They didn't read the things and if they did read them, they didn't understand what they were reading because I got [ridiculous] comments . . . back. . . . Now it's "You've got to write a professional [development plan]. You've got to write goals and objectives, you've got to have a plan for your school." . . . That's all good . . . but they're pushing too much, too hard, too fast. We're

trying to get the primary school going here. We're trying to get SBDM going. . . . We had like a two-week period to get our professional development plan going. It's just . . . they're coming down too much, too fast, with goals and objectives and plans and so forth. . . . [The biggest challenge I face in implementing these reforms is] just keeping up with the paperwork.

Practitioners also expressed concerns about the human costs of these pressures. Said another principal:

They have outlined [a good plan], I think, . . . but they're going to have to give us time to do [it]. . . . [Our] superintendent has said . . . several times, . . . and I've heard this from [others], too, . . . that they don't think anybody has ever worked any harder than . . . [Kentucky] teachers and administrators have . . . in the last two years. . . . [But] everybody is feeling overwhelmed . . .

Another . . . concern I have is that if we keep pushing at the same rate, a lot of [good] teachers . . . are going to retire or quit or burn-out. . . . And we've tried to get that across to the department of education and I think they realize that, too. . . . Some of [the people leaving] probably ought to get out. . . . But I think we're maybe forcing some out that probably . . . should stick around for a while . . . because they're skilled people. . . . On top of teaching their regular course load, [teachers] are working on committees now for the site-based program. They're having to take training for portfolios and develop portfolios as a part of the process. And I think portfolios are great except that that needs to become a part of the process and not something added on to. Over time this will all work out but . . . we're going to have [to help people survive in the interim].

Even in their frustration, however, at least some practitioners understand the KDE's dilemma, as one teacher said:

If I had the opportunity to give the department advice . . . on one level I would probably say, . . . "Slow down with the reform." But at the same time, I know that sometimes if you don't just wipe the slate clean that . . . it will never get done. . . . You still have a lot of [educational personnel] . . . out there . . . saying, "I've got 7 years to retirement. I am not going to do this. I'll do the minimum that they can let me get by with and that's going to be it." There's no doubt in my mind if you look at our test scores, . . . that . . . [something] had to be . . . done [about education] in the state of Kentucky. . . . I just . . . like

I said I feel overwhelmed and I'm very frustrated. . . . So for me personally, I wish they'd slow down! [laugh] [But] I can understand . . .
why . . . they are trying to push this and say, "We mean business and it
is here to stay."

Asking the KDE to know the schools and districts it works with reflects
practitioners' beliefs that context matters. Much of this advice was backed
by the complaint commonly heard in all states that department of education
staff have not been in the classroom for 20 years, do not understand the
current conditions of teaching, and therefore cannot understand the difficulties of implementation. While these complaints probably still have some
validity in Kentucky, one must point out that a number of the new KDE
staff have been hired directly from the field and consequently probably do
have a better understanding of the context of schooling than previous staff
members.

The more interesting turn of the "know us" advice, however, took the
form of "know *us*." Practitioners giving this advice were emphasizing the
importance of understanding not just the context of schooling writ large but
also the context of schooling in the individual schools and districts with
which the KDE works. These practitioners linked the importance of know-
ing individual schools and districts to the need for what some have termed
"differential treatment"—basing the treatment of districts on their individual
needs and performance, as opposed to global uniformity (Fuhrman & Fry,
1989). One principal said:

My advice to the state department of education would be that you
need to look at the districts you're dealing with in different ways. . . .
Some of the advisories that come from the state department to a district that is made up of three schools . . . are very different when you
need to carry them out on the grandiose scale [of our district]. . . .
And so I . . . think [it is] . . . very important to . . . know what audi-
ence you're speaking to and make sure that you understand the logisti-
cal problems that the districts can have.

Another principal said:

[I would tell the department] that schools need a tremendous amount
of help and support and understanding and assistance, and to be as responsive [as possible]. . . . And that it's important that they understand
. . . the dynamics that are operating inside of given schools. And it's
not all the same. The schools are not the same in [our county] as they

are in [other counties]. So different kinds of needs in different places makes one hell of a complicated job for them.

SUMMARY AND ANALYSIS: THE CASE OF KENTUCKY

This case shows that the culture and organization of the Kentucky Department of Education is reflected in the culture and organization of the implementation of KERA. In this case, the reflection of the KDE's culture and organization onto the reform implementation process has led to a process that is in many ways incongruent with the philosophy on which KERA is supposed to be based.

The parallels between the culture and organization of the KDE and the culture and organization of the implementation process are numerous. The first and most striking parallel is that department activities are rule- and oversight-driven, as is the implementation process of schools and districts. Department staff report that decisions are made at the top, allowing for little individual initiative and creativity. Extensive reporting on activities is required. Practitioners report that they are overregulated and that extensive reporting on process is required.

This regulation of process is incongruent with one of the tenets of the KERA philosophy—that schools will be held accountable for outcomes but will be given flexibility to achieve them. The case demonstrates the costs of this overly regulated implementation process. It slows the actual accomplishment of the work, both by putting the importance of accountability over the importance of implementation and by creating confusion in the implementation process.

Even more importantly, however, the compliance environment created by this overregulation threatens the commitment to reform of the very schools and districts working hardest to achieve it. This threat to commitment comes in two forms. First, schools working within the spirit but not the form of the law are judged to be out of compliance. Of the 131 shared decision-making schools in the early adopter district, only three are SBDM schools by the state's definition. And yet it seems probable that if the desired outcome of SBDM is to have genuine shared decision-making in schools (as opposed to simply a shared decision-making structure), some of the early adopter district's shared decision-making schools may be much closer to the desired outcome than some of the state's SBDM schools, simply by virtue of the fact that they have been at it longer and achieving true shared decision-making takes time.[32]

Second, commitment to reform is threatened by the fact that the most conscientious schools and districts, those working hardest to implement the reforms, will probably also be those that take the state's reporting requirements most seriously. This means that reporting requirements will be most onerous for the very schools and districts that need them the least, causing increased resentment and perhaps eventually reducing overall commitment to reform.[33]

When KDE staff are not themselves allowed flexibility in their work, as would seem to be necessary in order to successfully implement complex reform, it is hard to imagine how they can give much flexibility to schools. The implementation environment is not conducive to the deregulation called for by complex reform.

The second parallel between the culture and organization of the KDE and those of the implementation process is segmentalism at both levels. Even though restructured, the KDE is still organized into bureaus, offices, and divisions, and these are divided along the strands of the reform—School-Based Decision Making has its own division, for example. While some work takes place across offices and divisions in the department, the implementation process still reflects this segmentation. Two examples of this segmentation in the implementation process are the mixed messages from the department that practitioners cite as problematic and the fact that the majority of the department's professional development provides information on single pieces of the reform. Neither the structure of the KDE nor its delivery of services to schools and districts is integrated.[34] Integration of the structure of the KDE and, assisted by that structure, integration of the delivery of services would better help schools and districts to implement complex reform.

The final parallel is the feeling, present at both the department and local levels, that time lines are overly short. Department staff feel that they are "running as fast as they can" and that there is no time for reflection. This press to meet deadlines in individual areas of the reform discourages KDE staff from working with colleagues in other divisions and was one reason people cited for the department's organizational flux. At the local level, practitioners feel that the reforms are "too much too fast," leaving them insufficient time to actually implement the changes required. A study published in March 1993 found that primary level practitioners spent an average of 33.85 out-of-school hours per month on KERA reforms in addition to the time they would have normally spent on teaching and other professional duties. Intermediate-level practitioners spent an average of 26.98 hours per month, middle/junior high school–level practitioners spent an average of 20.1 hours per month, and high school–level practitioners spent an average of 18.86 hours per month (Kentucky Education Association & Appalachia Educational Laboratory, March 1993, pp. 19–20). People are concerned about burnout and as a consequence fear that the system will lose good practitioners, not just those who are uncommitted to their work.

At both levels, the goal of accomplishing the work on time is given precedence over human factors. In the KDE, there are metaphors of battlefields and sacrifice. At the local level, the metaphors are not as brutal, but concerns persist about fatigue and about how much can be accomplished in a given period of time without sacrificing quality.

In addition to the principal story line of the case just described, there is an important subtext that should not be forgotten: Practitioners want KDE staff to spend more time in schools for two reasons. First, they believe that spending time in schools will give department staff a better understanding of the current conditions of schooling and the difficulties of reform implementation under those conditions. Second, practitioners want someone in the department to know their *individual* schools and districts so that they may be treated differentially. The starting points and contexts of schools and districts differ, they argue, and the state's reform approaches need to take these local differences into account.

The fact that practitioners see the need to have KDE staff in their schools for these reasons only reinforces the principal story of this case: What happens within state departments of education influences the local implementation of school reform. In this case, the culture and organization of the KDE are in many ways impeding the full implementation of KERA.

UNDERSTANDING WHAT IS HAPPENING IN THE KDE

Because of their effect on reform implementation, it is important to understand why the current conditions in the KDE exist. I address this question by examining the actions of the department through two different lenses.

The Narrow Lens

If one views the KDE as a closed system (Peters & Waterman, 1982, p. 91), what is happening within the department is something of a puzzle. On the one hand, the KDE seems to have positioned itself to become a very different type of organization—one that is less bureaucratic and centrally controlled. It was given the freedom, in fact the mandate, to restructure in ways that would allow it to implement the KERA reforms more effectively. It was allowed to hire outside the state's personnel system, enabling it to pay competitive salaries, and was encouraged to do national searches to attract the nation's "best and brightest" to Kentucky. One commissioner described the KDE staff as follows:

> What you have is like a gathering of eagles here. . . . And everyone is used to being self-directed, self-motivated, high achievers, hard work-ers, visionary. . . . So we have people in roles here several levels maybe below what they're used to working in.

The KDE, faced with the uncertain and demanding task of managing complex reform, reorganized itself to align with the areas of the reform and hired the most competent people it could find to engage in its new work. By taking these steps, it seemed to be equipping itself to operate more like an innovative organization and less like a traditional bureaucracy. To be sure, the formal structure was still bureaucratic and hierarchical, but the informal structure was intended to be more flexible and matrix-like. Highly skilled staff were hired a number of levels down in the organization to allow for decision-making to be moved to lower levels and for creativity to be encour-aged at all levels—characteristics needed if an organization is to engage in uncertain, innovative work (Burns & Stalker, 1961; Kanter, 1983, 1988). It is true that a number of the newly hired staff lacked knowledge of state government and of the Kentucky context. They did, however, have pro-grammatic expertise and, one would assume, the ability to learn about what they had not experienced.

On the other hand, however, it appears that the KDE is more centrally controlled than ever before. The KDE does not seem to be profiting from its earlier positioning because its decision-making and control structures are preventing it from benefiting from the competence and expertise of the per-sonnel within it.

One possible explanation for this paradox is that it is indicative of an organization in transition—it takes time for trust and fluid working relation-ships to develop. While this explanation may have some merit, there is no evidence to suggest that the current decision-making and control structures are viewed as transitional, and there is still a perceived lack of trust in the department, even after more than a year and a half. Said one consultant, "The trust level is not built up there yet. You know, the commissioner hired me back and all that kind of stuff, but he's not sure really if he can trust me 100%." A director, when asked if this level of oversight might be transitional, said that while he could not say that it would be maintained forever, he could definitely say that it had remained consistent over the time he had been in the department.

Another possible explanation for this paradox is that it has more to do with leadership style than with conscious consideration of how an organization faced with this type of implementation task should be run. There is more support for this view. People who worked with Boysen in California said that his style there was also top-down and characterized by micromanagement. A KDE director said:

> I think there's that style, there's that approach, there's that sense of you know how to . . . lead this organization. . . . And then [the organization is shaped] by virtue of who is picked at the next level . . . [and] how their style interfaces with the top style . . . I'm not so sure, in thinking about it . . . how much of it is . . . "What would make this organization learn most?" . . . versus how much of it is, "This is my management style. When I come in, this is the way I know how to [run an organization]."

Viewing the KDE from this closed-system perspective provides some possible explanations of why the activity of the department diverges from that predicted by the framework. Given the complicated environment in which the department operates, however, this closed-system perspective alone is overly simplistic.

The Wide Lens

If one views the KDE as a more open system (Peters & Waterman, 1982, p. 91)—considering the organization in its context—its behavior is less puzzling. The task of implementing the reform act given to the KDE and its Commissioner has from the outset been difficult at best and impossible at worst. Many of these difficulties are the result of the context in which the KDE is situated.

First, according to a participant in the creation of KERA, the new KDE started out at least a year behind in implementation. KERA was passed in April 1990 and went into effect that July. Commissioner Boysen was not hired until January 1991, and the reorganized KDE did not open until July 1, 1991, a full year after KERA was passed. Worse still, while the new department opened on July 1, some of the staff were not actually in place until September, meaning that the KDE was even further behind.

As a result of this chronology, the Commissioner was faced with an almost superhuman task. He had only six months to design the new agency. Simultaneously, he was supposed to be familiarizing himself with Kentucky, working with the new State Board of Elementary and Secondary Education (also reorganized as a result of KERA), managing the old department, and making sure that KERA was being implemented in accordance with the time lines. And he was to accomplish all of this with a staff who were wondering whether or not they would have jobs once the reorganization was completed.

Also as a result of this chronology, many of the pieces of the KERA reforms had to be started prior to hiring the staff who would ultimately be in charge of them. New leadership came in partway through the design and implementation process, and because these people were new, they often did not even understand the law. Said a former member of the governor's staff, "I made more trips than you can imagine to Frankfort to explain the law to new people." He said he did this gladly, but that it just showed how much people had to learn when they came on board.

Second, the KDE is under close scrutiny and active oversight from the state assembly and its Office of Education Accountability (OEA). The Kentucky Supreme Court, in *Rose v. Council for Better Education, Inc.,* ruled that the General Assembly was responsible not only for establishing Kentucky's new education system but also for monitoring it on a continuing basis. The assembly created and passed the massive reform act along with a close to $1.3 billion biannual tax increase and is taking its charge of monitoring the reform very seriously. According to a member of the Commissioner's staff:

> In the stewardship of KERA, there are certain aspects that [the legislature is] watching very closely, where I think that is essential. So I'm not saying that it's necessarily good or bad, but it really makes for a different dynamic when they're that involved in almost . . . month-to-month operations. . . . Our interim committee structure is very, very strong. . . . [And] they take it seriously—particularly the education committees—and they expect to be briefed and to understand what's going on and to facilitate that if they can.

The Commissioner meets with legislators regularly regarding the intent of the law and sets the direction for the KERA strands based on this intent. (This practice was instituted after the KDE was criticized early on for interpreting the law in ways not intended.)

The OEA, an investigative arm of the legislature created through KERA, is one of the strongest aspects of legislative oversight of the reform. Housed in the Legislative Research Commission, the OEA is intended to be the "watchdog" of KERA, monitoring implementation to ensure that it is done correctly. In addition, the OEA is empowered to conduct covert investigations of school districts suspected of activities such as waste and mismanagement, corruption, and nepotism. However, once the OEA has compiled evidence against the school district, the file is given to Commissioner Boysen to act upon in conjunction with the State Board. This relationship to the OEA puts the Commissioner in the position of removing superintendents and board members in corrupt districts (accompanied by much media attention) while at the same time saying that his department should become more of a service and support agency.

It should be noted that Commissioner Boysen, while acknowledging that some might see these enforcement and service roles as contradictory, does not see them that way himself:

> The way I feel about it is that if we don't take care of the relatively small minority of problems like this it will undermine the whole reform, including the credibility of local boards of education. So it's like a rotten apple thing, if you don't get that out of there you . . . will spoil the rest of them. So I feel that I can believe as I do very strongly in local boards of education and remove one or two at the same time . . . to save the rest of them.

The KERA legislation also established time lines for the various reforms, and these time lines are short given the magnitude of the change required. Consultants to the legislative task force that created the bill predicted that implementation of these reforms would take 6 to 10 years. The legislation provides for six years, and all indications are that legislators intend to hold the KDE to these time lines. For example, early on, the old department interpreted the legislation regarding the ungraded primary program to mean that implementation would begin in 1992–93 and be fully phased in by 1995–96. Key members of the legislature said that that was not their intent and clarified that intent, through legislation, in the 1992 session. The ungraded primary program must now be fully implemented by the 1993–94 school year.

Commissioner Boysen does not object to this level of scrutiny and oversight from the legislature:

> People say, "Don't you mind that you get such close scrutiny from the legislature?" . . . But my attitude . . . is [that] as soon as . . . [the legislators] stop feeling . . . that they have a right to probe into this thing and [KERA] is theirs . . . that's when our trouble starts because then it's ours and not theirs. So we, as much as possible, try to keep their interest up and not complain about their inquiries and . . . most of the time they have good questions.

While this level of legislative interest is positive in many respects, it also seems likely that this level of scrutiny, particularly combined with the short time lines and the fact that the department started out behind, increases the feeling that all of the KDE's actions must be carefully controlled and that people cannot be allowed to make mistakes. This press for perfection, combined with the relatively immovable time lines, translates into intense pressure to get it done—the "it" being implementing the law.

This pressure in turn affects the internal culture of the department. That this is true is demonstrated by the metaphors used by the KDE staff to describe both KERA and their work to implement it. Some staff used war-like metaphors. For example, a commissioner said, "We keep our people under the gun." He later said:

> Strategic planning and all that [is] . . . a systematic way of doing
> things. And it's good if . . . the foundation . . . has been laid, the train-
> ing is there. But, you . . . must allow for flexibility in the plan . . .
> [and] informal linkages. . . . [But] we're under so much pressure. You
> know when you're being attacked by the enemy, you don't have time
> to do informal linkages. We get attacked all kinds of ways. . . . We
> might be in the foxhole together but the only thing we do is fire back
> and try to keep from getting killed and cover up. You know . . . you
> need to learn how to shoot this way. And you can't teach me how to
> fire my gun in a foxhole.

A director used a different metaphor that also conveyed the pressure within the KDE. In talking about the decision not to institute Total Quality Management throughout the department, he said:

> [The Commissioner] feels that people are too busy trying to imple-
> ment the reform to have a reduction in our productivity to learn this
> new process. . . . There is a real sense of the freight train is right be-
> hind us and we can't stop to learn how to do it more efficiently be-
> cause there is going to be a J-curve drop in our productivity.

The Commissioner seems to increase rather than decrease this internal pressure. When asked how the Commissioner was apt to adjust divisions' action plans, a director said,

> In the school council area, for instance, if the legislation says, ". . . All
> schools will have [councils] by 1995." He may move them up and say,
> "We'll have them by 1994." . . . That's pretty much a valid generaliza-
> tion. . . . He would be apt to speed [things] up.
>   I think he conceives of his role as CEO partly as . . . keeping a
> fire under people to get the thing accomplished. And he wants to
> stretch, doesn't want any drift. And if you think you can get to an ob-
> jective in 18 months he'll say, "You can do it in 12 months." And so
> you redo and you end up doing more. Sometimes it's a little harried

and hectic and the stress level is a little high sometimes but there's so much involved in the reform. If we tried to do it sequentially we'd never get there. You have got to do it all at the same time and he's got to push it.

Third, the KDE is faced with competing expectations and definitions of what they should be doing, perhaps most importantly for this analysis, from the legislature and the state bureaucracy. The KDE was told to reorganize through the KERA legislation, but then, because the legislated reform did not change the larger state bureaucracy, the KDE was told to maintain a traditional organizational structure with the lines and boxes understood by the state personnel agency. The legislature did not allow the department to establish its own personnel system despite the Commissioner's requests that this be done, due to its concern that the state personnel system would be undermined. The legislature did, however, recognize the need for the KDE to pay competitive salaries in order to attract the "best and the brightest" and so granted it some increased hiring flexibility.

Probably the most difficult set of competing demands and expectations that the KDE faces, however, are the demands that it on the one hand deregulate and give increased autonomy to schools, but that it on the other hand hold schools strictly accountable for implementing the KERA reforms and accounting for all dollars spent. These competing demands come from the legislature. According to the Commissioner:

> We identified some roles for the department as a part of our planning process. . . . One of them was to shift from a regulatory emphasis to a facilitative emphasis and . . . we keep working on that. We get a lot of pressure from the legislature to be more regulatory. . . . The extended school services program would be an example. . . . That's money . . . to be used to help students at risk of school failure outside of the normal school day. . . . [And the first year,] for example, some district was using 20% of it for instructional materials. Now nobody said it couldn't be used for instructional materials but the chairman of the appropriations and revenue committee [got] that information and . . . [got] very assertive . . . "Get out there and stop them from using that money for that purpose." So all of a sudden we get some limitations and guidelines in those areas [and] more reporting requirements . . . for all districts.

And another commissioner said:

> The focus of this department is to be more service oriented and less prescriptive. Now I have to tell you that the distance between that

statement and reality is pretty broad. And the reason why, I guess . . . is that the legislative process still occurs and that in legislation most often as it deals with the DOE, will be a statement. "The commissioner, or the State Board for Elementary and Secondary Education will promulgate administrative regulations to do X." So when superintendents say, "You're too regulatory," . . . our response is, "We are trying not to be too prescriptive in that regulation but the regulation still must occur because it's driven from the legislature."

This commissioner went on to describe testifying before a legislative subcommittee and being told that legislators were hearing that the KDE was too prescriptive, directive, and regulatory. She assured the committee that she and other KDE staff would like to be less prescriptive. She also pointed out, however, that when the department is asked questions such as, "How are you going to monitor this program? Where is that regulation that's called for in the statute? How are you assuring that this money went for the best purposes?" by the legislature and the Office of Education Accountability, the result is the institution of new regulations and processes to address these concerns. She continued:

> So we had a good conversation about it but I'm not sure they . . . understand [the dilemma]. . . . So . . . we're really caught in th[e] middle, . . . saying, "We're service focused, but here's your regulation on this." And . . . school people are saying, "Doesn't fly."

Yet, despite the frustrations of these competing demands from the legislature, the leadership of the KDE also understands the dilemmas that legislators face. The Commissioner, when asked if he'd had a dialogue with legislators about these competing demands, said:

> No, we haven't had this dialogue you mentioned. And it's a good point. It's occurred to me but . . . I didn't really have a solution . . . I . . . [could understand] their interest in making sure that these programs were fully implemented. . . . And I didn't want to tell them . . . [with] the primary program [for example], "Don't have a regulation."

And the other commissioner cited above said:

> And I don't know that there is a way to get out of [this dilemma], frankly, because . . . I understand the legislature . . . I'm not being critical of the legislature when they say, "We have constituents who say this is the biggest tax increase that's ever been passed. We've basically

not revolted but tell us what's happening with our dollars." And so the only way that all of us in our past paradigms know how to do that is to count something. Require it to be reported and then count it. So that's a real dilemma.

What explains these conflicting demands from the state legislature and bureaucracy, particularly when it was the legislature that crafted the KERA reforms that called on the KDE to be less regulatory and more service-oriented? First, the legislature is not a monolithic entity. The fact that KERA was passed does not mean that all legislators have identical understandings, desires, and interests in the reform. It seems safe to say that there are differing interpretations of what the role of the KDE should be under KERA.

Second, it may be that while KERA changed the vision and role of the KDE on paper, it did not change the societal myths that help to define both the structure and function of the organization. Meyer and Rowan (1991) argue that "the formal structures of many organizations in post-industrial society dramatically reflect the myths of their institutional environments instead of the demands of their work activities" (p. 41). The authors further argue that organizations have to reflect these myths in order to maintain legitimacy in their environments. As applied to the KDE, this would mean that while KERA did change the work demanded of the department—it is now expected to implement complex reform—it did not change the societal "myths" or understandings of what a department of education should look like and how it should do its work.[35] KERA also did not fully change the societal understanding of how schools should be held accountable for their work.

Support for this argument comes from three areas. One, although the KDE was told to reorganize in order to better implement the reforms, nothing was done to allow it to escape from the societal myths of what a government agency should look like that are embodied in the state personnel system. Two, although the KDE was told to become more service-oriented and to deregulate its control of schools, legislation pertaining to education still begins with "The State Board for Elementary and Secondary Education shall promulgate regulations such that . . ." Three, although at least some legislators apparently want the KDE to be less regulatory and the legislation calls for holding schools accountable for achievement outcomes, there is still an understanding of accountability in evidence that calls for counting inputs and instituting process-level controls. There has not been a complete shift from the process to the product notion of accountability, either in the legislature or the department itself. As it stands now, the societal myths or understandings of what a department of education should look like, be like, and do, held to some degree both within the legislature and the KDE, seem to conflict with the kind of institution that could most effectively manage and implement systemic reform.

PRELIMINARY CONCLUSIONS DRAWN FROM THIS CASE

It seems unlikely that the KDE will be able to change dramatically without its surrounding environment changing, either first or simultaneously. According to Scott (1992b), "From an open systems point of view, there is a close connection between the condition of the environment and the characteristics of the systems within it . . ." (p. 85). KERA has not changed the understandings that exist in the environment of what the department should be and should do to a great enough extent to change the norms, values, and incentives that influence the operation of the KDE. The department is faced with conflicting demands from the legislature, but demands for regulation and accountability are still of paramount concern, making it unlikely that the KDE will evolve into a more service-oriented, flexible organization any time soon.

At the same time, however, organizations can also act to change their environments (Scott, 1992a, p. 145). The responsibility for bringing about change does not rest solely with the legislature and the larger state policy context. It is at least possible that KDE leadership could influence legislators' thinking about both what is to be accomplished through KERA and how best to accomplish it. This might be done through more in-depth conversations about the contradictions between outcome-oriented policy and regulatory or process-oriented policy. Through such conversations, it might be possible for both KDE staff and legislators to come to new understandings about how best to accomplish their work. They might be able to move beyond the regulatory paradigm that both sides are operating in to varying degrees and come to some consensus about new principles to guide operation on both sides.

These new principles might take the form of a lens, framework, or set of guidelines used to examine action before it is taken, in order to ensure that that action is in line with the larger goals of KERA.[36] For example, the legislature, before passing any new legislation regarding education, might ask itself, "Does this law allow the KDE and the schools to pay attention to outcomes, or does it require them to engage in a monitoring process? Is this law designed to enable all schools to further their change efforts, or is it designed to prevent a small group of schools from abusing some aspect of the reform? And if it is the latter, is there another way to accomplish this objective, other than passing a law that will require more regulation for all schools, including the vast majority that are not abusing the system?"

Investing the time and effort required to hold these conversations and bring them to fruition would probably require a broader task definition than seems to be in operation in both the KDE and the legislature. Implementing complex reform, in this case KERA, is about more than simply implementing the law, which quickly translates into meeting the legislated time lines. It is also about implementing the law in such a way that deep and lasting reform takes place throughout the system. Achieving such deep and lasting reform requires changing fundamental beliefs, values, and approaches to the work in all parts of the system, including the legislature and the KDE— much more than mere compliance and adherence to time lines. Unless this broader task definition is understood and accepted, there will probably be little investment in conversations working toward new paradigms of how the state should interact with schools. Without reaching these new paradigms, the likelihood of achieving true complex reform seems slim.

CHAPTER 4

Vermont

Vermont is a small rural state of 576,000 people. The state's public school system has 285 school districts—grouped into 60 supervisory unions, 399 schools, and just over 8,000 instructional staff. The system serves more than 100,000 students, 98% of whom were white in 1992.

Supervisory unions are groups of small districts that collectively hire a superintendent and other central office staff. Larger school districts in Vermont hire their own superintendent. Because of the supervisory union relationships, Vermont has only 60 superintendents serving its numerous districts.

Vermont is a state of average wealth and above average expenditures in education. In 1992, per capita personal income was $17,800, ranking the state 26th in the nation. Per pupil expenditure for 1992–93 was estimated to be $6,944, sixth in the nation. The state's estimated average teacher salary was $35,726 for 1992–93, ranking it 20th in the nation. The state paid an estimated 31.6% of the cost of public education in 1992–93, ranking it 46th in the nation.[1]

THE HISTORY OF THE VERMONT REFORMS

Vermont has a strong history of local control that is reflected in its governance of education. The state has historically played a very weak role in education, with the majority of decisions being made at the local level. Prior to the recent reforms examined here, for example, there was no state-level assessment of student achievement.

Establishing Goals and Designing Assessments

When the State Board of Education hired Richard P. Mills as Vermont's new Commissioner of Education in 1988, they were looking for "a reformer who was capable of moving [the] system," according to one Board member. There was a confluence of factors supportive of reform in the state at this time, in addition to the arrival of Mills and the support of the Board: Numerous national reports on the need for education reform had been published in the 1980s; Mark Tucker of the National Center for Education and the Economy had addressed the state legislature the previous year on the need for school reform; and both education committees had new leadership.

Mills convinced the State Board and legislature of the need for state education goals soon after his arrival and established a participatory process involving hundreds of people to discuss what those goals should be. Four goals were established through this process:

Goal 1: Vermonters will see to it that every child becomes a competent, caring, productive, and responsible individual and citizen who is committed to continue learning throughout life.
Goal 2: Vermonters will restructure their schools to support very high performance for all students.
Goal 3: Vermont will attract, support, and develop the most effective teachers and school leaders in the nation.
Goal 4: Vermont parents, educators, students, and other citizens will create powerful partnerships to support teaching and learning in every community. (Vermont Department of Education, 1992–93, p. 4)

Discussions on the need for a state assessment system took place during this same time period. Developing an assessment and accountability system was one of the first assignments the State Board gave Mills, and this was again done in a consultative manner. The state was moving toward a traditional standardized test, but the reactions from teachers at public hearings were profoundly negative. According to Mills:

> In the middle of the third hearing we finally got the message when one teacher said it makes no sense to teach writing through a process approach and then test the result with multiple guess. We stopped, and rethought the whole thing. (VDE, Appendix 1, 1991a)

The Commissioner and his staff met with approximately 100 people in groups of 20. Each discussion was framed along these lines: "We've spent $X million, we know where every penny went, but we can't really tell you how kids are doing. How do you feel about that?" People invariably said something needed to be done; more information was needed. "Well, should there be a test?" "Well, not a multiple choice test." "What then? What do you want to see?" According to Mills, he and his staff listened hard during these conversations and then came back to people with draft assessment plans for reaction and critique. This process led to the state's current assessment system. In writing, this assessment system includes a portfolio, best piece, and uniform test. In math, it includes a portfolio with a letter from the student explaining the collection, and a uniform test.

Designing a Strategy to Reach the Goals

The Vermont Department of Education's (VDE) *A Green Mountain Challenge* outlines 13 initiatives designed to achieve Vermont's 4 education goals (VDE, 1991, September). Together, these initiatives work to transform all of Vermont's education system and have many of the elements of "systemic reform" (Smith & O'Day, 1990), including curriculum statements, assessments aligned with those statements, redesigning teacher preparation and certification, and encouraging additional decision-making at the school site. The initiatives include developing a Common Core of Learning—"a statement of knowledge, skills and values Vermonters say all students should achieve through their education" (VDE, 1991, September, p. 9); continuing to refine and provide training for the state's three-part assessment system; raising professional standards for educators through establishing Local Standards Boards, a professional development consortium, and redesigning the approval process for teacher preparation programs; reinventing schools for very high performance; deregulating schools for high performance; and re-structuring the department of education. In addition, there are initiatives intended to restructure special education, strengthen school-to-work transitions, build collaborative initiatives with human service agencies, promote full literacy in the state by the year 2000, and increase family and community involvement in education. A year's worth of activity under each of these initiatives is outlined in the *Challenge.*

A new *Green Mountain Challenge* (VDE, 1992–1993) was written for the subsequent school year. This publication assesses the current status of each initiative, restates its ultimate goals, and again outlines a year-long time line (VDE, Appendix 1, 1991a).[2]

Participation in Vermont's education reforms, for example, the state's assessment system and the use of the Common Core of Learning, is largely voluntary. According to Mills: "We avoid mandates and rely instead on a convincing case, continuous training, and the opportunity for all to participate at the design stage" (VDE, Appendix 1, 1991a).

An Analysis of Vermont's Policies

How likely is it that Vermont's education reforms will transform the state's school system with the goal of dramatically increasing student achievement?

On the one hand, as already discussed, education reform has historically brought about only incremental change in schooling and has generally failed to change the core processes of teaching and learning. Given this history, a prudent person would probably predict that Vermont's current efforts also would fail to transform teaching and learning.

On the other hand, Vermont's reforms do have some strengths that may make this reform effort more successful than those of the past. First, the reforms attempt to be systemic—to change all pieces of the system in coordinated ways so that they work as a coherent whole. The proponents of systemic reform predict that such coherent policy will succeed in changing teaching and learning where other policies have failed because the various component policies—for example, curriculum, assessment, and teacher training—will align with one another. These aligned policies will send clear messages and incentives that will prod and assist teachers in changing practice in the desired ways.

Second, the participatory process used in the development of the state's education goals, assessment strategy, and Common Core of Learning is designed to develop consensus and commitment. There is evidence that consensus was successfully developed, at least at the top of the system. The State Board of Education has adopted the education goals and approved the department's strategy for reaching them. The legislature passed a resolution in support of the goals and gave the department funds to design the assessment system. When the Reinventing Vermont Schools program was initiated, schools were challenged to reinvent themselves not only by the VDE, but also by the State Board of Education, the legislature, the governor, and key members of the business community. Developing consensus at the lower levels of the system is an ongoing effort, the success of which is more difficult to measure.

Third, the success of the policy depends on the state's developing a convincing argument and communities coalescing around that argument. These community coalitions in turn strengthen the argument because they will pressure schools to participate in the reforms and work to continually improve their performance. For example, when asked how schools judged to be weak through the assessment process would be responded to, a VDE staff member said:

> The first thing that happens next, we hope, is that those schools and communities have a real conversation about what the findings are, and that they decide to take some action. I mean . . . we haven't put any stakes on this stuff except reporting results. And then the Vermont environment, that seems to be pretty high stakes. I mean there are a lot of people who are uptight out there. . . . But . . . what I hope happens is that those communities will really start pushing professional development to a much greater degree in their schools. And . . . we're not only going to identify weak places, we're going to identify strong places. And if we can get the two linked then I think that we'll be much better off.

This dependence upon persuasion, while also a potential weakness—the policy is "toothless"—is a potential strength because participation will be the result of commitment and consensus rather than compliance with a mandate. It is commitment that is required for practitioners to examine and improve their practice on a day-to-day basis.

Fourth, the policy is flexible. While the VDE has made itself very publicly accountable for achieving its goals, none of the time lines is in legislation. This lack of legislated time lines at least potentially can give the department the space to make the intelligent adjustments that are bound to be needed during implementation. While the VDE will need to work to maintain the support of the Board and of the legislature as these adjustments are made, it will not have to work through the legislative process.

There are, however, potential weaknesses in this policy. While commitment to a convincing argument may ultimately be stronger than compliance with a mandate, the argument alone may be insufficient to sustain practitioners' change efforts as the novelty of reforms such as portfolios wears off and as the grind of implementation sets in. The state's argument will have to become increasingly convincing in order for practitioners to persevere during the inevitable "rough spots."

Maintaining political consensus through these rough spots will also be challenging. While the sluggishness of the legislative process may impede the making of intelligent adjustments in legislated reform efforts, it also can slow the undoing of those efforts. Any loss of consensus and support may be felt more quickly in Vermont's purely consensual environment.

In addition, Vermont's policy approach puts great weight on leadership. Leadership is important in any reform effort. In an environment like Vermont's where so little is formalized, however, and where numerous people interviewed attributed the building and maintaining of consensus to Commissioner Mills personally, the importance of leadership is even greater. While it is true that there has been broad public participation in many of the reforms and that the VDE is restructuring to better implement these reforms and is working collaboratively with numerous other institutions and players, it remains to be seen whether such participation and collaboration will be sufficient to institutionalize Vermont's reforms beyond the political life of Mills, their leader.[3]

Finally, successful implementation will require that numerous changes take place in the Vermont Department of Education and, ultimately, in schools and districts.

THE VERMONT DEPARTMENT OF EDUCATION

The VDE has a staff of 147 people—130 of whom work in K–12 and adult education—and occupies the third and fourth floors of a four-story office building. The department, led by Commissioner Richard Mills (Rick) along with the State Board of Education, in many ways has spearheaded Vermont's education reform efforts. The VDE and the Board led the state in its goal-setting efforts and the development of the portfolio-based assessment process. As these efforts evolved, so did Vermont's larger plan for complex change.

As part of this change, the department began to restructure itself, and this restructuring is still very new. The department's Restructuring Team began meeting in 1989, and the department's vision statement was developed in a department-wide participatory process. The Restructuring Team then developed a mission statement and plan for the department's reorganization. All department staff were assigned to teams midway through the summer of 1992, and all staff received introductory training in Total Quality Management (TQM) that same summer. People started working in their new configurations in the late summer and fall. The VDE is in transition when examined along many of the dimensions of the framework of predicted changes, as is described below.

Changes in the VDE's Work[4]

Product Development, Assistance, and Training. The substantive work of the VDE is in the process of changing considerably. The department's Public School Approval (PSA) process—in which schools are evaluated against specified inputs such as program offerings, certified staff, and library collections—while still in existence, is being substantially redesigned to allow for more flexibility and attention to outcomes. In addition, PSA coordinators report that the process has already been made more flexible in interpretation because they are now more attentive to the spirit, as opposed to the letter, of the law.[5] Teacher certification is still course credit–based, but the licensing process will be revised in the fall of 1994 "to reflect current research on best practices and authentic educator assessment" (VDE, 1992–93, p. 16).

There is increased emphasis on product development in the VDE. Two particularly strong examples of this are in the areas of assessment and curriculum. Assessment systems have been developed and are still being refined in the areas of writing and mathematics. Assessments are given in the 4th and 8th grades. The writing assessment consists of three parts for every student: a portfolio of different types of work, a best piece chosen by the student from the portfolio and accompanied by a letter from the student explaining why this work is his or her best, and a uniform assessment for which all students write based on the same prompt. The math assessment consists of a portfolio with a letter from the student explaining the collection, and a uniform assessment consisting of a multiple-choice section taken from the National Assessment on Educational Progress (NAEP) and a uniform prompt.

Committees of Vermont teachers, working with representatives of the VDE, developed the portfolio and best-piece portions of the assessment system, determining what the portfolios would include and the criteria for their evaluation, and choosing benchmarks from actual student work that demonstrated each achievement level. They also participated in the development of the uniform assessment and developed the scoring rubric and benchmarks for that piece. Outside scorers use the rubrics and benchmarks for scoring the uniform assessments. In addition, these committees have worked with the department in overseeing the implementation of the assessment system and developing networks of teachers to provide training for practitioners.[6]

In the area of curriculum, the VDE is working to develop a Common Core of Learning. Development of the Common Core started with more than 40 community focus forums held around the state, facilitated by department staff, practitioners, and community members. The forums were designed to generate Vermonters' answers to the question of what knowledge, skills, and qualities learners will need to succeed in the 21st century (Gross, 1991; VDE, n.d.-b., p. 4). The Common Core will ultimately consist of five reports describing the learning needs of students in the 21st century, the characteristics of successful learning and teaching, Vermont examples of successful learning and teaching, how communities can use the Common Core, and education systems that work (VDE, n.d.-b., p. 17). The first of these reports currently exists in draft form (VDE, n.d.-b.). In addition, the VDE plans to develop curriculum frameworks that "will contain the best thinking about what students should know and be able to do in particular disciplines or groups of disciplines" (VDE, n.d.-b., p. 15).

In addition, product development has been done in the area of school restructuring. A conceptual framework for reinventing schools has been developed, based on the experiences of schools that received restructuring challenge grants from the department in the fall of 1989 to reinvent themselves in order to improve student learning (VDE, 1991, October). In addition, seminars for restructuring schools are being sponsored by the VDE to allow schools to share effective practices and jointly develop strategies (VDE, 1992–93, p. 9).

There is also increased emphasis on assistance and training at the VDE. Training in the portfolio assessment process is being provided by networks of teachers established by the portfolio committees and the department. In addition, training directed at whole-school change has been and is being provided through the department's Reinventing Vermont Schools initiative, as well as through its initiatives sponsored by the New American Schools Development Corporation (NASDC) and the National Science Foundation

(NSF). Training for school change is also provided through School Development Institutes jointly sponsored by the department and the University of Vermont.

Overall, the VDE is working to shift away from providing assistance to individual teachers or portions of schools, as its curriculum consultants have traditionally done, and toward assisting whole schools or teams of practitioners interested in change.[7] These efforts are focused on building capacity throughout the state, as will be described further later in this chapter.

Rapidly Changing Work. In one respect, the work that the VDE is now engaged in does change rapidly. Some staff members make repeated references to "rebuilding the airplane while you're flying it," and the department's reform initiatives have evolved over time. In another respect, however, the VDE is faced with a demand for more long-term work than ever before. The accomplishment of reform initiatives that the department is now engaged in demands sustained, focused effort. Development of both the assessment system and the Common Core has already taken a number of years and will take still more. School restructuring does not happen quickly and will require prolonged effort on the part of both the department and the schools.

Engaging in sustained work presents new challenges to an organization that in many respects has historically had a crisis orientation, as was explained by one team member:

> We're definitely transitioning. We have initiatives we want to work on and some, like the Common Core, are moving very well. Unfortunately, we also tend to be crisis oriented and in trying to respond to the immediate demands of the legislature, governor and public, the procedures and processes for a quality organization sometimes go out the window.

Other staff members also spoke of the difficulty of finding the time needed for developing new programs and processes when they were still responsible for the jobs they had always done.

These comments demonstrate that in many respects the VDE's work still has not changed sufficiently to accomplish its reform objectives. The department is reaching a turning point where more far-reaching change will be required, as one manager explained:

> We didn't blow [the department] up [as some states have done]. We're going gradually, but we're coming to the point where there might be a small explosion because . . . there's not enough resources and not

enough of [staff] time. They're getting very frustrated but their frustration is, "The leadership is telling me to do new things and . . . I don't have time to do those. . . . Remember this other job I have?" . . . [And we haven't said to the staff,] "Don't you get it? Can't do that any more . . ."

And some of the things . . . [were very] specific in terms of the person's job title and . . . really the expectations and agreement under which they were originally hired, [so] it's going to be a radical change. . . . Unless we do this right process wise, [it could be viewed] as a violation of all that.

Changing the VDE's work to this extent has to be done carefully, not only for the staff's sake, but also so that the new work of the department is supported by practitioners in the field, as the manager went on to explain:

This is the point, too, where there's a part of the field that will possibly provide resistance to our change. . . . [As we've cut positions] in the last 2 or 3 years . . . [practitioners have] mount[ed] very effective letter writing campaigns and they . . . tell their legislators, ". . . The department of education [is] pushing the stuff on the Common Core and statewide assessment. I just want somebody that's going to help me teach social studies better." So you know the inertia of the status quo is . . . very powerful. So we've got to do this in a way so that the people here believe in where we're going, understand it, feel comfortable with the role that they will play and can communicate that to the constituencies that they relate to.

Making these changes in the department's work will require what one team member said was "talked about from time to time" as "planned abandonment." He explained that employing "planned abandonment" means ending what the Commissioner refers to as "wildcat operations":

[Wildcat operations are] those little services that some of us have fallen into the habit of providing that there really [aren't] funds for. . . . "It's not in the budget but you're doing it anyway. You say it doesn't cost anything but it took 40 hours of your week in the last three months, and [a] number of postage dollars. It's wild cat. And where is it in the plan?" So the dream is that we'll have planned abandonment. "No, we don't do that any more."

Ending the wildcatting may be difficult because, to an extent, it goes against human nature as well as the norms of the department, as the team member further explained:

I'm not sure that I've seen it in practice yet . . . I haven't said "no" yet to anybody . . . I'm so delighted when somebody asks my advice or wants me to come to a school. It's so flattering that if you can possibly do it, you're going to do it and . . . you're paid . . . to have that attitude.

The work of the VDE has changed, and staff are faced with new demands. Individual job descriptions and individuals' conceptions of their jobs need to change still further, however, before these demands can fully be met.

Organizational Capacity

The Vermont Department of Education has been faced with declining resources for a number of years. The number of VDE staff shrank from 173 in 1990 to 147 in 1992. Of that 147, 17 were in schools of practical nursing education, leaving 130 people working in K–12 and adult education. The department was asked to cut a further 5% from its budget for the 1993–94 fiscal year. Doing more with less is a refrain frequently heard in the department.

At the same time, however, the VDE is working to build capacity through building external linkages and partnerships and by pursuing outside grant funding. The VDE's total capacity, then, is the sum of its internal capacity—supported by state, federal, and grant funding—and the additional capacity generated through its external linkages. An internal document of the department states: "We have fewer staff but so many more partners that our total resources are actually greater than in the past" (VDE Transition Team, 1992, June 4, p. 4). The department's external linkages will be discussed in the capacity-building section of this chapter. The department's internal capacity is addressed here.

Skilled People. Commissioner Rick Mills saw "great opportunities" in the department he entered because he was able to fill a number of existing senior vacancies—including those of Deputy Commissioner, Director of Special Education, Legislative Liaison, and Counsel—with top-flight people, and he saw many strong staff members already in place.

Still, there are impediments to having the people with the necessary skills in the department. First, the overall number of staff in the department is declining, as has already been described. The VDE's capacity, measured in sheer numbers, has been reduced.

The second impediment is that it is difficult for the VDE to attract people with the desired level of expertise due to the low salaries dictated by both fiscal and civil service constraints. Entry-level consultants—positions for which the department wants people with master's degrees and 7 to 10 years of school experience—are paid less than $30,000 for year-round employment. Classroom teachers can earn an equal or greater salary for working only 180 days a year. In addition, working conditions in the department are not all that they could be. Support staff has been cut substantially, and there are few private work spaces, making concentration difficult.[8]

State and national interest in Vermont's education reforms offsets this second set of impediments somewhat, because the work is compelling to many educators. A team member of the VDE said that the collaborative nature of the work was very different from the isolation of the classroom, and that many Vermont teachers, university people, and policy people were willing to work on the reforms even if they didn't leave their jobs to do it. This was the first time numerous Vermont teachers had the opportunity to engage with their colleagues within the state and nationally around their work.

The department receives a number of calls from people out of state who are interested in working on the Vermont reforms, although one manager joked that they tended not to call back after they learned the salary level. The department did succeed in luring one expert away from another state, negotiating a higher than normal salary by arguing that the individual had extraordinary expertise and was currently making significantly more money. Still, this individual had to be paid with federal funds to make this solution workable and also had to take a pay cut.

The third impediment to having needed staff in place is how existing staff currently define their jobs, as was explained by one manager:

> We don't have the personnel to do all that we want to do. That's clear. But . . . there's a lot of brain power in [some existing groups, that needs to be used differently]. . . . They're high powered people. . . . And they could change [what they do] because the regulating that they've been doing needs to transform anyway. . . . But there's still a lot of people who say, "I can't do that. The federal government won't let me." Without ever really having pushed back that envelope [to] see if, in fact, they will be able to do that. . . . In some instances they may be right, but in some instances they're not. They're just not taking on the challenge . . . of looking at it and saying, "Yeah, . . . it does affect these students. I can do this."

The VDE has some talented staff in place and has attracted others in some instances, but the incentives of salary and working conditions are lacking.

Ongoing Learning and Training for VDE Staff. The VDE recognizes the need for training department staff. An internal department memo, outlining why change in the department was needed, stated: "We have not provided for our own professional development, but we have presumed to prescribe it for others" (VDE Transition Team, 1992, June 4, p. 4). The department has committed substantial time and resources to training all staff in Total Quality Management (TQM)—an approach based on organizational commitment to quality, data-based continuous improvement, and service to customers.

The TQM training was done under the auspices of the National Alliance for Restructuring Education, of which Vermont is a member.[9] The Alliance offers training in TQM to its sites, done by loaned executives from the Xerox Corporation. These executives trained a transition team in the VDE, consisting of the Commissioner and deputy, the department's four directors, some members of the department's restructuring team, and a couple of other staff members. This transition team, assisted by Alliance consultants, in turn trained all other members of the VDE. The transition team is currently charged with overseeing the further implementation of TQM in the department.

All VDE staff attended four days of TQM training during the summer of 1992. The goal of this training was to change the culture of the department to one that better fits with its new structure and goals.[10]

There is also some evidence that other types of training and capacity-building are available to department staff. One example of this is the Middle Grades Resource Team. As described by one team member:

> [The team is] interdisciplinary. . . . It's a model in the . . . department that's new. . . . The idea behind having th[e] team is that [the middle grades] project is for two years. There was no middle level consultant in the state department. . . . [So] the capacity need[ed] to be built. . . . And . . . it would be better to do that in a broad based kind of way than to do it with one person. [And] one of the commitments we made [as a group] was . . . that we would regularly do our own professional development and so we all, for example, . . . went together to the New England League of Middle Schools conference.

A member of another team said that the department has been "pretty generous" in making possible some special professional development that he wanted in a given area. He said that such requests were honored most of the time if kept "few and far between."

Even though there is a commitment to training, however, there are areas in which it is lacking. Many staff members said that the TQM training provided good exposure to the principles but that more follow-up and practice were needed. One manager who entered her first management position with the department restructuring said that new managers received no training before being "thrown into this." This lack of training is at least partially due to the press of meeting the ongoing demands placed on the department, as was explained by another manager:

> Ideally, if we had been able to forget some of the external happenings in the last 3 or 4 months and concentrate more on the team development and training ourselves in practicing the organization, we probably wouldn't have to worry about some of th[e potential conflicts that I foresee between internal and external managers] coming up. But at the same time we've been reorganizing we've also been dealing with internal and external things . . . that have not allowed us to have that type of an experience of working together. We've had . . . one day . . . so far where . . . both [the] internal and external [managers] spent time with [a consultant] to work out . . . the management team. . . . It would have been nice to have been able to have several of those by this time but it's [probably] not . . . realistic . . . to expect that that could happen, because life keeps going on.

Necessary Infrastructure.   There is unanimous agreement that the infrastructure necessary to give VDE staff the information they need to make data-based decisions about the education system is lacking. While the financial data that the department has is in relatively good shape, according to one manager, everyone agrees that other data on schools are inadequate. Said another manager, "Our data is bad—sloppy, piecemeal, incidental." The department does not have much of the data it wants, and much of the data it has are inaccurate and virtually inaccessible. Another manager said that the department had been collecting staff data from schools for at least 12 years and had never looked at it or reported on it:

> For at least 12 years these people were sending in these forms and when we got serious about it last year, . . . we actually [couldn't] report on it . . . because . . . when we finally looked at the reports [we] were getting an awful lot of teachers named Mickey Mouse. Because [practitioners] said "This form is crap. Why should I bother?" And if they weren't openly goofy about it, they just marked in whatever boxes and didn't take any time with it so the information was useless and probably the information we've been collecting for the last 12 years was useless.

Thinking has begun about what kind of information is needed by the department and by schools. One manager reported hearing again and again that schools wanted information on what other schools were doing and who they could contact to receive further information. He said that he and his co-manager hoped to interview schools in the middle of transformation and ask them what they would like included in school profiles. Ideally, he envisioned that such information would be placed in a database that would be accessible to everyone in the department and that could be updated over time. This information would also be easily transferable to a disk so that it could be made available to schools.

Achieving this vision, however, is limited by further infrastructure and capacity issues. First, while the availability of technology has improved in the department—most people have computers on their desks and access to e-mail—many of these computers do not have the capacity to access such a database. Second, the information collection activities of the department are understaffed and other priorities have taken precedence.[11]

Organizational Flexibility and Responsiveness

Hierarchy and Organizational Boundaries. The formal structure of the VDE has changed. The hierarchy has been flattened and may be flattened still further in the future. The original structure of the department comprised the Commissioner's office, four divisions, and nine units, with professional positions including the commissioner, deputy commissioner, division directors, unit chiefs, coordinators, program specialists, and consultants. (See Figure 4.1 for the VDE's original structure.)

The restructured department, headed by the Commissioner and deputy, has six Home Teams: Core Services, Family and Educational Support, Financial Management, School Development and Information, Teaching and Learning, and Career and Lifelong Learning. Each Home Team has an internal and an external manager. Internal managers are "responsible for implementing policies through organizing and managing the financial and human resources of the Home Team," and external managers are "responsible for policy formulation, budget development, and working with [external] partners." Together, team managers "have [the] ultimate responsibility for guiding [the work], setting standards and judging performance" (VDE, 1992, July 28 Draft, p. 1). Within each Home Team there are Work Groups responsible for some specific portion of the larger team's work—Special Education and Curriculum and Instruction are two examples. In addition, there are Focus Teams with membership that crosses Home Teams. These teams may focus either on long-term initiatives, such as developing the Common Core of Learning, or on short-term projects, such as planning for an upcom-

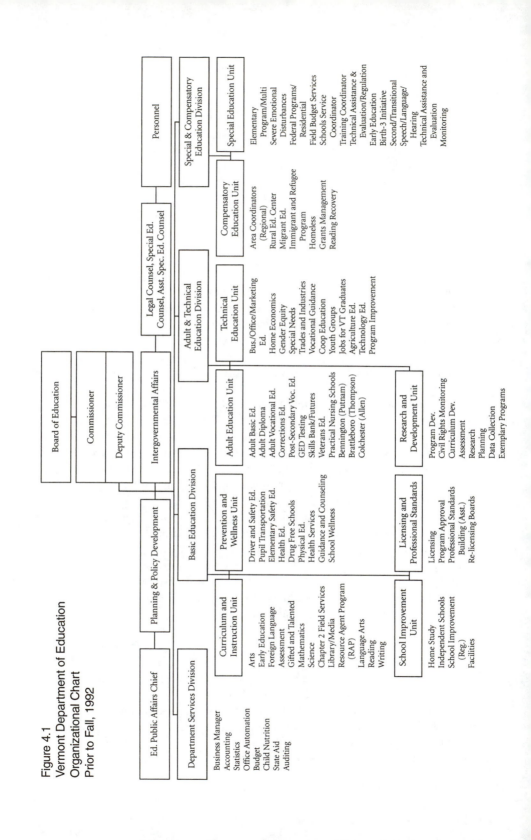

Figure 4.1
Vermont Department of Education
Organizational Chart
Prior to Fall, 1992

ing conference (VDE, 1992, June 18, pp. 10–11).[12] (See Figure 4.2 for the VDE's new structure.)

The department has taken the position that "a manager is a manager"— external and internal managers have the same level of responsibility and, consequently, the same salary schedule. Expectations are identical for managers no matter which Home Team they head. This position is still being negotiated with the state's personnel office. The department is also considering establishing one personnel level for work group and focus team leaders— leaders of smaller units within and across teams—one level for people currently called consultants—who serve on these teams—and one level for administrative staff.[13]

Organizational boundaries are beginning to be crossed in some areas of the department. A collaborative working environment was envisioned as restructuring began, as is demonstrated by the VDE's fourth Operating Principle: "The Department of Education, in all its work, shall insure that all Department efforts will be planned, developed, and implemented within a collaborative process that makes maximum use of staff and field input, talent, and skills," and also in its fifth Core Value: "We model collaboration in our work" (VDE, 1991, November 4, pp. 5–6). This vision of collaboration is being achieved in some portions of the department, as is exemplified in the description of one Focus Team. A team member explained that he thought his Home Team was a little large to really function as a team but went on to say:

> Each of us . . . have individual responsibilities and smaller teams called Focus Teams. . . . [And] that's where I've seen the biggest difference and I would say a very healthy transformation. . . . We now have 6 to 8 people meeting on a weekly basis to share the responsibilities of decision-making, and therefore to share in the ownership of the program. . . . Previously . . . each of us had a one-on-one relationship with [our director]. . . . And each of us would report to him individually and he would make the decisions in consultation with the Commissioner. And our advice might be considered but we wouldn't be part of the actual reasoning process always. . . . So this has been a major and a very healthy change . . . because all of us are invested equally. Each of us understands the reasoning behind what we're doing. And we have a common understanding so that [we're better able to answer questions that come to us individually].

Substantial collaboration has also taken place at the management level of the department. Internal and external managers meet together with the Commissioner and deputy on a weekly basis, and this group has spent the

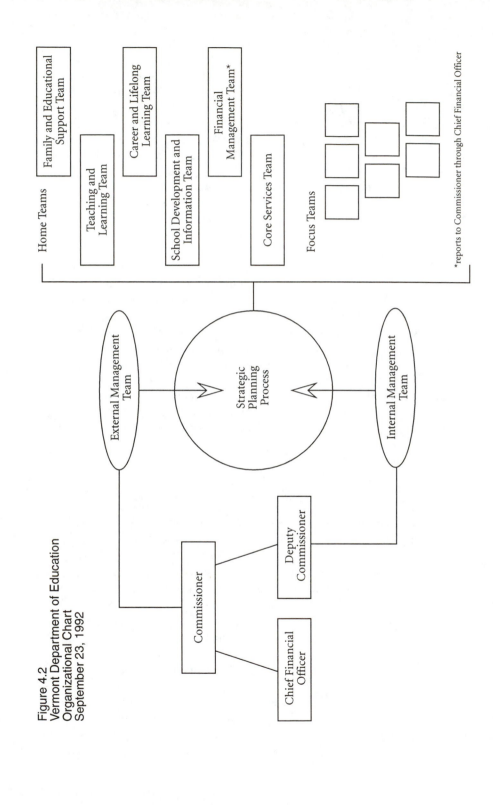

Figure 4.2
Vermont Department of Education
Organizational Chart
September 23, 1992

Home Teams

Family and Educational Support Team

Teaching and Learning Team

Career and Lifelong Learning Team

School Development and Information Team

Financial Management Team*

Core Services Team

Focus Teams

*reports to Commissioner through Chief Financial Officer

External Management Team

Strategic Planning Process

Internal Management Team

Commissioner

Deputy Commissioner

Chief Financial Officer

bulk of its time over the past few months constructing the department's budget for the 1993–94 fiscal year. The governor's office instructed the department to submit a budget that was 5% lower than the budget of the previous year and to follow a prescribed process in making budget cuts. The VDE was asked to describe each piece of its work and zone each of the pieces from one to four, in order of importance. Zone 1 work is the department's highest priority, zone 4 work its lowest. Funding requests were to reflect the priority of the work and whole programs were to be cut; simply taking 5% from all programs was not acceptable.

Following this process gave all managers an understanding of the full scope of the department's work and forced them to prioritize that work relative to the department's mission. The budget-building process was also an exercise in collaboration and consensus-building, as one manager explained:

> It was a totally different ball game [than in the past] because we were redefining what programs we should have. . . . And . . . we used the total quality skills. We met for hours upon hours upon hours and did consensus development. . . . Designing that process . . . was not easy, [because] in the past what it used to be was if you're the division [director], your job was to protect . . . the people in your division . . . as opposed to talking about the department . . . working as a larger entity.

In addition to these two examples, there are also some examples of Focus Teams working together and of Home Teams working together through the creation of Focus Teams. The Common Core and Assessment Teams have shared membership, for example, allowing for cross-fertilization between the two initiatives. And the School Development and Information and Career and Lifelong Learning Home Teams work together through the School-to-Work Transition Focus Team. One staff member also said that there was some information sharing on the various initiatives through e-mail.

Collaboration and boundary-crossing, however, are less apparent in other parts of the department. None of those interviewed thought that their Home Team was completely functioning as a team, and the members of one team universally described it as a team in "name only," although this team was planning to engage in a joint exercise that members hoped would help them begin to see the connections in their work. Other staff members said that they thought the various initiatives of the department should be better integrated—Common Core, Assessment, and redesigning Public School Approval, for example. Still other staff members said that they knew little about the department's reform initiatives, other than that they existed, and that they had little impact on their work.

Many staff members said that the department was in transition in terms of crossing organizational boundaries, as was explained well by one manager:

Links are being made slowly so as to not overwhelm or muddle. . . . We're trying to . . . bring people in at the right time when they have . . . some expertise. So they come in at a point where they know their entrance is helping the team and their inclusion is not just for sort of gold stars but for real purposes because we're all too busy otherwise . . .

We're starting to outreach [to other Home Teams]. . . . There's so much on our plate we haven't had time to pull that agenda forward very much. But I think the stage is set so that it can happen. . . . We are needing to be much more inviting and almost demanding of our invitations [to other teams]. Because if [these reforms are for] all kids . . . there are some real implications of what that means for [the work of other groups here].

Vision, Mission, Decision-Making, and Planning.   The VDE has explicit vision and mission statements. The vision statement of the VDE is as follows:

- We work creatively and collaboratively on issues that affect the education and well being of Vermonters; we are committed to the success of every student.
- We value each other, sharing information, solutions, and success; we challenge and support everyone to be their best.
- Our actions are marked by integrity, courage, and a high ethical standard.
- We embrace the constantly changing environment as an opportunity for leadership and dynamic growth.
- We develop and expand education partnerships to reach the best results, learning from and celebrating everyone's achievements. (VDE, 1991, November 4, p. 4)

The mission statement of the department reads:

Our mission is to lead and support educational transformation in a continuously improving education system.

We work as a partner with educational leaders and local decision-making teams to ensure that every student becomes a competent, caring, productive, responsible individual and citizen who is committed to continued learning throughout life.

To do this we will:

- promote diverse and powerful alliances and networks;
- create statewide expectations and measures of high performance for schools, educators, and all students;

- develop creative solutions to statewide problems;
- build local ability for setting and meeting goals and solving problems;
- provide timely, accurate information to guide state and local decisions;
- enforce essential standards and ensure the equitable distribution of funds so that all students benefit from a high quality education; and
- increase opportunities for effective professional development for all those involved in education. (VDE, 1991, November 4, p. 3)

To an extent, activity in the department is driven by its vision and mission, and there is evidence that it may become even more so in the future. Organizing around a vision and mission is a change from the past. Historically, department staff have tended to work autonomously, with their activities and approaches dictated by personal proclivities and styles, as opposed to an overall sense of mission, as was explained by one manager:

When I first came [to the department] it was a real kind of entrepreneurial environment. There were no real guidelines around what your job was. . . . Consultants would design their [own] job[s] . . . so that you'd have a fellow who established good relationships with [practitioners] . . . And he just really set up this . . . world . . . around him and teachers that he worked with and organizations that he worked with and so on. There was no real central sense of mission or connection in the department . . .

People just kind of moved in with their group. If your groups happened to be the same group, then you'd cross pollinate your ideas. But most of the time you were really working with a group of people that were a separate group. Not unlike say a secondary school, you know where the math people . . . get together and the history people and so on . . . But usually they don't talk to one another or in the past they haven't.

There is evidence that the department is striving to organize around its vision and mission, as well as around Vermont's four education goals. First, the VDE has organized and planned the bulk of its work in a series of initiatives that link to the state's education goals (see VDE, 1992–93). Second, the upper levels of department management are working to "live" the vision. A number of staff members commented that setting a vision, and organizing his own activities in pursuit of that vision, were one of Commissioner Mills's real strengths. Said one manager:

I think definitely Rick provides a vision, works hard to communicate the vision, continually goes back to it, behaves according to the vision . . . [in] how he spends his time. He's very consistent ad nauseam, you know . . . I don't know if anybody could be more focused and dedicated. He does not wander.

A team member said that one of the Commissioner's real contributions was setting the vision in motion—a vision that includes transforming schools and giving freedom to practitioners. He, too, commented on the Commissioner's dedication to the vision, saying: "If an earthquake destroyed the building, . . . knocked it to the ground, Rick would be outside saying, 'Don't forget the vision.'"

Managers also said that the department was *beginning* to live its mission. One example was the process used to develop the department's 1993–94 budget (already described) that required managers to prioritize and fund programs relative to their contribution to the mission. The mission statement was posted on three-foot-by-five-foot poster during this process.

From management's perspective, however, organizing according to vision and mission has not been entirely accomplished: Managers acknowledged that department staff needed to give up some of their current activities in order to devote more time to mission-related activities. Staff members need to stop doing consultations with individual teachers, for example, and instead work with teams of practitioners from one or more sites in order to expand the potential for reform.

Team members in the department were less sure that the department was working according to a shared vision and mission. Some team members, though acknowledging that the department had vision and mission statements, said that the department did not operate in accordance with them. One team member said that the vision talked about how well staff would work together and respect each other's work, and that that had not occurred. "I think it is a shared vision," she said, "[but] we all do it by ourselves." Another team member said that the vision and mission were a source of confusion:

> [The mission statement] was used as the basis for making some decisions regarding the budget and . . . I was told that . . . [the program I work on] . . . didn't fit into the department's . . . mission. . . . And that really surprised me because I think that . . . what we've been doing has been instrumental . . . to helping schools . . . find ways to improve their programs and services for students. . . . So I don't know if it's an interpretation of the . . . mission which I'm not understanding or that people are [mis]interpreting our program. I think it's probably really that they don't interpret our program the way that I interpret our program . . .
>
> I guess that's an area of confusion for me. . . . First of all . . . I

don't feel that I'm personally that clear on the vision and . . . I think
that perhaps there are many others like myself, and then, whether or
not it really affects our day-to-day operation. I think probably everybody in the back of their mind has the best interest of students in Vermont at stake but that there may be different perceptions as to how
that's best accomplished.

Reactions to and interpretations of the department's decision-making
process vary widely. Some staff members believe that the process has become
more collaborative, while others believe that it is more centralized than ever
before. The difference in interpretation seems to vary according to position
in the VDE's hierarchy and also according to which team or portion of a
team a staff member works on. One manager said that the way decisions
were made in the department was unclear at this point and that in the absence of clarity, things tended to gravitate toward the old organizational
model. The external managers "try to elbow the internal managers out of the
way to micro-manage," she said, even though "the point of having internal
managers was to take care of the day-to-day [operations and] to free up . . .
external managers so that they . . . could sit and think about [larger issues
of strategy]."

Most managers agreed, however, that decisions that affected the department as a whole were made either by the joint management team—the
internal and external managers, the deputy, and the Commissioner—or by
the internal or external management groups alone. One manager's description of decision-making at the various levels of the department was representative of the views of most other managers:

> Policy decisions are made pretty much by the managerial team, and
> more specifically the external managers with the commissioner . . . his
> legal counsel, [and] deputy. . . . That's a big part of the policy decision
> loop. There's other policy decisions that would include the internal
> and external managers where it was appropriate. . . . Internal managers
> have been very involved since they've existed. . . . So our management
> team is much larger and broader and brings together the operational
> side and the policy side. . . . A whole lot of [day-to-day] decisions . . .
> are made [between external and internal managers] within an existing
> policy and procedure . . .
>
> [And then teams like] the Common Core team . . . make deci-
> sions regarding activities, events, processes to get publications devel-
> oped, etc. The external managers and the commissioner would be deal-
> ing with the Common Core [around questions like,] What in large
> terms do we expect it to be? How does it fit . . . within the other

things that we're doing? What should it look like? What's the basic overall time line for developing it?

Another manager described the decision-making authority of Focus Teams as follows:

> Most of the technical stuff is theirs. . . . If we have the best people there they certainly should be able to conceptualize. It comes out to us [the managers] more in ways of are the human resources there? Are the financial resources there? . . . It's sort of almost like outward circles. If you make a conceptual decision, . . . the impact of that on . . . financial and human resources, then brings [the managers in].

Team members experience this new decision-making process very differently. Two members of the same Focus Team described broader decision-making powers for their team than had existed in the past. Said one of the team members:

> [Our Focus Team makes] scheduling decisions, training decisions, . . . you know, what would the nature of the training be for the teachers that we're asking to do this, certain financial decisions. I don't want to say we're all powerful but we have a voice in that. Rather than just being told, "here's your budget, work with it," we help to form the budget; rather than be told, "train the teachers," we sit down as a group and we decide what the teachers might benefit most from or what kind of schedule would work for them. And even certain areas of policy, of how will we ask the teachers to assess portfolios. We don't have the power of the decision but we're privy to the reasoning and we may contribute to that reasoning. And in that way, we're more fully invested in what we're doing.

This team, as well as others, also involves external teams of teachers in their decision-making process, as the same team member further described:

> I think it's fair to say that the department . . . set[s] the parameters of the program, and then we go to the teachers and say, . . . "These are the non-negotiable factors. It's going to have to be done this way in order for it to wash with the state board and to be credible to the psychometricians." Within these non-negotiable parameters, "How do we do it? What should be adjusted? Are we overwhelming the teachers? How can we make life a little easier for them?" So that the teachers are feeding back into our policy deliberations an element of reality as

well as the very practical means by which our policies can be delivered.

Members of other teams, however, while saying that they had significant decision-making authority in their day-to-day activities, expressed confusion over how decisions were made in the VDE and described the current process as more "top-down," "centralized," and "bureaucratic" than it had been before. These team members were disappointed by this development because their understanding was that restructuring was supposed to make decision-making less centralized, as opposed to more. Some of these team members also commented that people who had information germane to a decision were not consulted, nor were they consulted or even warned about decisions that would directly impact their jobs. One of these team members, when asked how decisions were made, said:

> I don't know. I have no idea. It's certainly not a group process. I mean we've lost two positions. It was never discussed here. They just announced it at the [department-wide] budget meeting. . . . There was no discussion with the teams. . . . One of them affects me. I had no idea. . . . There was no discussion . . . I heard nothing. I didn't get an e-mail. Nothing to say, "This could affect you." . . .
>
> The [other] part is at the same meeting [Rick] didn't say . . . that they're eliminating two and a half positions but creating others. And I think he owes that to people because the bottom line is they may cut three, two and a half, but they're enhancing one [in another area]. . . They ought to be more fair and say, "We're downsizing or cutting [in this area]" . . . because don't expect me not to know.

Another team member said that he thought part of the problem might be that the perspectives of management and nonmanagement staff could be in direct opposition. He said the Commissioner and deputy were more involved in shared decision-making with the management group than before the restructuring, so that the commissioners particularly might believe that decision-making had become more collaborative. But he continued, "The rest of the folks outside of that management circle . . . are less involved [in decision-making than previously]."

There is unanimous agreement among VDE staff that the department's planning could and should be improved. The department has taken and is taking some steps to improve its planning process. First, it has involved practitioners in the process. For example, teams of practitioners helped and continue to help with the planning and design of the portfolio assessments and the Common Core. In addition, the department had a two-day strategic planning conference in June 1992, with a group that was 60% VDE staff and 40% outsiders—including teachers, administrators, university people, and others. Conference goers broke into small groups around each of the department's initiatives and worked on them using the TQM process—identifying the current and desired states of the initiative and next steps that should be taken. The results of this work fed into the VDE's strategic plan for the following year (see VDE, 1992–93).

While this meeting was seen as a good start by VDE staff, one manager commented that it could still be improved: The meeting moved too quickly at the end and, even though the department got a wealth of information, that information was not sufficiently integrated into the work; meeting participants from outside the department told him on a few occasions that the discussions at the June meeting were not reflected in the final strategic plan. Another manager said that the meeting was a "jump-start" to the strategic planning process but that it had not worked to integrate the various initiatives.

Second, staff have proposed processes to improve the department's strategic planning. One proposal is to implement a meeting and planning process around how the individual projects and initiatives of the department fit together, and the second is to use a quality improvement process to determine how the department's strategic planning can be improved (Perry, Moore, & Walker, 1993).

One manager said that planning in the department is currently out of sync. The budget process used this year was at least linked to the mission, and he thinks it can be truly mission-driven next year. Bringing the public in to assist with strategic planning is in good shape, as are the efforts to involve committees of teachers and others to design different pieces of the work. What the VDE has not been good at thus far is translating the strategic plan into work plans:

> The piece that I think is really . . . missing . . . is . . . moving from a strategic plan into a work plan and then operationalizing it in a systemic way. So anticipating, for instance, in advance how many . . . full-time equivalents of work it's going to take to do a particular project; assigning people to that [and] letting them know.

There is evidence that plans are flexible once they are made. The Common Core was originally supposed to be completed in a few months, but staff and practitioners convinced the Commissioner that taking the time to use the broader-based community Focus Forums was necessary both to get the product right and to ensure its use. One manager explained the process used when time lines were not being met:

If a time line isn't getting met that goes to both [managers] because there's obviously internal and external implications. . . . And then it means you need to . . . sit and talk to Rick or Bruce [the Deputy Commissioner] and say, "You know, this isn't going to work if we're going to have this kind of quality." And the nice thing with the commitment to quality stuff is that we can say, "If you want a quality product this is the time to give us the time we need. Yes, we can rush it . . . , [but then we'll need] the time to do it over." And it's something that Rick has accepted. It isn't something that we say everyday and when we do, he believes it and that's nice.

Norms and Culture. When a group of VDE staff began planning for the department's restructuring, they discussed the need to change both the structure and the culture of the organization. Changing the structure would involve regrouping department staff into teams; changing the culture would involve helping staff to work together in new ways, shaped by the principles of Total Quality Management. According to one member of the Restructuring Team:

We have said to Rick that the reorganization, . . . the legal sheet with the boxes on it, even with the names, is nice, and . . . we think it's a good idea, but, for one it isn't going to work without massive training. And for two, . . . it isn't going to fix anything unless you change how people work. And that's what we see total quality management doing. . . . [Total Quality Management is] a massive part of our undertaking.

Adopting the principles of TQM involves changing the culture and norms of the VDE. The needed changes in the culture and norms of the department were summarized in a handout put together by the National Alliance for Restructuring Education, the group that provided the department's TQM training. The handout summarized the culture changes as follows:

From:	To:
Short term	Long term with successive short-term objectives
Narrow, parochial view	Participative, open style
Internal competition	Cooperation, common missions
Unstructured, individualistic problem-solving	Disciplined, participative group problem-solving

Constant rework	Right the first time
Ambiguous requirements	Systematic approach to customer requirements
Acceptance of status-quo "Not my responsibility"	Commitment to continuous improvement—Everybody's responsibility (VDE, 1991, November 4, p. 16)

Although this list was created by the National Alliance for Restructuring Education to apply generically to state departments of education, the VDE adopted it as its own, and the comments of many VDE staff supported its accuracy.

All VDE staff have received four days of TQM training, and follow-up sessions are supposed to occur, although they have not yet been planned. The extent of the impact of the training to date is the subject of some debate.

There is substantial evidence that the training has had at least some effect on staff work and interaction. The change most frequently mentioned as a result of TQM is that meetings are run more collaboratively and effectively. As one manager explained:

> When [the training] works there's . . . a noticeable difference in how the meetings go and how much is being accomplished. . . . Everybody participates. There's a whole lot more give and take. . . . Historically, . . . directors' meeting[s], for example, . . . were killers. Rick would come in and he'd say, "here's what I want to talk about today." And he'd talk about it and then we would leave. . . . And everybody . . . after the meeting would bitch and moan and complain . . . but nobody would say, "I don't agree with that." Or, "Have you thought about this?" And . . . [no director] would ever challenge something another director said in the meeting because . . . it was seen as . . . undercutting your colleagues in front of the boss . . .
>
> Now, . . . we [use] the quality management. There is a facilitator, there's a time-keeper, there's a reporter . . . there's always a note-taker and there's generally a recorder as well. . . . We build the agenda together and we say, "How much time?" and all of that. . . . And there's a constant flow of conversation and ideas and people will challenge each other appropriately, say, "I don't agree." And they'll challenge Rick. . . . And there are . . . pretty clear expectations at the end of the meeting of who is supposed to do what. And we just accomplish a whole lot more. The meetings are packed with real content and real policy.

Not all staff agree that TQM has had an effect, however, and there is unanimous agreement that the department is far from perfect from the standpoint of TQM principles and that more follow-up training and application of the principles needs to be done. A manager said that while the meeting skills were being used, implementing the principles of data-based problem-solving and being attentive to customer requirements posed a major challenge that the department was still working to address. Another manager said that the management team had "gotten grief" when the Commissioner picked the new managers because the staff—the customers in this case—were not consulted about what they wanted in a manager. A team member echoed this sentiment. She said she had seen no effects of TQM and continued:

> Again, it's supposed to be shared decision-making and you should ask your customers what you think. I'm a customer. No one asks. You know? And I'm not the only one. Has anyone asked outside whether they even like what we did with the new management? Is this really helping them?

Another team member said that the TQM training had only provided initial exposure and that more was needed:

> Unfortunately in a lot of ways I'm not sure that [the department has changed]. I think for some people at least there is . . . more of a sense of needing to work . . . collaboratively, but . . . [they don't] necessarily . . . hav[e] the skills or training to do that. . . . And I think there's also a sense of needing to be more . . . customer-driven in how we act and how we make decisions. But again, I'm not sure that in practice all that much has changed at this point.

One manager described the norms of the department overall and how they are changing:

> First, there are norms surrounding the way we treat different customers. Anything requested by the governor or legislature is priority red. . . . Then, there are [other] pre-existing norms that block restructuring and the use of TQM. One is the norm that the group that you're working in is the group you're working in. Everything else is secondary. There's no norm of looking at or being concerned about what other groups are doing. . . . It's hard to get cross-pollination across the different groups and levels of hierarchy. . . . The project driven atmosphere we're working for is going against pre-existing norms of sticking with your group. And hierarchical roles are *very* important to some people—they define themselves by how many tiers

up and down the ladder they are. This works against group problem-solving.

There are also what I think of as emerging norms. There are glimmers, *just glimmers* in some people that you hope will grow into norms of problem-solving and shared responsibility. And . . . there's [an] ease with which people can say what they believe. We had a team meeting today that was pretty brutal. Not a lot of complimentary things were being said. I think that's okay. We can deal with things out in the open. This norm has always been here, and it continues now in a healthier vein. More people are speaking out.

Whether the norms and culture of the VDE are changing in the right direction is also a subject of some debate. All staff members said that morale was either low or mixed, and many of them said it was the lowest they had ever seen.

A number of team members expressed concern over the way new managers had been selected and over some of the individuals ultimately chosen. One team member said some people already knew that they were going to be given certain management positions before the interview process even started. Some team members said they had no problem with the Commissioner selecting his management team but that if he had already decided, it should not have been presented as a fair selection process open to all applicants.

Some team members also commented that the Commissioner and Deputy Commissioner were less accessible than they had been in the past. One team member said that the Commissioner used to hold "stand-up" meetings to tell the staff what was happening around some initiative or piece of legislation and that he had developed good rapport with the staff through these meetings: "There were some laughs and some jokes, and they really sort of pulled the department together." The team member said that there had been no stand-up meetings since the restructuring. He thought that this was because the Commissioner felt tension in the staff, some people had told him that the restructuring was not going very well, and he was backing away.

Finally, some staff members felt that there was more room for individual initiative in the old department. According to one team member:

[The department's] much more stratified [since the restructuring]. . . .
When I first came to the department . . . there [was] a lot of flexibility.
Rick was accessible. Bruce was accessible. And I did a lot with both
of them. . . . I was a project manager for [one of the new projects,]
which I really loved. . . . I mean I still did my job, but that was in addition and I just loved it. And . . . I felt that . . . Rick, believed in *In*

Search of Excellence where you take somebody who's [got] an interest in [the work] and you give them an opportunity to excel. . . . That's not at all the case [now]. . . . It's been made clear to me that I now have a supervisor which I never had felt before. . . . Rick and Bruce are not at all accessible. . . And so now I do my job. Before I had an excitement of doing other things in addition to my job and I felt I was contributing. . . . [Now] I don't feel there's any trust. . . . Budgets are discussed without [consulting us, and] neither of our managers have ever had any experience in anything [that this team does].

Some team members said they had tried to express their concerns about what is happening in the department. Those who wrote memos to their managers and/or the Commissioner said that they had received no response.

TQM has made some inroads into changing the culture and norms of the department, as is evidenced by the changed meeting structures described. To date, however, these inroads do not seem to have made a difference for all VDE staff. While some staff members, primarily those in management positions, experience the working environment as collaborative and supportive, many staff in nonmanagement positions feel isolated from the decision-making process and key work of the VDE.

Collaborative Connections with Other Institutions

Building strong linkages with outside groups is an explicit part of the VDE's reform strategy. This strategy is new to the department since the arrival of Commissioner Mills, and he is widely credited with creating an atmosphere of collaboration. The department has developed strong linkages with practitioners and groups representing them, such as the Vermont Association for Supervision and Curriculum Development (ASCD) and the Headmasters' Association (now called the Vermont Principals' Association), state universities, the business community, the State Board of Education, and the legislature, among others. These linkages provide the VDE with programmatic advice, programmatic and political support, and increased capacity in a variety of areas. Examples of how linkages have strengthened the department in each of these areas follow.

The Vermont ASCD has worked in partnership with the department (and others) on the state's Common Core of Learning initiative. They strongly advised the department to move more slowly at the beginning of the design process, taking the time to generate ideas and support from the field. Now that this initial groundwork has been laid, they are pushing the department to move the initiative along at a faster pace so that momentum is not lost.

Practitioners and the associations that represent them have also provided the department with programmatic and political support. Teachers who work on the state's portfolio assessment committees, for example, provide the department with school-based advocates for the program. Further, it is hoped that practitioner involvement in the development of the assessments and the Common Core will lead to greater acceptance of the products ultimately developed. Practitioner associations have also provided the department with needed political support. During the 1992 legislative session, when the governor was advocating further cutting the department's budget, the heads of the superintendents', headmasters', and school boards' associations testified before the legislature, asking them not to make the cuts. The association heads argued that practitioners could not afford to have the department lose more staff when the legislature was cutting state aid to schools. The department's support was needed in the field.

Finally, creating strong linkages with outside groups has provided the department with increased capacity for leadership, planning, development, and training. When the Reinventing Vermont Schools program was initiated, challenging all schools to reinvent themselves, the challenge was issued not only by the department, but also by the State Board of Education, the legislature, the governor, and key members of the business community. Local leaders are relied upon as part of the department's strategy, according to Mills: "This is very much of a joint venture. . . . It's our job to provide strong leadership, but we expect strong leadership from local leaders too."

Outside partners also increase the capacity for planning. When the VDE held a two-day strategic planning conference in June of 1992, 40% of the participants came from outside the department.

Development of products is done with the assistance of outside partners. Teacher committees headed the development of the state's portfolio assessment system. Many practitioners and other community members have assisted with the design of the Common Core. Said one manager:

> [The department is] also a broker because we have 130 people, including every . . . data clerk . . . up to the commissioner. So we have to realize we don't have the ability to say, "This is our project and no one else can touch it." We don't have the staff, the capacity to do that. . . . And that's why our partnerships are so important. The Common Core, we [go] to ASCD. We have to have curriculum people from principals and other organizations that are interested in curriculum. We need to have higher ed. The same with assessment . . . [and] some of these others. And . . . they become part of the department's . . . strategy. It does two things. It gives us the manpower and probably

more importantly, they then feel a part of it and it's not something that's so difficult for them to accept when it is finally implemented.

Partnerships also increase the department's capacity to provide training. Two examples of this are the School Development Institutes and the Portfolio-Based Assessment Network. The School Development Institutes are week-long summer institutes for teams of school people planning for change in their schools. The Institutes are jointly sponsored by the University of Vermont and the VDE. The university donates the time of one full-time staff person to the program, and the department donates a portion of a staff member's time to each of the Institutes. The rest of the facilitators are paid from participants' tuition. The institutes increased from 4 to 10 in number in 1992 at the urging of the Commissioner.

The Portfolio-Based Assessment Network is really 17 networks of teachers in different parts of the state, charged with providing training in portfolio assessment, scoring, and improving instruction to improve student performance. These teachers provide training in topics such as introduction to portfolios, strategies of assessment, and using portfolios across the curriculum, for teachers, administrators, school boards, and parent and community groups (VDE, n.d.-a.).

Summary

The Vermont Department of Education charged itself with leading complex school reform in the late 1980s. The work of implementing this reform was dramatically different from the department's past work, and staff believed that change in the department's structure and methods of operation was required to make successful implementation possible, as was explained by one manager:

> There were a lot of new initiatives coming down the road and they were initiatives that we weren't staffed up to do . . . so that people were really just doing things in addition to what they already did. . . . So . . . it made sense . . . from . . . just the face validity of it to say times are changing, the department needs to change. But the reality was that the kinds of things that were being put on us for work to do were things that unless we changed, we couldn't do.

The department consequently began to make some changes. A vision and mission statement was constructed, reflecting the department's new goals. The organization restructured, hoping to attain a structure and culture more conducive to accomplishing the work they were undertaking. Staff were regrouped into teams, and all received four days of TQM training. The department began building stronger linkages with practitioners and other groups, thereby increasing its capacity for leadership, planning, development, and training, and also increasing the likelihood that the reforms that were ultimately developed would be accepted and implemented by practitioners in the field.

The VDE, by virtually everyone's admission, however, is a department in transition. While these changes are being attempted, none of them has been completed. The waning old department and the emerging new department are uncomfortably co-existing to varying degrees in different pieces of the organization.

While the mission of the department has changed, the work of some of its staff members either has not changed or has only changed through addition rather than a complete reorganization of the work to be done. The new organizational structure of the department has placed the staff on teams, but some of these are teams in name only. TQM has influenced the culture of the organization to a degree, but by everyone's admission, more training is needed for a complete change to take place. Strengthening external linkages may be the furthest along of all the changes undertaken.

Living between the old and the new has costs both for the work to be accomplished and for individual members of the staff. There are costs for the work because the new work, the priority of the emerging department, does not get the time, attention, and resources it requires. This problem was described by a manager when he discussed the difficulty of getting the data needed to effectively use TQM:

> That whole side of things has been underdeveloped. But I think our vision is there and our ideas are there but we just haven't been able to inch up to it. And . . . you can['t] do good, effective total quality management without good data. . . . [And] we need a great capacity to go get it and to do something about it. We're all trying but this is where the inertia of both change and to keep on doing what you have to do hasn't allowed us to go into those areas I think as quick[ly] as we'd like.

A member of another team talked about how frustrating it was to be unable to work consistently on planning a new initiative. She and her partner in the endeavor would carve out an afternoon, but then it might be a month later before their schedules allowed them to look at the plans for the initiative again. She said that there had been no tradeoff of old work for new; there was just more to do. Meeting once a month was not very productive.

The personal costs of living between the old and the new come in the form of emotional pain, confusion, and feelings of devaluation. One manager, when asked what she thought the restructuring meant for people not placed in management positions, said: "Mostly pain. That's what I'm hearing. There are a [very] few people, . . . and they stand out like sore thumbs and say, 'Wow, this is great.' I think it's wonderful but mostly it's pain." She said that she thought the pain arose from the fact that things were unsettled and that the choice of new management left people with their loyalties divided between their new and old managers, wondering exactly how they should respond to each. In addition, the declining budget would make this a painful time even without the restructuring, and the pain of the two has been lumped together.

These costs, both for work and for people, are of consequence. It is more important to ask, however, how the work of the VDE does or does not assist schools and districts in implementing Vermont's education reforms.

THE VDE's EFFECT ON LOCAL IMPLEMENTATION

The restructuring of the VDE is of interest to school reformers because it is supposed to be instrumental to implementing Vermont's education reforms. We must visit schools and districts, then, to get even a preliminary sense of how Vermont's reforms are progressing and particularly to judge the effects of the VDE's actions on local implementation.

The findings from schools and districts reported here should be treated as preliminary because of both the timing and the scope of the study. I visited the districts in January and April 1993, only two years into the full implementation of Vermont's assessment process, and even earlier in the life of the state's other reforms such as the Common Core. I visited three districts—a small portion of the total 285.

I did, however, choose three districts that represent something of the range of districts that the state is trying to change: 1) an "early adopter" district that was engaged in reforms similar to the current state-level reforms prior to the state's involvement; 2) a "status quo" district that delivered a more or less average traditional education to its students for years; and 3) a "low-performing" district that the state had been concerned about for some period of time due to its below-average delivery of educational services.[14]

In each district, I visited the schools that district personnel felt were furthest along in their reform efforts and interviewed the teachers most involved in the reforms. I chose schools and personnel with the greatest involvement in the state's reform efforts due to the relative newness of the reforms.[15] I reasoned that because the reforms were so new, I would need to look at the best-case scenario in order to see many signs of change. There was still wide variation in levels of involvement and change, even using this selection strategy. (See the Appendix for a more detailed discussion of sampling and methods.)

I visited schools and districts to answer four questions:

1) Is there evidence of reform-related activity taking place in schools and districts?
2) Is the VDE allowing schools and districts maximum flexibility to achieve the desired outcomes by holding them accountable for outcomes as opposed to process?
3) Are the actions of the VDE helping schools and districts to build the capacity needed to institute the state reforms in the envisioned manner?
4) What do local practitioners identify as ways the department could help them to better implement the reforms, i.e., what advice do they have for the VDE?

Reform in Vermont's Schools and Districts[16]

Some reform-related activity is taking place in all districts, with the state's portfolio assessment process the initiative by far the most frequently mentioned as having an impact.[17] Teachers in all 4th and 8th grades in the districts visited are keeping portfolios in writing and mathematics, although their comments on the process demonstrated a substantial range of understanding, compliance, and commitment to the reform. One teacher, interviewed halfway through the school year (in January), who was not a supporter of the reform, said that he would probably begin portfolio work with his math class the following week. A math teacher in another district said that many of his students did not take the portfolio work seriously once they learned that it would have no effect on their grade. He said that the portfolio problems did usually fit in with his other course material and acknowledged when asked that it "wouldn't be a big deal" to factor the portfolio work into student grades. When asked why he did not do so, the teacher responded:

> Basically, it's material that they've already done . . . a rerun of [a set of problems] they've done before. So they have been graded on it in the past but now they're . . . doing it and I'm asking them to add dimensions with different things. . . . And this has been tested on and it's stuff that's been already graded, etc., in . . . an earlier problem, and then I'm giving it to them again. See? So it's . . . a repeat of the problem [and] they've had time to reflect on it.

Portfolios are not an integral part of the curriculum for these teachers.

Other teachers, however, were enthusiastic about the portfolio process. For example, one teacher said:

> I think it's one of the best things the state department has come out with to help math curriculum because it's a good way to tie the math in with your other subjects because you're doing a lot of written communication. And it's changing the math to the way that I've always seen it done, where you're not just looking for an answer, [but] you're hearing and seeing their thought process. And if they just write an answer down, you don't know what they're thinking or how they get there. And it's also helping to get children away from this idea that the teacher knows the only way.

This teacher and a colleague had spent substantial time over the summer and tried to integrate their math curriculum with the portfolio problem-solving skills. She said further of the state's portfolio assessment efforts:

> I think it's great. The only thing I'd like to see them do, once they get it perfected, is to have it in every grade because to me it's not doing any good doing it in fourth grade and then waiting and doing it again in eighth grade. So what we're trying to do here is to get it on each grade level. And [another teacher] and I are trying to help the other teachers but it's really hard until we know what we're doing. . . . [So] I think to have that really effective the state's going to have to say something about it and start training these other teachers, too.[18]

Many practitioners said that more attention was being paid to writing and problem-solving as a result of portfolio assessment. Some practitioners said that they had been teaching this way all along and that the portfolio system had simply formalized the process. This was particularly true in writing; many Vermont teachers have been trained over a period of years in the process approach to writing through the Vermont Writing Program at the University of Vermont. The process approach to writing involves keeping writing folders for each student.

Some schools and districts are using the portfolio assessment process as a focus for their professional development activities. One district planned to train all its teachers in the portfolio process in both math and writing over the next three years. One school in each of the other districts was working to implement portfolios at all grade levels. The principal of one of these schools said:

> We've made a commitment to implement portfolio K through 9. We've made a commitment to train all teachers, not just writing and math teachers, but all teachers, gym teachers, everybody. Everybody will be trained in the portfolio contents, methods, instructional methods to create all the pieces, and assessment methodology. And so we're taking that really seriously.

This school planned to have a portfolio day when students, teachers, and parents would work on creating products in the morning and assessing them in the afternoon. Later in the year, when 4th and 8th grade portfolios have to be assessed for the state, all faculty in the school will do the scoring, while the 4th and 8th grade teachers oversee and facilitate the process. This will alleviate the burden on faculty at these two grade levels.

Practitioners' most frequent complaints about the portfolio system were the time required, the lack of reliability in the scoring,[19] and what many of them viewed as the competing demands of using portfolios to improve the teaching and learning process versus using them as a mechanism for state accountability. Fourth grade teachers talked about the burden of scoring portfolios for each of their students in both math and writing.[20] Eighth grade teachers talked of the near-impossibility of successfully using the portfolio process with student loads of 100, citing the lack of time to individually conference with each student as well as the burden of scoring based on state criteria. One eighth grade teacher who said the idea of keeping portfolios was not bad but that it was a "nightmare to deal with" continued:

> I took six sessions with a lady up in [town] about portfolios and she says, ". . . This should fit within your curriculum." And . . . "My students do a wonderful job." But it comes down to again, "Well, how many students do you do this with?" "Well, I do it in one of my classes with 18 students. . . . And I can read their work and I can write back to them and they can redo it a second time or a third time." I mean that's fine but when you've got a hundred kids you don't have time to read a hundred portfolio pieces and evaluate them and have them do it over. I mean even if you had the physical time to do it, you don't have the time block in 180 days to take that much . . . of your class time to do that. . . . I mean we have a curriculum that we have to follow so there are certain amounts of things that need to be done.

Scoring portfolios can be a time-consuming process. Each piece in a student's math portfolio is given a score of one to four on each of seven criteria. Writing portfolio pieces are scored from one to four in each of five areas.[21]

Practitioners also talked about having gone to multiple training sessions on portfolio scoring and scores still being "all over the map." Many felt that the state emphasis on using portfolios for accountability and its consequent emphasis on scoring reliability were misguided. Said one principal:

> I think that when we talk about portfolio assessment, I think that the state of Vermont is missing the boat trying to standardize it. The issue of portfolio is to create real assessment for children, and for teachers and parents to look at that real assessment. When you start using it as a standardized form of testing, I mean I've been working on this . . . with my staff to bring them to the state's standards. And every time we work on the criteria that the state gives us and we work on actual writing samples, no matter how long we work on those criteria the teachers are all over the board. And if you can't get a staff of 40 people to come to consensus, how are you going to get a state to come to consensus? . . . . I think trying to standardize portfolios . . . is a mistake.

And the superintendent of another district said:

> If [portfolios are] used to assess student progress as . . . one tool, it's very, very powerful. But when you try to move into some sort of an objective system for evaluating schools and individual teachers in it, it falls all apart. And I don't think it will ever, ever become that. The tragedy is going to be if we insist on pushing that as a state and it causes the whole system to . . . fall into disfavor.

In addition to using portfolios, there was evidence of attempts at restructuring in parts of all districts visited,[22] ranging from plans for whole school restructuring to team teaching to experimenting with interdisciplinary units. Some of this restructuring predated the recent Vermont reforms, while some was spurred directly by them.

Other state reforms mentioned by at least some practitioners as having an effect on local practice were the Common Core of Learning and the Local Standards Boards in charge of relicensure. The Common Core was just beginning to be acknowledged in most schools, since a draft had been mailed to all Vermont educators shortly before my visits. Some practitioners, however, did report using the Core as a resource in their schools' curriculum revision efforts. Practitioners who mentioned the Local Standards Boards felt that they had brought positive changes in the relicensure process and were a step toward teachers taking responsibility for the monitoring of their own profession.

The reaction to and attitude toward the Vermont reforms varies substantially according to type of district. The early adopter district's attitude toward the reforms is characterized by impatience and frustration, due first to the feeling that the state has not gone far enough fast enough, and second to the feeling that the state has not sufficiently recognized the district's reform efforts. These feelings were particularly apparent at the district level. The superintendent complained that the state reforms were not sufficiently forward-thinking, saying that 10 years from now we should be talking about school as a concept rather than a place due to the implications of the rapid expansion of technology. He also said that while some of the state reforms might serve as a part of the district's reform efforts, he was not sure how long the district would continue to work within the state framework because of the competing demands of politics and educating children:

> We think the portfolio . . . will form a very basic part of the kind of stuff we want to do. I guess if we have a concern about the portfolio, . . . and . . . I don't believe this is what Rick thinks left to himself, but he has now had to shift the focus of the portfolio . . . away from something that becomes a piece of dynamic stuff for a kid and a mentor to learn with and through and plan, to now making it an evaluative tool of how well do we teach math. And politically, that's important. . . . I understand that. . . . But that doesn't help our kids any. Not one damn bit. It doesn't help us develop the portfolio into . . . an instrument to plan and record the growth of each individual kid . . .
>
> [So] it's an aspect that we're trying to go along with. . . . [But] I don't know for how much longer, because it's so contrary to what we're talking about. It really is. . . . If we start from a point of view that we believe that every kid can learn everything we think is important to learn in school. . . . But they can't do it when you do everything in 42 minutes. . . . Then what it means is I've got to start building on each individual kid. And the main thing I'm concerned about is that I identify all the things that are important for them to learn and how well is a kid doing it, and I don't care how well you're doing it compared to this kid. . . . The thing is, . . . [are you] doing it? . . . And also, . . . you're going to get there in something more or less than 12 years, and it does vary. And therefore, I can't sit down . . . [and] say, "All 12-year-olds will know this." . . . And that's the base of the difficulty.

Other practitioners in this district agree that the state has not gone far enough fast enough. They expressed frustration at having to expend energy on the state's Public School Approval (PSA) process when it did not help them further their reform initiatives.

Practitioners in the early adopter district also feel unrecognized by the state at both the district and school level. While the state repeatedly sends important visitors to the district, according to practitioners, has invited the district or its schools to apply for numerous state grants, and has brought grant recipients to visit the district's schools, it has never awarded one of the grants to the district. One principal said that her staff "had had it" and that she was reluctant to keep asking them to make big application efforts. Another principal said that it was hard to figure out how to get involved in the state's efforts because it was viewed as a waste of time by the district office. She wished the VDE would be more proactive in inviting her. Both district- and school-level practitioners said that their district did not need the state's money. What they do need is the legitimacy that would be given to their reform activities through state recognition.

Despite this sense of impatience and frustration, most school practitioners in this district saw Vermont's recent reforms as largely congruent with their restructuring efforts, and there were a number of individual practitioners who had worked or were working with the VDE on some of its initiatives. The state seems to be moving in a similar direction as, albeit not keeping up with, their planned reforms, and different schools find different pieces of the reforms to be helpful. For example, a team in one school that predominantly felt that they had undergone their major restructuring despite the VDE still acknowledged that the portfolio assessment process had been very helpful to them.

Overall, the practitioners in this district are proud of their reform efforts, although openly admitting that they still have a long way to go, and feel empowered to use the state reforms when and as they see fit. Said one principal:

> I think there's a lot of faith in individuals within the state department and that those individuals will, in fact, be used as a resource and can be seen as a valuable resource. But . . . this is a group of very independent thinkers here, and they believe that their way is better than that. I'll give you an example . . . with the writing portfolios. We got involved with that and it was not summarily dismissed, but we took pieces that were appropriate and we expanded in other areas and said, "This is what we're going to do with our portfolios. So this piece matches what we need to do and this piece doesn't, and this is where we need to expand it to meet our needs."

There is evidence of congruence between state and district activity in the early adopter district, but there is little evidence of state push. The district seems to be pushing the state in most areas, rather than vice versa.

Activity in the status quo district has been shaped by the state's reform activity to a greater degree. The district has made portfolio assessment the centerpiece of its professional development activities. All teachers will be trained in the use of math and writing portfolios over the next three years.[23]

There are also plans for restructuring in the district as well as in individual schools. The restructuring planned in one of the schools was started by the VDE's Reinventing Vermont Schools Challenge Grants. School faculty wrote a grant proposal and continued with their conversations and work even though they did not receive the grant. In addition, this school has profited from participating in the School Development Institutes (SDIs) jointly sponsored by the VDE and the University of Vermont (UVM), using the Institutes to generate new ideas and involve faculty in intensive planning. Other restructuring efforts, while not started as a direct result of state initiatives, are receiving intellectual support and credibility from the state's reform efforts, according to one district administrator. A group of people involved in these efforts will also be attending an SDI.

This is not to say that all practitioners in the district joyfully embrace the state reforms. There was the wish and belief on the part of some, particularly in one school, that with time this would all go away.

The status quo district in many ways uses the state's initiatives as a framework for its own reform activities. A school administrator explained:

> We like the alignment [with SDI] because we want to feel that we are really using UVM and the state department as viable resources and that we are willing to share what we do here with them. So we want to try to have that kind of a relationship. So to the extent that we do anything that's successful here, we want them to feel free to use it as a means of encouraging others.
>
> . . . We['ve also] tried to align our work with the state department's . . . Common Core, where feasible. In fact, some of us have participated in the development of the Common Core curriculum. . . . There are also a set of four major goal areas that were stated by the state department. We've tried to keep those in mind when we're working. I mean we refer to them and we try to make sure that we're doing things consistent with those. . . . They're over-arching so it can be a formula for all kinds of things. But we try to be mindful of that so that we feel like we're working in concert with other people's efforts.

From the point of view of its leadership and of some of its teachers, the state reform efforts seem disconnected from the primary work and concerns of the troubled district.[24] Portfolio assessment was the only reform mentioned as having any impact on the district, and, as one district administrator said, "The assessments are here. I'm not sure what impact they're going to have."

The reasons district and school leadership articulated for the disconnection of state and district efforts differed substantially. The district administrator criticized the state reform initiatives, first, for being presented in a confusing manner and, second, for in many ways not going far enough to address the key problems in education. He said information was often handed out at School Report Nights that looked impressive but was not understandable to the general public. Further, he felt that the language of the state initiatives got in the way. "Focus forums" and the Common Core in general did not give the public enough to "hold on to":

> When you're sitting out in a town and you're the only educator, . . . and you want to talk about education, and if you really want [people] to listen to you, you better make sure it's at a level they understand . . . I could announce that we're going to have a focus forum. . . . Good grief, you know I'd have six people call me because they wouldn't know what the hell a focus forum was and they would come and see what it's about. . . . If I announce that at the next PTC [Parent Teacher Committee] meeting . . . we're going to talk about . . . some things kid[s] should know when they leave high school, or when they leave elementary school, I'll get some [response]. But I think terminology in some of these things . . . totally gets in the way.
>
> And I think the public wants some things that they can put their teeth into. . . . You know the state mandates that no child is going to enter high school until he can read at a 5th grade level. And that means reading out of Jimmy John's textbook. . . . That's a goal. It's clear-cut. It's out there. The public understands that . . . It's probably not called restructuring but it's getting something done. But . . . you know the Common Core to these people and. . . . Now, educators are having problems . . . really understanding what [it is] . . . I mean it's out there floating around. . . . It's kind of like catching that cloud.

But in addition to feeling that the state reforms were somewhat ephemeral and confusing, this district administrator also felt that in many ways the reforms did not go far enough:

> [If you] compare all 4th graders, automatically, you're putting a time limit on when that skill has to be accomplished. I think you're defeating your purpose. I think if they said, "Here's a skill. Let's look at the child and see how you're progressing toward that skill. And then we will tell you whether it's an A, B, C, or D." If they want to use let-

ters. So that I'm progressing toward that skill. I may not reach it until I'm 10 years old but I'm progressing at an A rate. Somebody else may be progressing toward that same skill. They reach it at 9. But they may be progressing at a D rate, based upon ability. Kids can learn if we get the pressure off that it has to be done at a certain time . . .

I know how to improve education but we can't do it [at the local level]. . . . We're not going to live long enough to accomplish some of these things. And I think those are the things that the state needs to look at. And if the state can truly say that we should eliminate grade levels and have skill levels. And kids start school and they work toward a skill and when they reach that skill, they move on etc. . . . And mandate it . . . then we can. The state can mandate. We can suggest, but the school boards have to approve it.

The school administrator felt that his school and community had to grapple with some very basic issues and that the state reforms were on another plateau that did not apply to their work. When he came to the school two years ago, he discovered a lack of community support for education and a faculty and curriculum in need of strengthening. He acknowledged that the Common Core of Learning was useful as one document among others to look at when thinking about curriculum revisions. He went on to say that he had heard Commissioner Mills speak at a number of meetings:

All he did was beat this Green Mountain Challenge and all these wonderful grants and stuff we're getting. And my thought at that time was "You don't have the foggiest notion of what's going on in the schools." Now when he came [to this area] it was like . . . [now] maybe you can see that you've got to get down and you've got to convince the people that one, education's important here. And you also have to show the people that the school is working, and if there are problems in it you've got to correct the problems. So to me, he was . . . up on the 20th rung [of the ladder] and we're down here on the 2nd or 3rd rung. . . . Those goals and those ideals that he was trying to preach really mean nothing here.

There is some reform activity in all districts visited, but the reaction to and attitude toward Vermont's reforms varies substantially according to type of district.

Giving Schools Maximum Flexibility

Relative to other states, Vermont has never had a strongly regulatory policy environment. The state has never had a statewide assessment prior to portfolios, and its Basic Competency program, while required of all schools up until the onset of the more recent reforms, allowed for local variation. The state identified the competencies every child should master, but it was up to local practitioners to determine how mastery was defined and when students had achieved it. The Basic Competency program was termed "wishy-washy as can be" by one superintendent interviewed.

When Vermont's Public School Approval (PSA) process was introduced in 1984, however, the regulations "had some teeth," according to this super-intendent. PSA was designed "to assure acceptable educational opportunities for all Vermont students regardless of where they live and to set in motion a mechanism for school improvement statewide" (VDE, 1991b, p. 1). Schools are to go through the approval process every 10 years and are judged on traditional input indicators such as explicit, written scope and sequences for all subject areas, coordinated with sending and receiving schools; quantity of materials in the library; art, music, and guidance programs available for all students; and staff who are properly certified for the areas they teach (VDE, 1991b). It should be noted that the PSA standards have been difficult for Vermont schools to meet; only 51 schools had been granted full approval as of June 1992 (State of Vermont Board of Education, 1992, June 16).

The VDE is attempting to change the regulatory environment established by PSA to one that allows for greater flexibility and local innovation. First, the traditional PSA regulations, while still in place, are being interpreted in a more flexible manner. Department School Improvement Coordina-tors say they are now holding schools accountable for meeting the intent rather than the letter of the law. For example, the standards requiring home economics and industrial arts were originally interpreted to require that schools have separate programs taught by individuals licensed in these areas. Some districts are now looking at providing these programs as integrated components of a school's broader curriculum, with portions of the subject matter being taught in science and social studies, for example, under the guidance of a licensed practitioner but not as a separate program. These efforts are being undertaken with the blessings of the state coordinators. Coordinators describe themselves as "more willing to accept creative solu-tions," while at the same time holding schools to the same high standards.

Second, the current PSA regulations sunset in 1994, and the process is being redesigned for subsequent years. The new PSA process is supposed to emphasize student performance, but it is still unclear exactly what form the process will take.

VDE staff are reluctant to dramatically change PSA before all Vermont schools have completed the process. School Improvement Coordinators feel that changing the standards before all schools have completed the process would send a message of inconsistency and be unfair to schools that worked hard to reach the standards.

Third, the VDE has developed a blanket waiver proposal that it will recommend to the State Board of Education. This proposal would offer to:

> waive all regulations not required by federal law [or specifically required by state statute] or affecting health, safety and civil rights . . . to schools that commit to sweeping changes in standards and assessment, curriculum and instruction, integration of education and human services, public involvement and evaluation. (VDE, 1993, January 12, p. 1)

Teachers in these schools would have to be licensed educators, but all specific endorsement areas could be waived, except special education. School districts applying for this waiver would be required to present "systemic school restructuring plan[s] based upon a shared vision and goals," including a statement of how results would be monitored and reported (VDE, 1993, January 12, p. 1). A team of people including VDE staff and local educators would periodically visit schools, using this visit to offer suggestions, support, and information.[25]

Vermont's regulatory environment is in transition, and practitioners are largely dissatisfied with their treatment by the VDE during this transitional period. Their reasons for dissatisfaction, however, are in almost direct opposition, depending on the type of district from which they come.

For the early adopter district and the schools within it, the continued enforcement of PSA is viewed as a frustrating and time-consuming impediment to change. Practitioners are frustrated by the fact that they are slowed in their implementation of a reform agenda that recent state reforms support by a set of regulations that the same state is enforcing. According to one district administrator:

> We've spent a lot of time with committees district-wide . . . looking at what are the outcomes and what are the essential behaviors and how can we implement these. Okay. And then you have [the VDE] come and do a PSA inspection and they say, "Well, you haven't had the math teachers K–12 meet. . . . You're supposed to have coordination of program." Well what they think about as program and what we think about as program are two different things. . . . They want to see our scope and sequence for [each subject area. We're trying to coordinate the whole learning experience to reach these outcomes.] . . . And we may have committees that are functioning across [disciplines].

A principal in the same district said that she had been excited about heading her current school because it "was as far out in front as any school [she'd] ever seen anywhere." This school began its reform efforts "in spite of the state," according to the principal. But, she continued:

What I recognize now, is that there is a lot of confluence between what the state thinks is important and what we think is important. . . . And I think for [this school] that is a brand new experience . . .

So . . . I'm hoping that over time . . . this staff will learn to respect the state department. . . . There are things the state department is doing, though, that are . . . hurting that goal of mine. . . . You know how when we change we still have vestiges of old systems or perhaps something far more than a vestige? And in our case we've got PSA—Public School Approval—which . . . has its place and had its place. It is now a major irritant. . . . Those standards were written 10 years ago and they reflect a very different reality than the one that is now here . . . I mean they don't even match the run of the mill middle school's reality, let alone our reality. And so while I see the state department bending over backwards to try to do the things that they quote "have to do" in order to provide us with final approval, it is very frustrating and it's embarrassing . . .

It's real clear that . . . they're going to make us jump through X number of hoops. . . . They're going to cause us to waste a fair amount of time, making responses to requirements that are irrelevant to anything that has to do with our success [and we don't have time to waste.] . . . [and] I saw incredible flexibility but it's still not enough . . . I mean [this PSA staffer] must be jumping out of his skin to be able to be this flexible because it's not like him. He's been one of these real dot the i's and cross the t's type of [people]. . . . It's [just] sad . . . that the response can't happen quickly enough. We're having to go in and spend a lot of time getting waivers on certification. We're having to produce bogus curricula [to meet the PSA requirements] . . . [when] we're in the process of . . . totally rethinking how we feel about scope and sequence, and we're moving very much in the same direction as the state's Common Core . . .

The principals of all three schools in this district had similar complaints about a PSA process that did not in any way help them to move their schools' reforms forward.

Added flexibility in the existing process is not enough, as is exemplified by the above statement, nor is the regulation-by-regulation waiver process currently available from the State Board of Education. This process is insufficient because it burdens those schools and practitioners who are seeking to be innovative, when being innovative in and of itself is a time-consuming and burdensome process. Said a district administrator:

Even the fact that there's a waiver process means that we have to do something which is kind of above and beyond. . . . In a sense, it's penalizing school districts that do want to step out there because it's another piece that you have to go through . . .

One twist to this story of the state's regulatory environment impeding reform, however, is that while there is evidence that early adopter practitioners feel impeded, there is simultaneously evidence that the State Board and the leadership of the VDE would like to see schools ask for more flexibility than practitioners feel they can responsibly exercise at this point in time. This twist was articulated by one principal:

> I think that you have from Rick, from [name of another VDE staffer], and from the State Board . . . it's almost a desperation. "Somebody come forward with something for us." . . . And yet schools are not in the . . . let me give you an example. When I go to a state board meeting, and we wanted to present this [idea of experimental status] as just a conceptual idea at that point, they said, "well . . . just ask us to get rid of Carnegie units." . . . My response to them is "I'd love to get rid of them. But being a responsible administrator, what are you going to replace them with?" And it's not that easy an answer. So if one moves to outcomes-based education and one moves to . . . a continuous progress approach, the state board has one piece of it. There's a parent group that has another piece of it. How do we report that to colleges or to the Air Force or to wherever this student wants to go? . . . Very easily the state would probably give us permission to do away with [Carnegie units] but to be responsible about it, to be accountable . . . is not as easy. [So there is a group of schools doing some work on this.]

While this principal and others in the early adopter district do want greater flexibility than the state's PSA process allows, it is far from clear that immediate, complete deregulation is what they are seeking.

Ironically, PSA seems to be more irritating and time consuming for schools in the early adopter district, where the problems identified through the process were comparatively minor, than it is for schools in the troubled district, in which the process brought serious problems to light.[26] In the troubled district, the prevailing perception of practitioners is that the state is backing away from the enforcement of PSA. Said a principal:

> We have a home ec. teacher who had an oven door one day just fall off, and luckily the kids . . . weren't under [it]. It could have burned them or hurt them. It's like you're trying to run a school and . . . townspeople will . . . come in here and say, "You know, there's noth-

ing wrong with the building." I mean we have wiring that['s] . . . not up to code. It could burn the place down. . . . [We're] not working with good equipment . . . in the science room [or the business program. We don't have art and music programs.] . . .

A lot of people feel that [PSA's] getting phased out . . . PSA did come in here and they . . . had probably I don't know . . . 8 or 10 pages of . . . things that need to be improved. You know the wiring and the home ec. room needs to be, and the science room and all these things. And some of them were improved and obviously some of them weren't. Because if the town didn't vote money to upgrade the building and the facilities then obviously you couldn't do it. And I think now because of the finances in the state and the finances in the country, they've backed off, and they can't hold these schools to those standards. . . . I think right now there's a period of uncertainty as to . . . what [the state] really want[s].

PSA is becoming more flexible, and, in the eyes of the superintendent of this district, that is unfortunate. He believes that flexibility will lead to a lowering of standards:

When [PSA] came out, it had some teeth in it. . . . And I . . . said, "fine." The state department has taken a stance. . . . And they started listing these PSA requirements and I thought, boy you know, this is good. . . . And now at this point, I'm just not sure and I'm not sure how many other superintendents are . . . out on a limb. We've been telling school boards, "You must, you must, you must." We need guidance counselors . . . PSA requires [them]. And now they're beginning to waiver on that requirement. And they're saying, "Well, if you can tell us how you might deliver those services and satisfy us, that's fine." And what's going to happen now is during times of budget crunch they're going to say, "Well, maybe we can get three volunteer mothers to come in and run our library for us. And we can eliminate the certified librarian." And I heard it last week at a board meeting, "Do we need a guidance counselor? . . . Can't the kids go to mental health if they have a problem?" And all of this. And I'm just afraid we're going to lose all of that, and we're going to be back to where we were staff wise and program wise 10 or 15 years ago.

Practitioners in the status quo district said little, positive or negative, about PSA.

Practitioner perceptions of the state's flexibility, or lack thereof, varied not only by department program but also in some cases from staff person to staff person. A district administrator in the early adopter district said that Mills "telegraph[s] that he's pretty flexible" but that other people in the department are "all over the spectrum." The trick is finding the right person who will focus on the intent rather than the letter of the law.

The VDE, however, receives substantial praise as well as criticism from practitioners. Many practitioners interviewed praised the department not only for going in the right direction with its reforms but also for listening to and involving practitioners more than they ever have in the past. Practitioners cited two problems that may prevent their peers from recognizing that the department is reaching out to them. First, there is a lack of resources in the VDE. Practitioners noted that it was underfunded, understaffed, and in a state of confusion as a result of its restructuring and the resulting job changes. Second, practitioners noted that while the department was making great efforts to involve practitioners and others in the reform process, not all practitioners have accepted the offer. One teacher commented:

> I think [the department's] much more inclusive of people in the field now than it ever was before. . . . Through the professional standards and through . . . the work in the committees . . . like Common Core, all those different subcommittees and subgroups of the state department, seem to be asking teachers for some input and being willing to listen. So . . . I think the state is attempting to include. I don't think people have taken them up on it. I think some people do and it's their voice [that] comes . . . quite strongly through in some of this stuff. I mean I know some of the people who have been instrumental in some of these reforms and the reform is that person or that small group of people.

Another teacher said:

> I think [the Common Core Steering Committee is] a really comfortable, open . . . collegial type of group. . . . I guess it's enhanced my belief in the individuals who are . . . in the state department, the whole bureaucracy of it. You don't really know what's going on, or what the responsibilities are, or how deep they are, or what their backgrounds are until you work with them . . . on this kind of level. And I'm really impressed. I mean I've been involved with . . . some national groups [and different states] in terms of reform . . . and it's pretty impressive. I mean I think we've got some people who are really on top of change . . .
>
> And I think the state department really truly wants to have grass roots involvement. They've had community forums. They've had con-

ferences. And they've had input from over 2,000 people outside of education as well as inside. So they've really made a valid effort. I don't think people in this building really know that because they haven't been involved.

The regulatory environment and the relationship between the VDE and schools are in transition. Right now, the old and the new are uncomfortably co-existing. Practitioners' understandings of the department's role vary quite dramatically according to the type of district they work in and their level of involvement in the department's activities.

Building Local Capacity

In the face of limited human and financial resources, the Vermont Department of Education is working hard to build state and local capacity through creating networks and liaisons with talented practitioners and other groups. Networks of practitioners have been created to provide training in portfolio assessment and support for restructuring in general. Vermont's Portfolio-Based Assessment Network is composed of 17 practitioner networks, each with a network leader, serving different geographic areas of the state (VDE, n.d.-c). These networks were established in 1991 to provide training in all aspects of portfolio assessment. However, training for the 1992–93 academic year focused predominantly on the reliable scoring of portfolios (VDE, 1993, January). This focus was due to the release of the Rand report the previous year that criticized the reliability of the portfolio assessment system (Koretz et al., 1992).

The Vermont Restructuring Corps is a group of approximately 100 people—practitioners as well as other interested citizens—brought together by the VDE and the University of Vermont. These people have been trained to provide periodic support to restructuring schools and districts. The corps is an extension of the work done in School Development Institutes (SDIs) that is further described below. Members of the Restructuring Corps work throughout the year with school teams that have attended these institutes. According to a SDI staff member:

What we want to do [through the Restructuring Corps] is two things. We want to cut short the thing we call the implementation dip. . . . And the second thing is we want to help people anticipate problems and search for resources before the problem gets out of control for them. And so the role of this corps member is to act in a facilitating capacity. And that takes on a lot of dimensions. And so . . . their job is to go to the district at least three times during the year and meet with the team. . . . We'd like it to be more, but we felt that there was a fine edge over which we wouldn't have any volunteers. . . . Our hope is that they'll catch the fever and want to go back more. But it . . . also is a means for myself and the site coordinators to be in touch with the site . . . on a regular basis and know what's going on. . . . It's only through direct contact that you can really sense the real issues, not the stated ones.

The VDE has also joined with the University of Vermont (UVM) in sponsoring School Development Institutes. SDI is 10 years old. It expanded from 4 to 10 locations in 1992 at the urging of the Commissioner, making a SDI location no more than 30 minutes from nearly all Vermont schools. UVM donates the time of one faculty member, who serves as full-time director of the program. The VDE donates the time of one staff person to work with each Institute. In addition, this year the department has also set aside some money to provide school teams with implementation grants to assist them in carrying out their action plans in their schools.

The SDI philosophy is built on the concept of team building and the values of fairness and cooperation. These values mean, in part, that the staff works to ensure that all stakeholders are included in a school's decision-making process. SDI is designed to introduce people to best practices and national trends and to assist practitioners in determining the best course for their schools. One SDI staff member explained:

> One of our roles is to inform people about what the options are for them. And what's available to them. We don't start out with a set of premises about what people ought to do. We start out with the belief that the decision rests with them. We certainly give them guidance, but we don't start out with the premise that . . . we know best what they ought to do, in terms of [their] project.

Schools send a team of people to SDI with the goal of developing an action plan for some kind of school change. Teams have varied in size from 3 to 40 people. Schools may attend SDI for as many years as they like. One school has sent a team for eight years.

The Institutes are at least loosely linked to the state's reform agenda. The Commissioner and Deputy Commissioner speak at the sites, and staff talk with practitioners about linking their development projects to the state reforms. The SDI staff member admitted that these connections were probably not made as well as the staff would like. He explained:

> Certainly [the connections between the interests of the school and the state's reforms are] made. It's just that there's always a balancing act be-

tween the agenda of the school, and the agenda of the state. . . . And we have to be . . . sensitive to that. . . . [So] it may be more subtle sometimes than it is direct.

In addition to joining with UVM in SDI, the department is also seeking to foster coherence in the other professional development offered around Vermont through the formation of the Professional Development Consortium in the fall of 1991. The consortium is a voluntary group of professional development providers throughout the state, working to provide equitable, accessible, and high-quality professional development statewide.

The concern for statewide access to quality professional development grew with the introduction of teacher relicensure through Local Standards Boards overseen by Vermont's Professional Standards Board. All Vermont teachers are now required to submit Individual Professional Development Plans to their Local Standards Board for relicensure every seven years. The boards approve these plans and also look for evidence that plans for the previous seven years were satisfactorily completed. The requirement of these plans increases the demand for quality professional development, as well as providing data on local professional development needs. Local Standards Boards write an annual report for the Professional Standards Board with information including the kinds of professional development activities approved and the number of teachers participating in these activities (VDE, 1990, September 14). Someone who worked with the Professional Development Consortium described how the group should function as it evolves:

If, [for example,] there was a school leadership dimension that we wanted to deliver in professional development, the question to the consortium should be, "How can we deliver what's needed? What's the full range of it, and how do we define quality? And then, how do we deliver this out where the needs are?" And hopefully that will arise because locals are saying, "Hey, we need help in X, Y, or Z." And the consortium should be saying, "How do we get it out there?"

The VDE also has focused on building capacity outside the department with each new initiative. An example of this is the department's approach to its New American Schools Development Corporation (NASDC) grant, as described by a VDE manager:

And what we've done systematically in all these [initiatives] like National Science Foundation and New American Schools is that . . . we focused on building . . . state [and local] level capacity . . . [that's] outside of the department. . . . You know, the quotable quote is that

we're going to do a lot more steering than rowing. But even if you're
going to steer you need some capacity . . .

The notion behind . . . [the] NASDC proposal is that if you
could take some schools that were really out there already and had already gotten by some of the basic stuff. . . . Had a clear sense of direction on where they were going. You could identify those schools and
you could put them in contact with the best resources in the world on
the best cutting-edge ideas on what had to happen. And give them the
resources . . . that they need and the time that they need to take that
information and to make it theirs . . . and to change their school. . . .
That that's a start. But then if you could create the resources to bring
school teams from other schools to visit those schools, not for a visit
but for 4 to 6 weeks, and to live in those schools with the people.
Team teach with them, you know co-administer with them, and
so on. And have them go through a planning process at the same
time, that you could roll this out, that you could create a sense of momentum . . .

Practitioners are divided on whether or not enough training is being
provided overall and also on the quality of that training. The SDIs were
universally well received by practitioners who had participated in them. The
quality of training in portfolio assessment was praised by numerous teachers,
and practitioners said that the training had improved over the past year. One
of the most positive aspects of the training cited by teachers was the opportunity to learn from colleagues, and teachers called on the state and districts to
provide as many such opportunities as possible.

There is at least preliminary evidence, however, that the department's
strategy of using practitioners for providing training has limitations. Teachers,
as well as others, said that using practitioner networks for training, while an
important strategy to generate involvement and share expertise, was straining
the system. School boards have complained of pulling "the best and brightest" from their classrooms. In addition, tight local budgets make the money
for the substitutes, phone calls, and so forth, required to allow teachers to
work with others difficult to find.

There is also substantial agreement among practitioners that the portfolio process, particularly in math, was rushed by the state, with little attention
paid to giving practitioners adequate training before beginning the process.
For example, one district administrator said:

I think what happened last year was, when we sort of jumped in with
both feet, it was a process of learning as they were going. So really
most people didn't have any kind of formal instruction in how to do

the assessment, in our district anyway until October of 1991. . . .
[And] there were very few actual dates that our district people were invited to as part of a network training session. And then all of a sudden
. . . the portfolios had to be scored . . .

My . . . frustration with this was not with the idea of a portfolio
assessment but with what I considered the mad rush to get it done.
You know, the lack of training and the lack of practice time and the
lack of attention, I think, to let people feel competent in what they
were doing. And that's the sense of frustration that I heard from the
teachers.

Considerable pressure was placed on schools and districts to participate
in the assessment process, despite practitioners feeling unprepared. One large
district, in response to teacher sentiment, opted to keep portfolios in writing
and math but to participate in the state scoring only in writing, using the
1991–92 academic year as a pilot year in mathematics. This decision incurred
considerable wrath from the state and the press. District leadership was pres-
sured by the Commissioner and the State Board to participate in the scoring
of the math portfolios, and district teachers were attacked in the press.

The rush to implement portfolio assessment incurred costs in terms of
teacher support, according to some practitioners. Said the superintendent of
another district:

I guess to some extent the problems have been more in the lack of resources and the implementation, and maybe trying to move ahead
with time lines that really weren't viable. And . . . I see that as having
caused definitely friction at the local level. And in some respects with
the people that needed to be the most vested. [They] became the
people who are asking the most questions and starting to really. Especially after the Rand report came out saying the whole training protocol, the whole scoring protocol may [need to] be changed. [They
asked,] "Why are we continuing to be trained"?

An administrator in another district said:

I understand the argument that says that, boy, look at the change that's
happened, and it's been profound. But by the same token I also know
that I believe that there was some damage done that will take a long
time to repair in terms of teachers feeling like they have been hurt pro-
fessionally . . . [because they] need[ed] to be better trained and more
competent to be able to do the kinds of things that we . . . asked them
to do. . . . I mean some of the more experienced teachers who've

been in 4th grade . . . certainly not all, but some of them have sort of shrugged their shoulders and kind of heaved a sigh and said, "You know, here's just one more thing."

There is some evidence that the VDE is now more attentive to the time and training needed to successfully implement portfolio assessment. The department is allowing the implementation of portfolios at the high school level a longer pilot period. Said one high school teacher:

> There's been some evidence that [the way the state department works with practitioners] ha[s] improved. I think, well you take a look at what's happening with us and what happened in grade schools, and it is very, very different. Of course, the other thing is it's a simple fact of life, and I'm not doing this to blow my own horn, but you can't push high school teachers around the way you can grade school teachers. I don't know why that's true but it is. And they got shoved around pretty hard and pretty badly. And for some reason, and [name of department staff person] may be part of the reason, we're not being pushed around nearly as much. In other words, the time lines are a little more realistic. They're not saying, "We said on August 15th that this is the way it was going to be. Don't you dare change them." We have changed them.

Finally, there is some evidence that the emphasis on achieving reliability in scoring may be causing disillusionment with the portfolio process as a whole. Teachers talked about their frustration that reliability did not seem to improve and were skeptical that it would ever be achieved. One teacher said:

> I came to a realization today. Fourth grade teachers have been meeting for two years now. Today was the day that the fourth graders' portfolios needed to be scored. . . . And the first thing we did was . . . all of us in the room scored the same piece, which was very short. . . . And the differences in the room were amazing. You know, you've been doing this for two years so . . . I guess what I'm saying is, this is a very subjective mode of whatever and . . . you're not going to get agreement. . . . We each scored it. Then we raised our hand if we [scored it a certain way] . . . Usually there was one thing that the majority of people said . . . but quite often we did not agree with quote, "the state." And you know the state is only other people just like us.
>
> And . . . I just came to the realization today that this whole thing is stupid. . . . You're not going to come to any consensus so why try? I mean I can see encouraging writing. I can see teaching . . . details and

purpose and all those things that you're trying to score. But . . . trying to get human beings to agree to a score is as far as I can see, a waste of a lot of time and energy. . . . [And math is] even worse. . . . [And the training sessions are] not really that helpful . . . because of . . . not being able to come to a consensus. It's just more frustration. You know you just go and do the same thing again and it really isn't any better.[27]

There is an additional catch-22. While teachers want more training, they do not want to spend more time out of the classroom. One teacher suggested summer training. This tension between the desire for training and the desire to minimize time away from the classroom exists not only in Vermont but in virtually all teacher training efforts.

Practitioners' Advice to the VDE

Vermont practitioners have numerous pieces of advice for the VDE. By far the most frequently mentioned advice, offered by 35%, was to get out into the schools. Other frequently mentioned pieces of advice were to focus the efforts of the department (26%), include practitioners to a greater extent in the decision-making process (19%), put resources into developing model restructured schools (14%), and to keep going—this is the right track (14%). Most of these pieces of advice have a number of components, and many of these are interrelated.

Practitioners who recommended that department staff spend more time in schools did so for a number of reasons. One, they believe that the conditions of teaching have changed dramatically over a period of years, and that department staff are out of touch with today's realities. Practitioners feel that spending more time with them, in classrooms, would help VDE staff to be more realistic about both their reform proposals and the time it will take to implement them. The difficulties of implementation will be apparent.

Two, practitioners want VDE staff to recognize that many good things are happening in Vermont schools and classrooms, to celebrate and validate these good things, and to explicitly and publicly honor and value classroom teaching. Said a group of teachers teaching in a pilot program:

First of all, [the state should] recognize we could use support. It would be nice if the Vermont state department of education said, "Hey, look at these guys. They're right on." . . . I mean if we are let's get some backing . . . so maybe other schools, or towns, or whatever would take a look and we'd have a little validation . . .

Education is one of those things that it's real easy to kick. Everybody and his brother can complain about education and it's a real easy band wagon to get on. And even the state department has a tendency to start everything they say with "We're in trouble so this is what we're going to do." And . . . we're not in trouble. You know we're learning. We're working. We're trying to figure it out but it's a process. It's not a product that you're trying to fix. It's a process that you're trying to get better at and get a grasp on. And I really think they have to get off the easy political side of saying, "We're in deep squat. If we don't do this nothing's going to happen." . . . I'd like them to lead positively.[28]

This team of teachers explained that they had spent all the previous year defending their pilot program with no outside support. Parents were suspicious that their kids were being "experimented on." It would have been helpful for parents and the larger community to hear the VDE tell them that these teachers were moving in the right direction and deserved support. One of the team members concluded:

Probably if the state department needs to do anything, it needs to be positive about education. . . . That's what I see their job is. I mean I'm a guy that knows how to teach. I don't need them telling me. I need them making it possible for me to, I need them helping me. I need them coming up with new things to have me think about so that I can interpret that into what I do. . . . Being educators, I think, rather than politicians is important. . . . I think the state department should almost be a resource for teachers, . . . not the people that are my boss. . . . I get the feeling, [at times,] that they think they're superior.

Three, practitioners want VDE staff to know schools so that they can customize their work with them. Schools are starting in different places and need to be worked with accordingly, as one principal described:

I think it's a general type of thing that [the department's] trying to do. Maybe it's the only way that they can do it. I've never been at an administrative level that high. But to me, [change is] individual and that's why you have, you know, commissioners in different states, and that's why you have superintendents of certain districts. To me, you go to them and you have them present needs and so forth . . .

It doesn't seem like it would be that difficult to do if someone wanted to stop and think about [working with districts individually]. . . . And . . . find[ing] out what the needs are for each district because you can't, you just can't be general about schools and about people and about education. Different needs and different [people] and different situations. . . . The big thing that I would [recommend] is to find out the different needs and wants and problems and strengths of each individual district and then go from there as far as setting goals.

Practitioners who advised the VDE to focus their efforts also presented a number of variations on that theme. First, they recognize that the department is working with limited resources and consequently urge that it be clear on what it wants to do and what it can do, given those resources. Second, practitioners urge the department not to make any more changes but instead to focus on implementation and institutionalization of existing change efforts. They expressed concern that often a new initiative is started before an old one has had time to gel.

While a number of practitioners did acknowledge and compliment the department for including them in the decision-making process more than ever before, a number of teachers still said that the department should make greater efforts to include them. One teacher suggested:

What might work with schools is to set a day aside every month and have field representatives, if you want to call them that, to come around. Or even invite a teacher from a district once a month to take an afternoon off, a professional day or whatever, and go to the state department and just sit down and talk about a list of concerns or problem areas or direction. . . . Because teachers know what they need . . . but they don't always have the method to get that information across to someone who will listen . . . and can do something about it. And they often feel that "Well, no one's going to listen to what I say." Or, . . . "the state doesn't care."

Practitioners also urged the state to expend its resources on developing model restructured schools. They do not want a single model that all schools would be expected to emulate, but a variety of models that they could visit and learn from. One school administrator envisioned these models as follows:

The state department could do a lot of service to all communities if they used, in different locales, schools for pilots in which they really tried out their ideas, as a research station. And then when things work[ed] they made recommendations throughout the state, not a dictum. But "this worked here. If you want to try it, try it. Talk with the teachers. These are the people who did it. These are the parents that support it. These are the results that the kids had. It looks like it's working. Check it out. . . ." And have . . . 3 or 4 different demographic research stations going on, demographically different because what's appropriate for one is certainly not appropriate for another except in certain ways . . .

And . . . rather than trying to do everything for everybody I would give extra attention to those [research stations]. . . . And it takes a lot of encouragement because we're in a system that is resistant to change. And state departments . . . could encourage change that was genuine and qualitative, not just change for its own sake . . . but real change. . . . If somebody learns something really great, one of the benefits of the larger organizations is that they can disseminate that in an appropriate way and share it.

Finally, a number of practitioners advised the VDE to keep going, saying that the state reforms were on the right track. Even a number of practitioners who were quite critical of the department's implementation still agreed with the fundamental direction of the reforms.

SUMMARY AND ANALYSIS: THE CASE OF VERMONT

This case highlights three important themes as well as a key challenge, not only for the implementation of the Vermont reforms, but also for the implementation of complex reform in general.

Turning first to the themes, this case demonstrates that the internal condition of the Vermont Department of Education affects the way department staff work with schools and, consequently, local implementation. This is most clearly seen in the tension between VDE attempts at deregulation and VDE enforcement of the existing Public School Approval process. Just as the hopefully-waning old department and hopefully-emerging new department are uncomfortably co-existing inside the organization, they are also uncomfortably co-existing in the department's messages to the field—"Just ask us, and we'll get rid of Carnegie units" versus, "Where is your scope and sequence for bicycle safety"?[29]

Ironically, this uncomfortable co-existence seems to have counter-intuitive effects on local implementation, varying according to type of district. The early adopter district, with relatively minor PSA infractions, reports that the time spent trying to comply with PSA detracts from its change efforts, while the troubled district, with some relatively major infractions, reports that state enforcement of the standards is unlikely. The mixed messages resulting from the co-existence of the old and the new do not appear to be serving anyone well.

The pinch of insufficient resources is a second example of internal organizational conditions affecting state-to-local implementation. The internal reality of having less people to do more work creates at least the perception (and probably also the reality) that department staff can only be less responsive to practitioners' needs. In addition, the lack of resources in the department has resulted in pushing greater costs and responsibilities onto localities, according to practitioners. Practitioners, too, feel that they are being asked to do more with less.

The second theme that emerges is that practitioners want VDE staff to spend more time in schools for two reasons. First, practitioners want VDE staff to understand the current conditions of teaching and consequently the difficulties of implementing proposed changes. Second, they want VDE staff to understand individual schools and districts so that they can work with them differentially. Schools and districts start in different places and are located in different contexts. Practitioners argue that strategies for change need to reflect these differences.

The third theme that emerges is that indirect leadership from the state can work to bring about local reform. While department of education activity and state reforms cannot be said to be directly responsible for all of the reforms taking place in the schools and districts visited, the state's establishment of powerful ideas and a climate for change do seem to be important for all of these efforts. One district administrator described it this way:

> Vermont schools are very definitely shaped and controlled by local forces, and the state board, in the past, has been largely on the fringe of that. And what I think has happened is that as important as the actual initiatives [are] . . . I think the largest effect . . . has been the power of the idea. I think . . . slowly but surely . . . the concept that change is vital to improve student learning has infiltrated the culture of the people that are involved . . . . And I think it's awakened people to possibilities . . .
>
> The actual initiatives themselves were accepted by some and ignored by others and rejected by others. . . . [But] I think [raising this set of issues] has energized people at various points in the educational system. . . . It has energized administrators probably more than anybody. . . . So that it's sort of become . . . something in their craw they can't spit out. . . . And so, I think in time, boards are becoming more willing to acknowledge the need for change. And . . . it's touched the nerve among some teachers. . . . And this is sort of like top seeds growing.

Finally, this case exemplifies a key challenge in complex reform—maintaining flexibility in the new structures and products created, such as assessments and curriculum frameworks, so that they do not become impediments to future local reform efforts. In many ways these structures and products need to remain "living" processes, or documents that continually evolve.

The need for this evolution was alluded to many times in the case. Practitioners talked of developing interdisciplinary units and of the desirability of moving away from age grading, both changes that are advocated by reformers (for example, Sizer, 1984). If teaching practice evolves to such an extent that the VDE's current conceptions of portfolios are no longer appropriate, this could be a very real sign of success of the state's overall reform effort. The challenge for the VDE will then become making the portfolio assessment process flexible enough to accommodate these further reforms in education. Because participation in the assessment system is not mandatory, schools and districts do have the option of opting out of the process, but doing so will undermine the VDE's goal of statewide accountability. Only by maintaining sufficient flexibility in the assessment process can the state's dual goals of improving practice as well as achieving statewide accountability be accomplished. Vermont's forthcoming curriculum frameworks will face a similar challenge, although this challenge will not be quite as strong, since the frameworks are to serve as exemplars and are not part of the state's accountability system.

Elmore and McLaughlin (1988) argue that variability in teaching practice "is a key ingredient of effective [teaching] performance," and that variation in practice is at least partially conditioned on teaching context (p. 39). This understanding of effective teaching leads to the conclusion that changes in approach and practice of both individual teachers and schools are not only to be expected, but also to be encouraged, as teaching and learning contexts change over time. This means that if the state's goal is to produce reflective practice focused on student-appropriate teaching, then the state's mechanisms for improving practice (in this case assessments) must be sufficiently flexible to allow these changes in practice to occur over time.

A variation of this challenge is whether or not the assessment process can accommodate local adaptation. A principal in the early adopter district described her faculty as "a group of very independent thinkers" who did not fully accept the state's definition of portfolios and their contents but, instead, took the pieces that met their needs and expanded and adapted their portfolios in other areas. From the standpoint of fostering practitioner engagement in the improvement of teaching and learning, I would characterize this use of the state's portfolio process as an unqualified success. Good teaching is all about adapting methods and materials in ways that will best meet the needs of your particular students. From the standpoint of state accountability needs, however, such adaptation presents a problem, because in order to reliably report assessment results, each school must participate in a common process.

The school described here is a high school, so it has not bumped up against the state's requirements. But since adaptation is in many ways desirable, a tension still exists between the requirement of good teaching practice and the requirements of state-level accountability.

UNDERSTANDING WHAT IS HAPPENING IN THE VDE

It is important to understand why the current conditions in the VDE exist. Examining the actions of the department through two different lenses helps to address this question.

The Narrow Lens

Much of the unevenness of VDE activity can be explained by viewing the department as a closed system (Peters & Waterman, 1982, p. 91). There are largely internal explanations for staff members' differing understandings of how the department works—whether or not teams are effective, boundaries are easily crossed, vision and mission are a driving force, and decision-making is a collaborative undertaking.

First, team formation takes time, and some of the VDE's teams have been in existence longer than others. Teams that existed at least informally in the old department, such as the groups that worked together on assessment and the Common Core, have been strengthened by the restructuring. These, now called Focus Teams, have an obvious joint task, the accomplishment of which has been made easier by the new structure that formalizes and facilitates their work. Other teams, however, formed as a result of the restructuring without having a joint task that was readily apparent. Such teams were described as teams "in name only" by their members. It is possible that joint tasks will emerge for these groups over time, but at the moment they are not apparent.

Second, restructuring is commonly recognized as painful for all involved, even in the best of circumstances. There is tremendous uncertainty and also the perception that different groups have gained or lost power. This pain was heightened for some members of the VDE staff due to the perception that the management selection process was not as fair and open as it was portrayed to be. Said one team member:

> There was a very elaborate . . . interview process, which was pretty much a farce. People knew they had their jobs and said they had their jobs prior to the interview process. . . . And so [for management] to turn around and say, "Isn't this wonderful? We picked the best people

and we did it in a fair process," has never ever been dealt with. . . .
You know, if you've already got somebody in mind just say that. I really don't have any problem with that. I do have a problem with you
trying to tell me that this has been a fair process.

The restructuring has also led to an insider/outsider dynamic in the
department. The people who are in the new management positions or are
on effectively functioning teams working on priority initiatives for the
department are considerably more upbeat about the restructuring and its
effects. The people engaged in the "old" work of the department—work
that at least in part entails enforcing regulation—feel that their work is mis-
understood and devalued. One team member said of his program:

> [Our program has] a regulatory function. There's just no way around
> that. And the vision for the department, is to deregulate. So [our pro-
> gram] is really a dinosaur in the department and no one wants to pay
> much attention to it. It's sort of viewed as a necessary evil, but not
> something that people want to give priority to. Actually our unit does
> more than [this regulatory function] but few people understand this.

A member of another team commented on the difficulty of maintaining
enthusiasm for doing work that was ranked a low priority during the bud-
geting process:

> It's tough. I mean I know my job [was zoned a 3]. It makes it real
> hard to come in here and talk to [the public] and be positive when
> you know that they don't value or care about what you do. . . . And
> I'm not given an option to work on anything else, you know. And I
> think I've demonstrated that I can work on a lot of things. I mean
> there's a lot of things in action. It's not like, "What you do no longer
> fits and these are the new options. Where do you see yourself fitting?"
> That's not it. That's not been there. It's been, "You no longer fit but
> you have to do the job."

Third, understandings of what currently exists are always relative to
what existed in the past; the judgments of VDE staff about the way the new
department functions are relative to the functioning of the old department.
The feeling of some VDE staff that decision-making has become more centralized and bureaucratic than it was in the past may be due, in part, to the
fact that there was almost a complete absence of work coordination and
structure in the old department at some levels. This lack of structure is reflected in the descriptions of staff members about individuals coming to de-

partment jobs with little orientation or guidance, and being left to their own devices in shaping their positions. One team member described her arrival in the department a number of years ago as follows:

> When I arrived in the department, I was surprised. I sat at my desk and was expecting someone to orient me. There was no discussion of expectations, no setting of goals, no evaluation. I just flopped around and did my own thing. I think that's what most people did.

When the basis of comparison is almost total decentralization and individual autonomy, establishing any structure will lead to more centralization.

On the other hand, staff reports that the department's new structure discourages individual initiative and participation in the decision-making and planning process give cause for concern. To date, the VDE has not achieved an organizational balance between encouraging personal initiative and empowerment and achieving coherent action.

Finally, having to do more with less, while the result of external budget exigencies, puts added stress on the internal dynamics of the department. Many staff members are trying to continue carrying out their old responsibilities, while at the same time undertaking new responsibilities—responsibilities that require training and planning to carry out. Efforts to build the capacity to undertake new tasks are slowed by the need to continue with current work. The internal stress caused by budget cuts is compounded by the stress caused by the VDE's restructuring. According to one manager:

> I think [the pain of restructuring comes] from things being unsettled, and I think from the management still being unsettled and undetermined. There are people who are feeling pulled [by their loyalties to old and new management] . . .
>
> Plus, . . . the incredible shrinking budget is killing us. If we had money and support and help, you know in bodies, it wouldn't be as hard as it is, I think. And if we were in our old organization and you were otherwise secure, the budget cuts would be a little easier to handle. I think that you know they're resonating against each other and . . . I think people are blaming the restructuring solely and in fact . . . I think it's the budget [that] is just making everything worse because we have too much to do. We don't know what . . . who's responsible for what and all of that. And as I see it, part of that reality is we just don't have enough to do what we need to do. And even if there was no restructuring this would be a very painful time. . . . It all gets lumped together. And Rick is pushing. He never stops pushing. "Do more, do more." And people don't have the energy to do more and

they don't have the resources to do more and so they're feeling very, very stressed out. Very painful.

Viewing the VDE from a closed-system perspective explains much of what is occurring in the department. This is an organization in the throes of restructuring, and it is caught between old and new paradigms and practices in many respects. The work, the structure, and the norms of the department have all changed, but they have not yet changed to the degree envisioned prior to the restructuring. The VDE is partway along the restructuring continuum, and this is an uncomfortable position for nearly all concerned.

The Wide Lens

The VDE, largely through the efforts of its Commissioner, works hard to manage its external environment and appears to have a substantial degree of success. Mills was repeatedly described by informants as a powerful consensus-builder and facilitator. A member of the State Board of Education said that Mills was known as a consensus-builder in New Jersey, the state from which he had come, and that he had lived up to that reputation. A state legislator, remembering the early discussions of Vermont reforms, described the legislature as a "remedial classroom" instructed by Mills on the need for education reform. Mills built consensus not only in the legislature but also with others, according to the representative:

> The commissioner was not stupid. He involved local boards from the beginning, local people, local business, whatever, so that it would come as an agreement from the ground up, even though the ideas started at the top. And it is unique when you can have that kind of shared ownership. It was shared so deeply that basically the governor at the time . . . received a lot of credit for the statewide goals, when in fact, she came in at the same level the rest of us had. "These are some ideas, bounce them around, see what they are . . ."

The department also works to manage its external environment in other ways, as is illustrated by two examples. First, the department worked with the State Board of Education to develop a *Policy Statement on Deregulation*. This statement includes a set of standards against which the Board will measure all proposed legislation and regulations prior to endorsement or approval. One of these standards defines the role of the VDE vis-à-vis schools, saying, "Any rule or law should place the state education agency in the position of assisting local schools" (State of Vermont Board of Education, 1992, January 21, p. 4). This standard, as well as the others, works to ensure that state policy sends a consistent message to the department regarding its role, and in turn to the schools. The complete list of standards is as follows:

> All proposed legislation and regulations that come before the State Board should be measured against certain standards prior to endorsement or approval. Those standards should be as follows:
> - Any rule or law should advance student performance, but not in such a rigid manner as to foreclose alternative means of achieving goals.
> - The law or regulation should permit local education agencies to implement local policies, consistent with state education agency goals, in a manner that allows for results to be measured. The law or regulation should not prescribe *how* to educate students but *how well* they should be educated. The State Board or Department should intervene only when a school fails to do well by its students.
> - Any rule or law should place the state education agency in the position of assisting local schools.
> - The law or rule should be cost effective. (State of Vermont Board of Education, 1992, January 21, pp. 3–4)

Second, the department is working to make its external customers more thoughtful about their requests for information by detailing the costs of providing that information in its response. Information requests, from legislators and others, often consume substantial staff time. But obtaining this information is costless to requesters, and free goods are readily demanded. The VDE is working to make people more cost-conscious as they consider making information requests. The cover sheet of each requested report lists the requester, the preparer, and the cost of preparation. The costs include staff time as well as materials. One manager explained that a three-page report might cost $1800, once staff time for data analysis, writing, and production were taken into account.

Still, for all its efforts, the VDE cannot control its external environment entirely. It is a public agency and as such must meet certain ongoing demands and obligations even as it is trying to redirect its work. It does not have the option of "closing the plant" while it "retools." It also must meet some demands that cannot be predicted in advance. As one staff member put it, "Anything requested by the governor or legislature is priority red."

Finally, the VDE cannot control the economic condition of the state as a whole. This state context of declining resources complicates the department's work on a number of levels. The internal complications and stresses of doing more with less have been described above. The VDE staff is stretched, and valuable time is spent cutting the budget. In addition, the department is working to convince practitioners to change in an atmosphere where they, too, are doing more with less. Some practitioners commented that the department was pushing some of its costs and responsibilities onto districts at a time when they could ill afford to absorb them. There are fewer consultants available to visit schools and districts, and practitioners are being "borrowed" from districts to staff the state's professional development offerings. While it is true that economic retrenchment can at times force restructuring, retrenchment also takes resources from the system that could be devoted to change.

As Fullan and Miles (1992) say, "Change is resource-hungry" (p. 750). They argue that additional resources are needed for schools attempting change, so that they can buy training, substitutes, materials, space, and, most important, time. I would argue that the same is true of state departments of education attempting change.

PRELIMINARY CONCLUSIONS DRAWN FROM THIS CASE

The VDE is partway through its restructuring process. The department is grappling with difficult questions of what the new work of implementing complex reform implies for its internal structure and culture as well as for its external relationship with schools—questions that have never before been raised in the organization. It also is trying to change in ways that accord with the answers to these questions.

Even though the VDE is working to change in ways that seem likely to better equip it for its new work of implementing complex reform, however, the transition from the old department to the new has been and continues to be difficult on a number of levels. Inside the agency, the old and the new uncomfortably co-exist, leaving staff members confused about both their work and the functioning of the larger organization. The internal transition is incomplete.

Raising these questions prior to the department's restructuring created a new vision for its staff of what might be possible in the department. While change has occurred in the VDE, the new vision has not yet been achieved, and the gap between the real and the envisioned creates dissatisfaction. The VDE is partway along its restructuring continuum, and this is an uncomfortable position for nearly all concerned.

As an organization partway along the restructuring continuum, it is conceivable that the VDE could move in either direction along the continuum. It could revert back to the department it once was or become the department it has envisioned being.

Neither outcome can be predicted with certainty, but I would point to the following as hopeful signs that the VDE would continue along its restructuring path: 1) There are indications that the teams that have been working together for longer periods of time are working as well-integrated teams with substantial decision-making authority. 2) Management in the department seems to want to move in a coherent direction, as envisioned by the restructuring team. While this direction has not yet filtered down to all department team members, management seems to be cognizant of the difficulties in the current organization, and to be making attempts to address them. 3) The department enjoys substantial support from the State Board, the legislature, and professional organizations for the direction in which it is moving.

Even with these hopeful signs, the remaining restructuring of the VDE and the larger implementation of complex reform will not be easy. There is much work to be done, both with staff and practitioners, to make the reasons and direction of complex reform clear and compelling. In addition, more resources will be required, and at this point, where they will come from is not apparent. Complex reform seems achievable in Vermont, but achievement cannot be accomplished without further work, resources, and support.

The case of Vermont is very different from that of Kentucky. Looking across these cases and examining their differences and commonalities is consequently instructive.

CHAPTER 5

Conclusions and Recommendations

State-level complex school reform, orchestrated through the traditional state bureaucracy, puts tremendous pressure on state departments of education. The cases of Kentucky and Vermont chart the struggles and successes of two SDEs as they attempt to implement complex school reform, and the effects SDE actions have on local reform implementation in a small sample of districts.

In this chapter, I draw a common set of conclusions from these two cases. In addition, I use these specific cases to give better definition to the general problem facing SDEs engaged in complex school reform. While these two cases can in no way be called a representative sample, they do differ sufficiently on a number of relevant dimensions to begin to flesh out the intricacies and difficulties of the general problem and some useful approaches to solving it. Finally, I conclude by recommending some basic approaches that SDEs might use in implementing complex school reform.

CONCLUSIONS

The cases of Kentucky and Vermont are similar on some dimensions but also different in significant ways. It is important to understand these similarities and differences when comparing the two cases and trying to draw conclusions from the set because contextual factors shape SDEs' responses to complex reform implementation.

The key similarity between Kentucky and Vermont, for the purposes of this research, is the ambitious nature of the complex reform agendas they are undertaking. Both states are struggling to make their reform efforts genuinely systemic—to achieve a coherent policy environment that will promote and support school reform on a level never before seen. Both states were early leaders in this type of reform effort, and only a few states in the nation had equally ambitious agendas so early on.

As leaders in complex reform, the SDEs in both states and the Commissioners who lead them are breaking new ground in virtually every area. They are working at the boundaries of knowledge and understanding about school and system reform and in a very real sense are having to expand those boundaries as they go along. "Rebuilding the airplane while you're flying it" is an apt metaphor in these cases.

Working at the edge of competence is courageous and risky business. The SDEs of Kentucky and Vermont and their leaders are still held accountable by the external environment for short-term results, even as they have been asked by that environment to take on long-term agendas. The SDEs of Kentucky and Vermont and the Commissioners who lead them represent an elite set. This should not be forgotten, even as I critique their efforts.

Importance of Contextual Factors

Within this frame of similarity, a number of contextual factors differ in the two cases. The contextual factors influence the SDE's response to the work of implementing complex reform. This response takes the form of both the internal operation of the department and the implementation strategy employed by the department.

Six contextual factors seem to influence the Kentucky and Vermont SDEs' responses to their charge of implementing complex reform:

1. the role of the SDE in designing the reform;
2. the role of key external policy players, in these cases the legislatures and state boards of education;
3. the policy history and regulatory environment of the state;
4. the SDE's evaluation of local school and district capacity;
5. agency leadership; and
6. scale.

The two states differ on most of these factors. These variations, in combination, help to explain the differing responses of the two departments in implementing complex school reform.

Role of the SDE in Reform Design. The KDE was almost completely uninvolved in the design of KERA, which was done by three legislative task forces. A few KDE staff members testified before the task forces, but no staff were task force members. The KDE was viewed by legislators as part of the problem that needed to be solved through reform. KERA mandated that the department be closed down and reopened with a new staff and structure.

In contrast, Vermont's Commissioner Mills, and through him the VDE, played the role of "policy entrepreneur" (Kingdon, 1984, p. 129) in Vermont. According to a member of the State Board of Education, Mills was specifically hired as a reformer who could turn Vermont's system around. There were no major reform efforts going on in the state when Mills arrived. It was up to Mills and the VDE to work with others to both design and implement the reforms.

Role of Key External Policy Players.   The state boards of education in both Kentucky and Vermont are viewed as competent, reform-minded bodies that support their Commissioners. The difference between the two states is in the relative weighting of power between the board and the legislature.

In Kentucky, the legislature was judicially charged not only with redesigning the state's school system but also with monitoring the implementation of the new design. The legislature takes this role seriously and monitors the activities of the KDE through an interim committee structure, as well as through the Office of Education Accountability, charged with monitoring all aspects of reform implementation. In addition, there is a regulatory review process in Kentucky in which all state regulations, including those promulgated by the State Board of Education, are reviewed by the General Assembly. When the interim regulation review subcommittee reviews a regulation, it may either do nothing, in which case the regulation goes into effect, or it may attach a letter. If a letter is attached, the regulation sunsets at the end of the next regular session of the General Assembly unless the assembly enacts the regulation as statute during the session. The legislature ultimately can overturn a State Board of Education regulation if it attaches a letter and then lets the regulation die in session.

In Vermont, the State Board of Education has primary responsibility for the direction of education in the state. The state does have a regulatory review process in which all regulations are reviewed by the Legislative Committee on Administrative Rules to see if they square with legislative intent. If this committee flags a regulation, it may still go into effect, but the burden of proof falls on the agency, and the rule probably would not stand if challenged in court. This flagging has never occurred during the recent reform efforts, but, according to a VDE staff member, the department goes over all regulations with the legislature, and numerous changes are made as a result of these discussions. The support of the legislature is clearly important for education reform in Vermont for approving the rulings of the State Board, for maintaining political consensus in the state, and because the legislature controls the purse. But in comparison with Kentucky, little of Vermont's reform agenda is legislated, and the legislature is not engaged in the same level of oversight of department activities.

Policy History and Regulatory Environment of the State.   Kentucky has historically had a strong state presence in education. In the 1980s, following publication of *A Nation at Risk* (National Commission on Excellence in Education, 1983), the General Assembly passed legislation that required testing of new teachers, specified the percentage of time to be spent in schools on the development of basic skills, required basic skills testing of students, and provided for state takeover of educationally deficient districts (Legislative Research Commission, 1984).

Vermont, conversely, has had little state presence in education prior to its current reforms. Virtually the only state regulatory program has been Public School Approval (PSA), in which schools are evaluated once every 10 years based on criteria such as curriculum, materials, physical plant, and certified teachers. If schools do not comply with PSA standards in the period of time established in their improvement plans, they may lose a portion of their state aid. In addition, since state law says that no Vermont student may attend a disapproved school, students in these schools would have to be tuitioned out to approved institutions, but neither of these steps has ever been taken. There was no state testing program of any kind. The state's former Basic Competency program serves as an example of the nondirective nature of state policy. Although all students were required to master basic competencies prior to graduation, mastery was defined and tested at the local level.

The SDE's Evaluation of Local School and District Capacity. While staff in the KDE acknowledge that there are high-capacity school districts in Kentucky, they find that there are many districts in which basic capacity for reform is lacking. Staff cite poor to nonexistent decision-making processes and lack of curriculum and professional development as examples of areas in which local capacity needs to be built. Capacity is lacking in many districts, even in the traditional sense of the term. This lack of capacity is even deeper when ambitious reforms of teaching and learning are being attempted.

The VDE staff also talks of the need to build local capacity, and there are some low-capacity districts in the state. The overall impression drawn from interviews with VDE staff, however, is that local capacity needs to be developed because current state reforms are aiming for a type of teaching and learning that is very different from the traditional definitions. Most districts in Vermont are viewed as in good shape when judged by traditional measures.

Agency Leadership. There are different conceptions of the Commissioner's role operating in these two cases. This is evident from the Commissioners' responses when asked to describe the role they play. Boysen of Kentucky responded:

> I would say [I'm] sort of like the contractor on a construction project where the architects have already laid it out, and the design is there,

and now you have to bring it into being. And you're trying to stay true to the original design and stay within the budget. And then every once in a while you get a change order, . . . something has got to be different from what was contemplated and you have to get that processed. . . . It's . . . sort of a technical and professional role. There's a political role, too, which is being a spokesperson for it. And . . . I'm probably the person, by virtue of the position, who is called upon the most frequently. But . . . there are [al]so many other spokespersons.

Mills of Vermont responded:

My role is on all occasions to project a vision and to keep in front of people a picture of what it could be like, to create opportunities for more and more and more people and groups of people to be a part of that vision . . . to see their own part in it. My part is to tell the truth about what's happening. And one of my responsibilities in the law is to report to the public on the condition of education. I do that formally through a written report and conference but I do it also every time I have a microphone in front of me. If I'm on television, or if I'm talking to a reporter, or if I'm talking to a legislative committee, a group of business people, a group of parents, or just one person over coffee, they end up hearing the story about how the schools are. . . "There are a lot of champions out there, but schools are not as great as a lot of people think. Massive radical change is essential and here's how we do it. Join in," is the message.

Two different forms of leadership are described here. Mills assumes responsibility for creating the vision and coherence for the state's reform effort. Boysen believes that the vision and coherence come from the reform design itself—the KERA legislation. His job, then, is to manage implementation in a way that is true to that design.

Scale.   Kentucky and Vermont are attempting complex reform on very different scales. The KDE is four times bigger than the VDE in terms of number of staff and serves just under four times the number of schools that the VDE does. Kentucky's schools are also spread over a larger geographical area.

One VDE staff member, when asked how the department had strengthened its linkages with external partners, while acknowledging that an atmosphere of collaboration had been built over the last few years, said:

> To be honest, I think . . . one of the great advantages we have in Vermont is everybody kind of knows everybody else and what they're doing. I mean that's sort of a gross overstatement . . . but it's kind of true.

The precise effect that scale has on the reform process is difficult to measure. My sense from these two cases is that while Kentucky and Vermont face similar challenges in trying to bring about complex reform, the larger scale of Kentucky makes addressing those challenges even more difficult. Developing the personal relationships that engender trust and facilitate the coordination of work, for example, is that much harder both in the KDE itself and in the state of Kentucky as a whole.

Additional Conclusions

In addition to demonstrating the importance of contextual factors, these case studies both point to a number of additional conclusions. First, what happens in SDEs should matter to people interested in school reform because the internal culture and organization of the agency are reflected in the implementation relationship between the agency and the field. Staff in the Kentucky department report little autonomous decision-making; Kentucky practitioners report that they are overregulated and that extensive reporting on process is required. The "old" and "new" conceptions of the Vermont department are uncomfortably coexisting within the agency, causing confusion for staff as to which of their work is the priority; Vermont practitioners are receiving both "old" and "new" messages from the department, creating confusion over the department's priorities in the field. SDEs are key players in the implementation of complex reform, and as such, they set the tone and parameters for the process. How the agencies themselves function seems to have important implications for the success or failure of complex reform.

Second, given the first conclusion, we must also conclude that leadership of the SDE matters. This leadership must focus not only on presenting and leading reform externally but also on building departmental capacity internally. There cannot be a disjunction between the principles and goals of the reform effort and the principles and goals of the department because one reflects the other. This is not to say that the Commissioner personally has to take responsibility for internal operations, but it does mean that the Commissioner needs to lead the department in ways that are congruent with the goals of the reform and also needs to make internal operations of the department a priority, even if that means giving someone else primary responsibility for them. As Gideonse says:

What is needed is a consciousness on the part of top management on down that the daily life of the organization is at least as important as the deliberations on high policy, for it is in the daily life that that policy is implemented. If the atmosphere is sour, so will be the implementation. (Gideonse, 1980, p. 67)

Third, implementation of complex school reform seems to require a more activist definition of the Commissioner's and department's role—one that is more analogous to that played by Mills and the VDE than by Boysen and the KDE. Mills and, by extension, the VDE have taken on reform design as well as implementation. They are the architects and the contractors, with the help of many allies. They take responsibility for shaping their external environment, such as their relationship with the Board and the legislature, rather than simply responding to it. To Boysen and by extension the KDE, implementing complex reform is about implementing the KERA legislation. They are the contractors. They implement the reform according to the specs of the legislation but do not seem to take responsibility for shaping either the grand design or their external environment.

It is true that the two Commissioners entered very different states under very different circumstances. Mills entered a state with some readiness for reform but no design in place. This meant that he and the department, along with many others, could play the role of architect as well as contractor.

When Boysen came to Kentucky, the design work was done, at least to the extent that the grand design had been established. Still, the architect/contractor metaphor seems to break down in the discussion of policy design and implementation because in a real sense, policy is continually designed through implementation. This is particularly true in the implementation of complex policies because of the high degree of uncertainty about what precisely should be done at all levels. Legislation, no matter how thoughtfully written, cannot possibly foresee all of the problems and challenges that will arise during implementation. It is up to the department, then, as the implementation arm of the state, to make the intelligent adjustments needed in the implementation process and to manage its external environment so that it has the political space in which to do this.

What follows from the department's key implementation responsibility is that it also is at least partially responsible for forging agreements with the legislature and board of education that will allow it to do the necessary work coherently.[1] These agreements might take the form of the Vermont State Board of Education's standards for judging new legislation or regulation (see the list of standards in Chapter 4). Making intelligent adjustments and forging agreements with policymakers are more proactive definitions of the department's role than waiting for a "change order."

The Vermont case demonstrates that it is at least possible for an SDE to exert some control over its external environment. It is undoubtedly true that this task would be more difficult in Kentucky. Boysen was hired to implement the legislators' reform design rather than to be one of the reform designers as was Mills. Kentucky legislators felt tremendous ownership over the reform. In addition, they distrusted the KDE, which was viewed predominantly as part of the problem that needed to be fixed rather than as a potential part of the solution. It would be difficult for Boysen, or anyone, to exert control or forge consensus in this environment, especially initially. Boysen is performing his job as the legislature envisioned. He is implementing the law.

The question is whether or not implementing the law is sufficient to genuinely implement complex reform. I argue that implementing the law is too narrow a definition of success. It would be possible to implement the law as written, enforce compliance with many aspects of it—such as SBDM and ungraded primary—and still not have dramatically improved teaching and learning. While some might argue that schools will not be able to meet their assessment thresholds without a dramatic improvement of teaching and learning, I would argue that if the vast majority of schools continually fail to meet their thresholds, Kentucky will not be able to uphold them.

The KDE and others need to work to generate practitioner commitment to the reforms, and the KDE needs some flexibility within its external environment in order to do this. While it would be difficult for Boysen and the KDE to exert some control over the external environment, I am not prepared to say that exerting control would be impossible, and it would seem to be an important goal to strive for over time.

Fourth, local practitioners are looking for greater involvement of SDE staff in schools. Practitioners urge this involvement for two reasons. First, they want SDE staff to understand the current conditions of schooling—both positive and negative—and consequently to understand the difficulties inherent in the implementation of complex reform. Second, they want SDE staff to know their *individual* schools and districts. Every school and district starts in a different place, surrounded by a different context, these practitioners argue. SDE staff have to know the conditions in each school and district and work with each school and district accordingly.[2] Practitioners are calling for "differential treatment"—treatment that is appropriate to the conditions of their individual sites (Fuhrman & Fry, 1989).

Fifth, these cases call into question the efficacy of any widespread use of mandates, regulation, and oversight. The fact that in both cases state mandates and reporting requirements appear to be most onerous for the districts who need them the least calls their value into question, at least when used nondifferentially. Regulation and oversight may have a place in school reform, but they are counterproductive when they impede good-faith change efforts.

PROBLEMS FOR SDEs ENGAGED IN COMPLEX REFORM

Understanding the complexities of Kentucky and Vermont also allows us to better articulate the general problem SDEs face when they engage in complex school reform. SDEs engaged in complex reform are faced with implementing a reform whose success depends on multifaceted layers of change (Elmore & Fuhrman, 1993, September, pp. 8–10). Change needs to occur in the external policy environment, the department itself, schools and districts, and the community at large.

The problem of bringing about change in all of these areas is even more complicated because of the reciprocal uncertainty present. Neither the SDE, nor the schools, nor anyone, knows exactly what should be done over a period of time. Complex school reform is, to a large degree, uncharted water for all concerned.

Within this context of multilayered uncertainty, the question for the SDE (as well as for others engaged in this reform) becomes how best to push, support, and manage change on all of these levels. I in no way mean to imply that SDEs can take sole responsibility for all of the needed changes. However, they, in addition to others, need to think strategically about how to move change forward at a variety of levels. Finding the best way to do this represents a balancing act for the agency in a number of areas, leading us to the first characteristic of the problem SDEs face in trying to implement complex school reform.

Numerous Dilemmas

SDEs walk a fine line between a number of dilemmas in complex reform efforts. Negotiating these dilemmas requires finding a balance between them, and achieving this balance requires flexibility on the part of SDEs.

Too Much Leniency Versus Too Much Stringency. If SDEs choose leniency by providing too little pressure for change, they may find practitioners to be so complacent that change never occurs. This complacency is captured in practitioner statements such as "This, too, shall pass." If SDEs choose stringency, however, change may never occur due to system overload. If the work cannot realistically be accomplished according to state-mandated time lines, then practitioners may burn out and/or revolt.

Another example of the leniency/stringency dilemma exists around listening to practitioners. If SDEs change course every time a practitioner or group of practitioners objects, change will never occur. If, however, SDEs listen to practitioners insufficiently, dumb or harmful policies that impede the reform of teaching and learning may be implemented. SDEs must develop a strategy not only for seeking practitioner input but also for filtering it. Such a filter might be provided partially through developing close working relationships with a number of reform-minded practitioners. In addition, more detailed knowledge of the majority of schools and districts would help SDEs determine the relative validity of different feedback from the field.

Being Inflexible Versus Frustrating Schools and Districts with Mixed Messages. As one practitioner interviewed said, "Change needs to be carved in play dough." Because of the newness and uncertainty of complex school reform, we have to expect that mistakes will be made, and that state approaches will need to be modified and reconsidered. If SDEs do not make intelligent adjustments as implementation progresses, then less than optimal policies will be implemented. These intelligent adjustments, however, may frustrate some practitioners who view the changes as mixed messages and/ or capriciousness.

SDEs will never be able to please everyone no matter how responsible and flexible they seek to be in implementation. There are some strategies, however, that may help departments please more people more of the time. One strategy would be entering into a dialogue with practitioners around not only needed reforms but also the nature of the change process itself, so that adjustments are expected. In addition, allowing sufficient time for reform would make these adjustments more palatable. Changes in an assessment system are easier to accept, for example, if stakes are not attached to them while the adjustments are being made. Finally, publicizing not only the changes made but also the reasons for them may help to build empathy in the field.

Providing Insufficient Training Versus Providing So Much Training That Practitioners Are Never in Their Schools. There is a fine line between providing training that builds capacity and taking practitioners out of schools for so much training that capacity is undermined. The most obvious example in the cases studied was the Kentucky principal who had 30 off-site meetings having to do with KERA in the month of February—a 28-day month. A principal cannot be an instructional leader if he is constantly pulled from the building. A number of teachers in both states said that they did not like to miss class time for professional development. In addition to the concern over pulling practitioners from their schools too frequently, there is the additional point that people need time to fully absorb, practice, and implement the training given. Multiple training sessions done in rapid succession may not be the most effective for changing practice. SDEs need to strive to make building capacity a practice-based activity rather than an add-on for practitioners.

Changing Too Little of the System Versus Changing So Much That There Is an Insufficient Foundation for Change.   Complex school reform is about changing the whole of the system. At the same time, there is some evidence in these cases that reform requires some underlying stability. Practitioners in both states said that the restructuring of the department of education caused confusion; they no longer knew whom to call. A practitioner in Kentucky commented that the integrated professional development series probably would have continued if the director of the KDE's Division of Professional Development had not changed. And a KDE staff member commented that it was difficult to keep reform moving when key positions turned over in the department. None of these examples are an argument against change. They do, however, collectively argue for strategic thinking around which elements of the system should be changed at what time and how much stability is needed to serve as a foundation for reform. In other words, SDEs need to consider how much change the system can tolerate before the quantity becomes counterproductive.

The cases of Kentucky and Vermont suggest a range of possible strategies to change the system on a number of levels. Since I have focused particularly on the relationship between SDEs and schools, I will now pose a way of conceptualizing the problem of changing *all* schools.

Changing a Broad Spectrum of Schools[3]

The second characteristic of the problem facing SDEs engaged in complex reform is that *all* schools need to be changed. Departments consequently need to have a strategy that takes the spectrum of schools they are working with into account. They are faced with the problem of moving the spectrum of schools in the desired direction. Not only do SDEs want to move the whole distribution of school achievement upward, they also want to narrow that distribution by moving the vast majority, if not all schools, to the positive, high end of the achievement spectrum. In other words, these SDEs want all schools performing at a similarly high level, as measured by student outcomes.

The next questions are: What does this distribution of schools that the state is trying to both move up and narrow look like? And what are the state's goals in approaching and working with schools that fall along each portion of the distribution? I posit that schools can be very roughly categorized into three broad types and that the SDE's approach to working with schools should differ according to these types.[4]

The "Early Adopter" Schools.   On the high end of the distribution, there are the "early adopter" schools, which may or may not be located in generally high-performing districts. These are schools that were engaged in the type of reforms that the state is advocating early on, before the state's initiative began. The state may have even looked to them for ideas when shaping its reforms. These schools do not necessarily have every facet of the state-envisioned reform in place, but they have some in place or at least have made significant strides in those directions. These schools will probably make up a relatively small portion of the distribution.

I argue that the goals of the SDE in working with these early adopter schools should be three:

1. *Not to impede their reform efforts in any way with state policies designed for less forward-thinking schools and districts.*

   Making available rule-by-rule waivers or other policy options that put the onus on these schools is insufficient for meeting this goal. The state needs to proactively deregulate these schools, not simply establish a lengthy process of which schools may avail themselves.

2. *To do everything possible to help these schools move forward at a faster pace than they could on their own, so that they can become (or remain) exemplars of what state reformers have in mind for all schools, and also so that the state and others can learn from the progress and pitfalls of these schools.*

   Meeting this goal involves not only getting out of the way of these schools but also in some way positively helping them to move forward. Ways of moving these schools forward might include recognizing their efforts, both to draw attention to them and give them the legitimacy of state approval. This attention and legitimacy would help early adopter schools win community support and attract additional resources, such as grants. Providing technical assistance and support in areas needed by these schools could also help to further their efforts. This might be done by people at the state level if they have the skills and expertise, the state might bring assistance in from outside, or assistance might come from networking with other practitioners—something that could be facilitated by the state. Finally, the state might provide these schools with additional resources through providing grants or through other mechanisms.

3. *To do everything possible to make these schools allies, bringing them on board to work with and support state efforts so that other practitioners can learn from the work of the early adopters.*

   The state needs to make early adopter schools valued partners in the work. Doing so will give the state partners from whom it can learn more about the nature of reform implementation. It will also give the state a group of practitioners and schools who can serve as advocates, professional developers, and reform exemplars.

   Meeting this goal may also pose a problem, however, as may some of the strategies proposed under goal two above: The state may be reluctant to recognize early adopter schools for fear that these schools themselves, as well as others in the state, will take this recognition to mean that these schools represent the "reform ideal" in all areas, which the vast majority will not. Somehow these schools need to be recognized, supported, and brought on board while at the same time challenged to continue striving for self-improvement. The state needs to develop a relationship with these schools that, while recognizing their efforts, will also encourage and maintain self-critical practice.

The "Status Quo" Schools.   The vast majority of schools in a state are status quo schools. These schools have delivered decent to high-quality, traditional education for a long time but are not known for taking the lead in major reform efforts. I argue that the SDE's goals in working with these schools are also three:

1. *To convince them of the need and desirability of change.*

    This could be done through exposing these schools to new ideas and information on the need for change. It would also be helpful to put these schools in contact with early adopter schools so that status quo practitioners could see some of the state's proposed reforms in action. The state might also work to generate broad-based community support for reform, which would in turn pressure practitioners in status quo schools and support their nascent change efforts.

2. *To assist them in moving the desired change forward with all possible speed, while at the same time doing a quality job.*

    This might be done through providing technical assistance, putting these practitioners in touch with other knowledgeable people who can serve as resources, and providing additional resources such as grants to plan and implement reform efforts. It would also be important for the SDE to be cognizant of the effect of state regulation on the reform efforts of these schools and to help them deregulate (as would be done with the early adopters) at the point where state regulation becomes an impediment.

3. *To treat these schools as early adopters when appropriate.*

    This rough categorization of schools for the purpose of targeting assistance should not become a rigid classification system. The categories need to be permeable and flexible. School reform efforts should not be impeded by state rules and regulations. Proactive deregulation should be available to all schools willing to demonstrate that they will and are using it wisely, or perhaps to all schools that request it, until such time as they demonstrate that they cannot use it wisely.

An argument could also be made for deregulating these schools up front, with the reasoning that this deregulation might spur on and free the change process (Consortium for Policy Research in Education, 1992). Deregulation, however, is not an obvious or easy solution to the problem of encouraging responsible innovation. Fuhrman and Elmore (March 1995) found deregulation to be only one of a number of policy approaches to enabling school improvement. They also found that state deregulation efforts, by themselves, had mixed effects and contained a number of difficulties and quandaries within them. Deregulation might need to be considered on something like a case-by-case basis, in consultation with the practitioners involved.

The "Troubled" Schools. A small minority of schools are probably in the "low-performing" or "troubled" category. These are likely to be schools that the state has been concerned about for some time due to their poor delivery of educational services.

In many ways the state has the same goals in approaching these schools as they do in approaching the status quo schools, but they may need to meet these goals in different ways. For example, the state may need to be more authoritative in its demands for change and also in its enforcement of existing state regulation. This will be particularly true if a school is truly recalcitrant or corrupt, as opposed to simply lacking in knowledge and other resources. The state may also need to connect these schools with stronger assistance efforts so that they can catch up to other schools and move forward quickly. Finally, if a disparity in resources is the major problem these schools face, it would be up to the state and/or district to take measures to equalize available resources. Resource disparities are not problems that schools can address by themselves.

The above description of a potential differential treatment strategy for schools is simplistic. It may be difficult for the state or anyone to identify which category each school falls under, the relevant category for a given school may change quite suddenly, and so on. Still, categorizing types of schools is a helpful construct, even if used largely informally. The construct can remind SDE staff and other policymakers that they have to know schools and that one policy size does not fit all.

Using such a categorization of schools implies that SDE staff or their representatives need to know schools well in order to make joint judgments with practitioners as to what level of assistance would most help to move their schools forward. Some of the practices that might help SDEs to have this knowledge of schools are outlined in the recommendations below.

Using such a categorization to define treatment of schools also diverges somewhat from the body of research that calls for broader-based, blanket deregulation (Consortium for Policy Research in Education, 1992). This research argues that if deregulation is good for successful schools, it will probably also be good for others—"persistent compliance shirkers or 'bad apples' aside" (Consortium for Policy Research in Education, 1992, p. 4).

My argument differs from this slightly because I am calling for differential treatment based on the progress of reform in general, as opposed to based only on student achievement. This method of at least rough categorization would mean that traditional schools with high test scores would fall into the "status quo" category, while schools with lower scores but more ambitious reform agendas would be in the "early adopter" category. I find that the Kentucky and Vermont cases add a cautionary note to the recommendation of immediate, broader-based deregulation. In Kentucky, there are a number of low-capacity districts, and it is unclear that total deregulation prior to building capacity will serve students well. In Vermont, the superintendent of the troubled district viewed state regulation as necessary for forcing the community to provide at least some minimal level of educational services, and even in the early adopter district, a principal expressed concern over dropping Carnegie units with nothing to replace them.

Still, the relative weakness of mandates that was also demonstrated by these two cases cannot be forgotten. While the enforcement of regulation may be necessary in some cases, it will never be sufficient for achieving reform.

Finally, it should be pointed out that this strategy of differential treatment of schools and districts, and indeed any change in the relationship between SDEs and schools, may cause political problems for departments and will also have to be legally defensible. A staff member of the Vermont department talked about practitioners lobbying legislators for the maintenance of subject matter consultants. School people view these positions as important supports even though the one-on-one work of consultants with teachers is not a sensible reform strategy because of the small number of teachers affected. In addition, even though practitioners interviewed, particularly in Vermont, called for the creation of model schools, it seems likely that if the creation of such models meant that some other schools got fewer resources or even reduced access to additional resources, someone would be sure to complain, maybe even through the legal system. As SDEs seek to change their relationships with schools and districts, they need to realize that even the most justifiable changes may not be immediately embraced by practitioners.

SDEs need to listen carefully to these concerns from the field. But they also need to separate the needs of the field from the provision of those needs as they listen. Practitioners may well need the assistance of subject matter specialists, for example, but this does not mean that this particular assistance has to be provided by SDE staff, even if a historical precedent exists for this type of service provision.

Limited Resources

The third characteristic of the problem facing SDEs engaged in complex school reform is that the resources of SDEs are limited in a number of ways. They have few staff, especially relative to the number of schools with which they are expected to work. It is impossible for SDE staff to make numerous (or maybe even one) site visit to every school in the state. Staff generally have limited, if any, expertise in working with reforming schools. SDE staff are more likely to specialize in a certain curriculum or regulatory area than in whole-school change. SDEs have limited funds, and many of their funds are tied to specific, categorical areas such as special education, complicating flexible spending (Council of Chief State School Officers, 1983, pp. 63–64). SDEs have traditionally had limited relationships with schools, often focusing on oversight, making it difficult for practitioners to believe new SDE messages of a willingness to provide nonevaluative service and support.

RECOMMENDATIONS

Given what we have learned from the specific cases of Kentucky and Vermont, as well as the more general problems facing SDEs engaged in complex school reform, what recommendations might be given to SDEs in other states embarking on this type of work? I propose seven:

1. The modus operandi of the SDE, both in terms of its internal operation and its implementation strategy, needs to model the desired values, norms, and goals of the reform effort. If what happens inside SDEs is reflected in the implementation relationships between departments and schools, then the internal workings of SDEs need to model the desired results of state-level reform efforts to the maximum extent possible. If policies are intended to be integrated and mutually reinforcing at the school sites, for example, then the SDE's design and delivery of these policies must also be integrated and mutually reinforcing. If one part of the department is asking schools to "break the mold" while another is demanding traditional scope and sequencing of curriculum, it is hard to see how integrated implementation can take place.

Cohen, McLaughlin, and Talbert have proposed the metaphor of policymaking as pedagogy (Cohen, McLaughlin, & Talbert, 1993, Chapters 7 and 8). One aspect of good pedagogy is modeling the desired behaviors, attitudes, and approaches that you wish to see your students adopt. Extending this metaphor to SDEs means that not only their message but also their approaches to delivering that message must be congruent with the reform. Increased local control through school-based decision-making loses some of its meaning if the SDE proceeds to direct the process and time line for making those decisions. Modeling the desired behavior and approaches within the SDE can help to create the ability to model those same behaviors and approaches in the field.

A potential tension in this call for modeling exists when SDE staff do not believe that schools and districts have the necessary capacity to implement the reforms in the desired manner. In Kentucky particularly, policymakers, both in the KDE and outside, do not trust practitioners to use their new discretion wisely, and regulations and reporting requirements proliferate as a consequence. Even though KERA was supposed to entail a shift to outcomes accountability, the state does not trust that all schools can develop processes to reach those outcomes. Thoughtful, data-based differential treatment of the kind proposed above could alleviate the tension caused by this lack of trust.

2. SDEs need to know schools and districts to improve initial policy design, plan for its successful implementation, and make reform initiatives locally appropriate so that change can occur. SDE staff need to know the conditions of schooling in order to design sensible and effective policies and plans for their implementation. They need to know *individual* schools and districts in order to make reform initiatives locally appropriate—in other words, to make differential treatment a self-conscious and data-based strategy.

A tension arises from this recommendation: There are many more schools than there are SDE staff. Indeed, SDE staff have been criticized at least since 1967 for using the inefficient strategy of giving one-on-one assistance to teachers (Campbell, Sroufe, & Layton, 1967). On the other hand, it is impossible to really know individual schools and districts without being in them.

One way to address this tension is for SDEs to use other partners to visit schools in addition to SDE staff, as Vermont is attempting to do with its Restructuring Corps. By building partnerships with university professors and graduate students, other professional development groups, practitioners, and other community members, it seems at least conceivable that each school could have a department liaison.

This solution to the problem of limited staff would still require that these external liaisons have a close relationship and easy access to SDE staff. Someone *in the department* will still need to know each school, or at a minimum each district, in order for differential treatment to be thoughtfully applied.[5] A reorientation of the work of SDE staff will still be required.

I am not arguing, however, that simply having outside partners report to SDE staff on the conditions of individual districts and schools is sufficient. In fact, I argue that having SDE staff themselves spend some time *in schools* is necessary to the development of appropriate policy. Spending time in schools is necessary because it is easy to lose the perspective of school-based practitioners without walking in their shoes to at least some degree.

I offer an experience I had in Vermont while doing this research as one small example of why it is important to spend time in schools. The Vermont assessment system makes no allowance in its procedures for special needs students, based on the reasoning that every school has these students, and when school performance data are reported, the percentage of special needs students also will be included in the report. Sitting in the VDE, this policy made perfect sense to me. On one of my school visits, however, a teacher told me how frustrating it was for her to have spent a year building up a special needs student's academic self-confidence, only to have him sit helplessly for 90 minutes during the uniform writing prompt because he was unable to do the assignment and she was not allowed to help him. Sitting in a school, I thought that this policy would make me extremely frustrated as a teacher, and angry if I were the parent of a special needs child.[6] What seems sensible often depends upon context.

3. SDEs need to proactively shape their external environments in contextually appropriate ways.   Judging from these two cases, the successful implementation of complex reform seems to require that SDEs take a proactive stance toward shaping their external environments. Complex reform requires change of the entire education system and consequently requires the long-term support of policy players outside of the SDE—particularly the legislature and state board of education in these cases.

There is a fine line, however, between the support of these players and overdirection from these players. The SDE must reserve for itself the power to make intelligent adjustments to the reforms and their implementation in wide consultation with external policymakers and, especially, with practitioners. Designing complex reform is new and uncertain work even for "expert" educational consultants. No legislature, state board, or SDE can possibly foresee all of the issues and problems that will arise during implementation, no matter how carefully the initial reforms are designed. SDEs are closer to the work of schools and districts (and will become still closer if these recommendations are taken) than are legislatures and state boards. Consequently, SDEs, probably largely through the work of their Commissioners, need to be proactive in their efforts to maintain flexibility.

4. SDEs need to develop and/or strengthen different policy instruments and approaches in order to implement complex reform. SDEs have a policy "tool kit" that is ill-suited to implementing complex reform. The policy tools that currently are used most frequently are mandated process regulation and monetary inducements (McDonnell & Elmore, 1987). The use of this tool kit is characterized by an emphasis on uniformity of treatment, little individual contact with schools, and a set of habits and attitudes geared toward monitoring, as opposed to promoting change in practice.

McDonnell and Elmore (1987) argue that states have two other generic types of policy instruments at their disposal: capacity-building—"the transfer of money for the purpose of investment in material, intellectual, or human resources"—and system-changing—"transfer[ring] official authority among individuals and agencies in order to alter the system by which public goods and services are delivered" (p. 134). However:

> Political pressures mean that policymakers usually use a narrow range of instruments, resorting primarily to mandates and incentives, which promise short-term results or provide inexpensive ways to get new programs underway. More long-term strategies aimed at building the capacity of schools and districts to provide quality instruction are much rarer. (Elmore & Fuhrman, 1993, September, p. 9; citing McDonnell & Elmore, 1987)

The goal of complex reform is specifically to improve instruction, and thereby student achievement. Bringing about this type of reform is long-term work requiring additional capacity at both the state and local level. It is also work that no one to date has had much success with, particularly on a statewide scale. No one knows exactly how to bring complex reform about.

Because of these characteristics of complex reform, I argue that not only do SDEs need to expand their use of the instruments of capacity-building and system-changing in the implementation of complex reform, but they also need to add two additional policy instruments or approaches to their tool kits. The approaches that need to be added are persuasion and joint learning.

"Persuasion" includes the power of the idea, which was cited in Vermont, establishing a climate for change, and "winning adherence to norms" (Barzelay with the collaboration of B. J. Armajani, 1992). The use of persuasion is required for two reasons. First, successful implementation of complex reform requires commitment rather than just compliance, meaning that practitioners and others need to be persuaded of the desirability of this type of reform. Second, it is unlikely that SDEs by themselves will ever have sufficient capacity to bring about this type of reform (Elmore & Fuhrman,

1993, September). This means that SDEs must establish a direction for schools to move in, a climate that works to push them in that direction, and an approach that wins adherence to the norms of complex reform—including promoting high achievement for all students and designing local practices appropriate to that end.

The increased use of persuasion by SDEs would have a number of advantages. First, it would help to generate the commitment that complex reform requires. Second, it would reduce the need for rules and their enforcement, the effectiveness of which is questionable anyway due to the nature of teaching. Good teaching and schooling require a myriad of decisions on a daily basis. The "right" decision is context-specific; the most successful approach for one student may not be the most successful approach for the next. Consequently, rules of good teaching and schooling cannot be prescribed. Instead, the goal of the SDE should be to help practitioners make their myriad decisions in accordance with the norms of complex reform.

> Since achieving adherence to norms requires people to make choices among alternatives under conditions of complexity and ambiguity, compliance strategies should empower compliers to apply norms to their particular circumstances. Compliers become empowered, by definition, when they feel personally responsible for adhering to the norms and are psychologically invested in the task of finding the best way to comply. Taking personal responsibility for results is as crucial to making good compliance decisions as to delivering quality goods and services. (Barzelay with the collaboration of B. J. Armajani, 1992, p. 125)

My argument for increased emphasis on winning adherence to norms should not be construed as an argument for completely eliminating monitoring and enforcement. "Some people may not respond adequately to efforts to win their compliance. For this reason, enforcement remains an indispensable function even when the focus is on winning adherence to norms" (Barzelay with the collaboration of B. J. Armajani, 1992, p. 126).

"Joint learning" encompasses all strategies that team the SDE with outside organizations and individuals for the express purpose of bringing about learning on both sides. One such strategy is developing "critical friendships" between SDE staff and schools.[7] A critical friend is "a knowledgeable outsider who can ask the crucial questions and help schools find the answers. The critical friend can see potential problems and upcoming challenges, bringing a new perspective and a certain distance to the issues at hand" (Lusi, 1994, p. 119).[8] Establishing critical friendships between SDE staff and individual schools can help practitioners to become more reflective about their change process, its goals, and how it can be furthered. These friendships will also encourage joint learning: Practitioners will learn more about the process of school change and also the work of the SDE; SDE staff will learn more about the school change process and the difficulties of policy implementation. These learnings will help the SDE to refine both the policy and the strategies for its implementation.

Professional development will be needed by many SDE staff before they have the skills and abilities to engage in critical friendship relationships with schools. It will also probably take time and experience before school practitioners really believe that SDE staff want to engage them in a joint learning relationship. In short, implementing this strategy will not be easy.

5. Nearly all state education policies should be designed with an eye toward building local capacity for change.   Because the need to build local capacity is so great and because the resources of SDEs are so few, nearly all state education policies should be designed with an eye toward building local capacity for change. There will still be a need for some monitoring of schools by the state, but ideally, even monitoring should work to create further local capacity. Such monitoring would give schools useful feedback on their performance, generating dialogue around aims and the success of meeting those aims. This process would build the capacity and habit of self-reflection and critique in schools. Examples of such combined monitoring and capacity approaches include New York State's School Quality Review Initiative (Nathanson, 1993) and Vermont's deregulation policy, which includes visits by a team of VDE staff and practitioners (State of Vermont Board of Education, 1993, March 16, p. 2).

At the same time, however, SDEs must be cognizant of the tensions that may arise in "dual-purpose" policies, designed to fulfill both accountability and capacity-building needs. Vermont's assessment program is an example of these potential tensions. The assessment program and the VDE's approach to implementing it were specifically designed to "encourage good practice and be integrally related to the professional development of educators" (Koretz, Stecher, & Deibert, 1992, p. 2). This is why the VDE has worked to train all teachers in portfolio scoring, rather than only a small, intensively trained group of scorers. The assessment program is also designed, however, to be a mechanism for state-level accountability, and the VDE hopes to report results at the state, district, and school level. This level of reporting requires interrater reliability, the accomplishment of which is more difficult as the number of scorers increases. There was at least preliminary evidence in the Vermont case that the VDE's emphasis on interrater reliability, necessary to meet the accountability goal, was creating teacher disillusionment with the portfolio process as a whole. SDEs need to study their dual purpose policies carefully as they are implemented to ensure that the two goals are not working at cross purposes.

6. State policymakers need a touchstone that guides their reform efforts. A touchstone, be it a statement of principles, a series of questions, or something else, can help to make a state's reform efforts coherent. The Vermont State Board of Education's "Policy Statement on Deregulation," for example, works to ensure that policy and regulation send a consistent message both to schools about the goals of the state and also to the VDE about its role in assisting schools.

Another example of such a touchstone comes from Minnesota's Information Policy Office, in an altogether different type of agency, in which administrators posed these questions to themselves as they shaped the structure and operation of the office:

> What would happen if we based our actions on the premise that 95% of state employees would be willing to comply fully with norms if only they knew what was expected of them and why?
>
> Can we design a control system that does not shackle most employees, while making use of techniques that will be fruitful in dealing with the minority who are unwilling or unable to comply?
>
> Can we exercise control in ways that help managers succeed in fulfilling their agencies' missions? (Barzelay with the collaboration of B. J. Armajani, 1992, p. 66)

In Kentucky, where such a touchstone does not exist, in contrast, both schools and the KDE receive mixed messages from the legislature. The reform rhetoric speaks of deregulation of schools and a service-oriented department, but much of the legislation requires reporting, monitoring, and oversight.

7. SDEs need partners in their work. SDEs need partners in their work of implementing complex school reform for at least three reasons. First, they do not have the capacity to do the job. They do not have sufficient staff to work with all schools or to develop all products such as assessments, and existing staff do not necessarily have the skills and knowledge necessary for doing the work required.

Second, complex school reform efforts are working at the knowledge frontier. SDEs need to learn from multiple partners, and their partners from them. All available knowledge and resources must be utilized.

Third, complex school reform requires a high degree of consensus over an extended period of time. SDEs need the support of legislatures, state boards of education, professional organizations, practitioners, business, and others in the community in order for the reforms to remain viable.

Even in building partnerships, however, SDEs must be aware of the potential strains they are placing on the larger system. Practitioner-led professional development is highly desirable, for example, up until the point that providing this professional development takes practitioners out of their own classrooms so frequently that their teaching begins to suffer.

State departments of education are pivotal players in complex state reform efforts because of their key role in the implementation of these reforms. SDEs are the state entities closest to the work of schools and districts and, as such, are key interpreters of state policy and the agents of its implementation.

In addition, the cases of Kentucky and Vermont demonstrate that what happens inside SDEs influences the implementation relationship among departments and schools and districts. What happens in departments is consequently of importance for all those interested in school reform.

Epilogue

The research presented in this book was completed in early 1993. Considerable time has elapsed between the completion of this research and this writing, and a number of changes have occurred in the education reforms of Kentucky and Vermont during the intervening period. I have updated some of the specific changes in the reforms discussed in this research via footnotes throughout the text.

In this epilogue, I will attempt to "hit the highlights" of the relevant changes in each state. The word "highlights" cannot be overemphasized here. It was clearly impossible for me to duplicate the depth of my original research in order to update it. What follows is a gloss on the major changes that have occurred in each state that are relevant for this research. The information presented here comes from more or less readily available sources.[1] For the purposes of this research, the relevant changes in each state fall into two categories: 1) changes within the state department of education itself; and 2) major changes within the pieces of the state reforms discussed.

As already mentioned, a change in leadership has occurred in both state departments of education. I have not attempted to study changes that have taken place in either department subsequent to these leadership changes. I have only looked for evidence of change prior to the departures of Boysen and Mills.

KENTUCKY

Changes in the Kentucky Department of Education

Existing evidence seems to indicate that the conditions described in the KDE during the time of this research remained largely the same for the duration of Boysen's tenure. Because staff morale and satisfaction were not priority concerns of the upper-level management of the KDE during my research, it stands to reason that there has been little effort to address these issues and consequently that there has been little change.

News articles written from 1993 through the date of Boysen's departure from the KDE on June 30, 1995, while crediting Boysen for his dedication to the KERA reforms and successful efforts overall, also have mentioned criticisms of his management of the department. Kentucky's State Board of Education awarded Boysen a 5% pay raise in the fall of 1994 and a performance evaluation that praised him for doing an "excellent job." At the same time, however, some board members expressed concern over Boysen's management style and the high turnover rate of staff in the KDE (Associated Press, September 8, 1994; May, September 10, 1994). A 1995 *Education Week* article at the time Boysen announced his resignation commented that while Boysen had won "high marks" for many of his efforts within the state, "the commissioner has repeatedly frustrated many reform supporters with what they see as his inability to court state legislators, his micromanagement in the education department, and his failure to retain some of his chief assistants" (Harp, February 22, 1995, p. 11).

The capacity of the KDE has been reduced somewhat due to state budget cuts. The department's budget was cut by 10% for the 1993–94 fiscal year; 29 jobs were eliminated, and budgets for equipment purchases and travel were reduced (May, August 27, 1993).

Changes in Kentucky's Reforms

Kentucky's reforms were initially designed to support student achievement of 6 Learning Goals and 75 Valued Outcomes. The six Learning Goals remain, but the 1994 General Assembly voted not to assess the attainment of Goal 3—"Schools must develop students' abilities to become self-sufficient individuals"—and Goal 4—"Schools must develop students' abilities to become responsible members of families, work groups, or communities" (Prichard Committee, 1994, p. 1). These goals were objected to by conservative opponents of KERA. In addition, the Valued Outcomes have been revised into 58 Academic Expectations that were approved by the State Board of Education as administrative regulations in 1994. "The intent and meaning of these expectations has not changed" (Prichard Committee, 1994, p. 1).

There is a considerable amount of new information available on Kentucky's assessment system. More recent assessment scores have been released, two external reviews of the assessment system have been done, a number of adjustments have been made to the system both prior to and as a result of these reviews, and the first round of cash rewards has been awarded.

The 1993–94 assessment scores showed considerable improvement. The percentage of students at the proficient level or above in mathematics, reading, science, and social studies increased from the previous year in all grades tested (grades 4, 8, and 12) (Olson, October 5, 1994). Statewide, 38.4% of all schools exceeded their improvement goals and were eligible for rewards, and an additional 8.1% of all schools met their improvement goals (KDE,

February 1995, p. 5).[2] The first round of rewards were awarded to qualifying schools in 1995.[3]

However, two independent reviews of the assessment system have questioned its reliability and validity. A study commissioned by the Kentucky Institute for Education Research advised state officials not to give schools rewards or sanctions based on test results until the reliability of the results was proven (May, February 18, 1995). A study done for the Office of Education Accountability (OEA) generated the following major findings:

1. The misclassification rates of schools in some reward categories are high and therefore the rewards and sanctions may be difficult to defend.
2. Although limited, evidence from other assessments (National Assessment of Educational Progress and the American College Tests) fails to show any reflection of the large gains observed on KIRIS.
3. Repeated use of ad-hoc, judgmental procedures of linking or equating assessments in 1992, 1993, and 1994 result in an accumulation of equating errors which make year to year comparisons of KIRIS results of questionable validity.
4. The setting of performance standards was seriously flawed.
5. For numerous reasons, the Panel concluded that the KIRIS portfolio assessments are currently inappropriate for use in the KIRIS accountability system. (Hambleton et al., June 1995, pp. 5–6)

A number of changes have been made in the assessment system both prior to and as a result of the findings of these reviews. In 1994, the written test and performance task portions of the KIRIS assessments were moved from 12th to 11th grade. Portfolios are still assessed in the 12th grade. Mathematics portfolios have been moved from Grade 4 to Grade 5 (Prichard Committee, 1994, p. 2). In 1995, the KDE announced that it would adopt 10 of the 12 suggestions made by the OEA's review panel. These suggestions included: develop an ethical code of conduct to ensure the integrity of the tests; expand research to make sure the test is measuring what students should know; ensure that the tests are comparable from year to year; redefine the standards that students are expected to meet; make sure reports to parents and schools are clear; provide the public with all the possible alternative explanations of results; establish routine auditing procedures; include multiple-choice items on the test; improve the documentation of decisions on testing for review purposes; and reconsider giving more emphasis to the content questions on the test (Schaver, June 28, 1995).

Finally, Kentucky's Educational Professional Standards Board is working to establish a primarily performance-based teacher preparation, accreditation, and licensing program. Work on this project has included the adoption of new teacher and experienced teacher standards for preparation and certification. In addition, superintendent and principal administrative standards have been adopted. Work continues to establish accreditation of college/ university education preparation programs based on assessment of product and process. A pilot program for performance-based accreditation has been developed with National Council for Accreditation of Teacher Education, and the first accreditation was conducted in November 1995 (Office of Education Accountability Annual Report, December 1995, p. 53).

VERMONT

Changes in the Vermont Department of Education

Concerted effort has been made to improve and track the internal workings of the VDE and to focus the department on its mission and strategic plan. Staff surveys have been done each year from 1992 through 1995 in the areas of "Living the Vision," "Organization Style and Culture," and "Work Team Effectiveness." The department was restructured in 1993.

There has been significant improvement in the percentage of positive scores—scores of 5–10 on a scale of 0–10—in each of the three areas from 1993 to 1995, although there is still substantial room for growth, and the percentage of positive scores has not returned to its 1992 level in any category.[4] The percentage of positive scores increased from 36% in 1993 to 51.2% in 1995 in the category of "Living the Vision," from 24% to 50.7% in the category of "Organization Style and Culture," and from 40.3% to 66.6% in the category of "Work Team Effectiveness" (VDE, 1995, p. 5).

The 1994 survey data were disaggregated by team, and Commissioner Mills asked that the team data be publicly posted within the department so that staff could see how their team compared to the rest of the department. In addition, a system of quarterly reviews was established for each team. Team managers were required to attend these reviews, along with the Commissioner, Deputy Commissioner, and Chief Financial Officer. Anyone else who wanted to attend was welcome. The reviews were about an hour and a half in length and focused on points including: the contribution of the team to the mission of the department; its contribution toward the management of the budget; its contribution to making the department a better place to work; and its contribution to fulfilling the strategic plan.

A former team member of the VDE reported that Home and Focus teams had solidified and become better defined since the time of this research. She thought that this was probably because people started to understand why they were teamed together as they engaged in the department's new work.

In addition, she reported that her team did a lot of work on improving morale. The team did systematic morale surveys and created a morale sub-team. There was also a team retreat focused on improving morale. All of these efforts resulted in people feeling that the issue had been paid attention to and addressed, according to this team member.

This team member and the Commissioner reported that departmental "stand-up meetings" had been reinstituted shortly after the completion of this research.

The organizational structure of the VDE is not quite as flat as staff originally intended. The department fought for its "a manager is a manager" position without success. External managers continue to have a higher grade in the civil service system than do internal managers.

A final change in the VDE has been cutbacks due to budget constraints. When Mills arrived at the VDE in 1988 there was a staff of 178 people. When he left the department in 1995, the staff had been officially reduced to 129 but because of forced vacancies was actually 123. (The VDE had a staff of 147 at the time of this research.)

Changes in Vermont's Reforms

The Vermont reforms studied here have in large part proceeded apace. Work in the areas of standards and assessments has continued. Both the Common Core of Learning and the Curriculum Frameworks have been completed. Three commissions wrote the frameworks to connect the Common Core with national content standards, describe the level of student performance expected for the content standards, and outline the learning experiences that would enable all students to meet the standards. The student performance standards address communication and literacy, problem-solving, personal development, and social responsibility across three fields of knowledge—Arts and Humanities; Science, Mathematics, and Technology; and Social Sciences (VDE, June 1995, p. 10). The curriculum frameworks were passed by the Vermont State Board of Education on January 15, 1996.

The state's assessment system has generated new achievement data. The 1993–94 assessment results on the uniform assessment in mathematics showed that Vermont 4th and 8th graders outperformed the 1990 National Assessment of Educational Progress (NAEP) sample.[5] Portfolio results in mathematics and writing have been relatively flat over three years with some exceptions such as substantial improvement in writing grammar and mechanics (Vermont Assessment Program, 1993–94).

The assessment system has been expanded and adjusted over time. Math portfolios are now kept at the high school level as well as in the 4th and 8th grades, and 5th grade teachers are now keeping writing portfolios so that their 4th grade colleagues are not overburdened by keeping student portfolios in two subject areas.

The reliability of the portfolio scoring has improved, particularly in mathematics. Reliability in scoring 8th grade mathematics portfolios increased from .53 in 1993 to .83 in 1994. Reliability in scoring 8th grade writing portfolios increased slightly, from .60 in 1992 to .69 in 1994 (Viadero, April 5, 1995).

There is also substantial evidence that the portfolio system is having a positive impact on instruction. A RAND survey of 80 Vermont schools participating in portfolio assessment found that:

> Of the math teachers in the sample, more than half said that, as a result of portfolio assessments, they had devoted more time to teaching problem-solving and communication in their classes. Three-fourths reported having students spend more time applying math knowledge to new situations; roughly 70% devoted more class time to making charts, graphs, and diagrams; and a similar proportion allocated more class time to writing reports about math. (Viadero, April 5, 1995, p. 9)

In addition, the survey found that the use of portfolios was being expanded beyond 4th and 8th grade math and writing in many schools: Principals in approximately half of the sample schools reported that portfolios were being used in their schools in some form beyond the grade levels and subject areas used in the state assessment program (Koretz, Stecher, Klein, & McCaffrey, March 8, 1994).

The tension between the demands of improving practice and the demands of state accountability has remained a continuing theme, however. A 1995 study by Stecher and Mitchell concluded:

> Ultimately, these results speak to the fundamental conflict between good instruction and good accountability-oriented assessment. While good instruction should be responsive to the individual needs and capabilities of students, good assessment for accountability purposes should yield data that are comparable across units of interest. When instruction and assessment are intertwined—as they are with portfolios and other forms of embedded assessment—these two principles are in conflict. At present, Vermont teachers appear to place greater value on instruction than accountability assessment, and Vermont policy makers seem to place greater value on local flexibility than on comparability. (p. xii)

A former team member of the VDE had a somewhat different view. She explained that consensus improved dramatically as teacher investment increased. She said that teachers initially thought of reliability as for the state, rather than for the kids. They soon realized, however, that common standards required reliability and consequently became more invested in consensus.

A major change in Vermont's reform efforts was the creation of the Vermont Alliance in August 1995, after the state's withdrawal from the National Alliance. The Vermont Alliance was created "to network schools that are (or want to be) involved in significant education reform with each other and with state, regional, and national level organizations, and higher education" (McNamara, June 24, 1995, p. 1).

The Vermont Alliance currently has 100 member schools. Its work focuses on three areas: 1) teaching, learning, and assessment; 2) leadership and accountability; and 3) community development and engagement (B. McNamara, personal communication, July 17, 1996).

Public School Approval (PSA) did become more flexible in interpretation, as already described. The State Board of Education concluded, however, that the process could not be substantially redesigned until all schools had met the current standards. The process was winding down by the fall of 1995 with only a very few schools still needing to pass the existing PSA requirements. The new PSA approach will stress student progress and the conditions, resources, and practices that enable all students to achieve the Common Core. The process is to be in place by September 1996 (VDE, June 1995, p. 12).

Finally, Vermont's licensing and teacher preparation program approval processes have changed. Teachers are now licensed based on demonstrated competence in five core areas: content knowledge and skills; instructional knowledge and skills; ability to work collegially; community partnerships that support student learning; and accountability for personal performance. Teacher preparation programs are approved based on the demonstrated knowledge and skills of their graduates. Programs prepare institutional portfolios that include examples of student work and clear linkages between course outcomes and the five standards for Vermont educators. Every teaching candidate develops an individual portfolio for use in the interviewing and hiring process (Mills, personal communication to John Anderson, President, New American Schools Development Corporation, December 8, 1994, pp. 8–9).

As this epilogue is written, the reform efforts of Kentucky and Vermont continue to evolve. I wish the practitioners and policymakers in both states continued success. They have more than earned it.

Susan Follett Lusi
April 11, 1996

Methodology

This appendix explains the research decisions I made and the research approaches I used. These issues are addressed under the categories of state selection; research approach, sample, and sample selection within each state; and data analysis.

STATE SELECTION

I chose the states of Kentucky and Vermont using "purposeful sampling." "The logic and power of purposeful sampling lies [sic] in selecting *information-rich cases* for study in depth" (Patton, 1990, p. 169, emphasis in original). Specifically, I searched for states engaged in complex school reform. In addition, while no states had been involved in this type of reform for extended periods of time, I searched for states where reform implementation had been underway long enough to expect at least beginning changes in local practice. In addition, I took the issues of state scale and personal capacity into account at the margins of my selection process. By this I mean that I recognized that I was but one researcher and consequently had limited capacity for collecting and analyzing information. These capacity limitations would have made adequate study of extremely large states, such as California or New York, difficult to accomplish.

Within the above criteria, I chose Kentucky and Vermont based on the recommendations of knowledgeable observers of and participants in state-level education reform. I consulted with education policy researchers affiliated with the Consortium for Policy Research in Education who had been studying systemic school reform, as well as other researchers who had been examining the efforts of particular states. In addition, I spoke with people at the Education Commission of the States and the Coalition of Essential Schools—the partner organizations in the Re:Learning initiative. Finally, I talked with people in the recommended states, both SDE staff and others, trying to gain a basic understanding of the nature of the reform efforts taking place and to determine whether or not a particular state met my sampling criteria.

I ultimately chose the cases of Kentucky and Vermont because they met my sampling criteria, were interesting cases in their own right, and made an interesting and informative pair. Kentucky is an interesting case because it is the most far-reaching state-level reform effort in the country. As is explained in Chapter 3, the Kentucky Supreme Court ruled the state's entire education system unconstitutional, opening the door wide for complex reform.

Vermont is interesting because it is what Patton refers to as a "critical case":

> Critical cases are those that can make a point quite dramatically or are, for some reason, particularly important in the scheme of things. A clue to the existence of a critical case is a statement to the effect that "if it happens there, it will happen anywhere," or, vice versa, "if it doesn't happen there, it won't happen anywhere." (Patton, 1990, p. 174)

Vermont exemplifies the latter statement; it is being looked at as a "best-case scenario" by researchers around the country. Complex reform will be difficult in Vermont, to be sure, but it has the advantages of being a small, homogeneous state without the added complications of large urban areas, extreme poverty, or extremely low levels of local capacity.

Kentucky and Vermont are an interesting and informative pairing of cases because while the two states are attempting similar reforms, they are using very different implementation approaches. Kentucky's reforms are legislated, and participation is mandatory. The majority of Vermont's reforms are not legislated, and participation is voluntary. Vermont relies on making a convincing argument to bring about participation. I thought that local responses to these differing approaches would reveal much about the potential of state-level reform to bring about school change.

RESEARCH APPROACH, SAMPLE, AND SAMPLE SELECTION WITHIN EACH STATE

I spent just over four weeks in each state doing on site data collection. These site visits were spread over the period of approximately a year. Site visits to Kentucky took place in July and November 1992 and February 1993. Site visits to Vermont took place in March and July 1992 and January and April 1993. Additional telephone interviews were done in each state between site visits.

I used open-ended interviewing and some limited observation as my primary methods of data collection. In addition, I collected and read numerous documents from each state.

My cases are based on a total of 195 interviews, 102 in Kentucky and

93 in Vermont. I interviewed SDE staff members, local practitioners, and knowledgeable others in each state. "Knowledgeable others" included members of the state board of education, legislators, university people, and others in some way involved in the reform efforts. The distribution of interviews in each state is as follows: In Kentucky, 38 interviews are with SDE staff, 48 are with practitioners in 3 districts, and 16 are with knowledgeable others. In Vermont, 37 interviews are with SDE staff, 46 are with practitioners in four districts, and 10 are with knowledgeable others. The criteria I used to select my sample in each category and the questions I asked are outlined below.

SDE Staff

Within each state's SDE, I interviewed people who worked in areas engaged in changing the whole department, for example, leadership, personnel, department restructuring, and people who worked on the reform initiatives most likely to directly impact teaching and learning for all students, for example, curriculum, assessment, school restructuring, and decision-making. Within these targeted groups I interviewed people at all professional levels of the department, from top leadership to program consultants.

My earliest interviews with SDE staff were designed to orient me to the activity in each state and the history of that activity, beyond what I could learn from existing documentation. I also sought to learn how each department had changed in general terms. My subsequent interviews focused on how the individual's job had changed and how the department had changed as a result of the reform initiatives. In addition, I asked what the individual's sense was of the reform activity taking place in local schools and districts, and how he or she would describe the role of the department in reform implementation.

My generic interview protocol for SDE staff was as follows:

I. General information
   - Mind if I tape?
   - Please tell me if you wish to speak on or off the record.
   - Name?
   - Position?
   - How long in this position?
   - How long in department?
   - Previous positions? Where did you come from?

II. Your job
- Has your job changed over time as the reforms have taken place and the department has restructured?
- How do you and your staff spend your time?
  —What proportion in schools and districts/with practitioners?
  —What proportion on reporting to higher-ups?
- How do you work with schools in your job? Exactly what do you do?
- Does this differ in any way from the way you worked with schools in the past? How?
- Is the way you work with schools indicative of how this division/office as a whole works with schools? Please elaborate.

III. Department
- Is there a vision that guides this department? What is it?
- What has restructuring the department meant for you?
- How does the new department differ from the old?
- How does your division/office work? How do you work together?
- Does your division/office work with other divisions/offices? How?
  —How much do you know about what other offices and divisions dealing with other areas of the reform are doing—curriculum, assessment, etc.?
  —How does communication occur?
  —What kind of information is shared?
  —How do you get this information?
- Are there connections between the work of the different divisions?
- How does your division work with other divisions doing trainings and working with schools?
- How are decisions made in the department? What is the process?
  —What kinds of decisions can you make yourself and what kinds have to be passed upward?
  —If a problem is raised by a school or district, how quickly can you give them an answer/help them resolve it?
  —If you make what might be a controversial decision do you worry afterward, or generally assume that you will be supported?
  —What kinds of decisions can the people who work for you make on their own?
- How does planning occur in the department?
  —What is the process?
  —If it becomes clear to you and others in your office that an aspect of some plan needs adjustment, what do you do?

—Can plans be adjusted fairly easily? What is the process?
- Is it easy to hire the people you need and want to work with?
- Are there ways for people in the department to learn new knowledge and skills—professional development?
- Do you have the information and technology you need to do the job?
  —Computers?
  —Easy access to information on the state education system?
  —Easy access to other parts of the system, e.g., schools, universities, other people involved in this kind of assessment and training?
- What is the Commissioner's role in the department?
  —What is he like to work for?
- What are the norms that exist in the department?

IV. Schools
- What do you hear from people in schools and districts?
  —What challenges are they facing in trying to implement KERA/ Vermont's reforms?
  —What are they struggling with?
  —What would help them in meeting these challenges?
  —Where could/should this help come from?
- What changes have you seen in these districts as you've been working with them?
  —Concrete examples?

V. How would you describe the role of the department in implementing the reforms?
- How would you describe the way the department as a whole works with schools?
- Does the current relationship with schools differ from the relationship that the old department had?
- Do you/how do you work with others doing trainings in schools, e.g., universities, private consultants?

The reader should bear in mind while reading this protocol that in open-ended interviewing, unlike in survey research, questions are not asked of each individual in the same order and in exactly the same manner. The answers to some questions emerge in the discussion of others, and the interviewer follows up on pertinent topics mentioned, even if they do not directly address one of the questions in the protocol. In addition, I adjusted the protocol in light of the individual's particular position and areas of expertise, and also as needed to meet with his or her time constraints. I generally asked informants for an hour of their time, but if they only had 30 to 45 minutes available, I took it and adjusted my questions accordingly. All of this is to say that this interview protocol should be viewed as a rough guide to the conversations that took place.

District and School Practitioners

I chose three districts to visit in each state that represented something of the range of districts that SDEs are trying to change: 1) an "early adopter" district that was engaged in reforms similar to the current state-level reforms, prior to the state's involvement; 2) a "status quo" district that had delivered a more or less average traditional education to its students for years; and 3) a "low-performing" district that the state had been concerned about for some period of time due to its below-average delivery of educational services. This sampling strategy falls under Patton's category of "stratified purposeful sampling" (Patton, 1990, p. 174).

I also visited a fourth district in Vermont, to add a larger district to my sample. My findings in this district, however, did not vary significantly from those in the other districts. Consequently, I used the data from this district as supplemental information, rather than developing a fourth category for it in my Vermont sample.

I selected the districts in each state based on the recommendations of people both inside and outside the state department who were closely acquainted with numerous schools. I chose districts on which there was some consensus as to the category they fell into. In addition, I chose districts in different regions of each state.

I spent approximately three days in each district. I visited the elementary, middle, and high school that district personnel felt were furthest along in their reform efforts. I interviewed the principal and three teachers in each school, in addition to the superintendent and at least one other district-level staff person in each district. I asked principals to select teachers who had been the most involved in the state's and the school's reform efforts.

There were a few exceptions to this strategy. In one or two schools, I interviewed less than three teachers due to scheduling difficulties, and in one district there was only one administrator (the superintendent). Also, in some cases districts only had one elementary, middle, or high school to choose from. In addition, given the exigencies of school schedules, it is probably fair to say that principals chose teachers on the basis of their availability to talk as well as their involvement with the reforms.

I chose schools and personnel with the greatest involvement in the state's reform efforts due to the relative newness of the reforms. I reasoned that because the reforms were so new, I would need to look at the best-case scenario in order to see many signs of change. Even using this selection strategy, there was still wide variation in levels of involvement and change.

My interviews with practitioners focused on how the state's reforms had affected their own activity and practice, as well as the activity and practice in the given school and/or district, the relationship between practitioners and the SDE, and the role of the SDE. In addition, I asked district-level staff about the role of the district in these state-level reforms. My interview protocol for Vermont practitioners is listed below:

I. General information
   • Mind if I tape?
   • Anonymity is promised.
   • Name?
   • Position?
   • How long in this position?
   • Previous positions?
   • How long in Vermont?

II. History
   • When do you consider the current Vermont education reforms to have started?
   • Describe what was occurring in your district/school prior to that time.
     —Were there reforms already under way/in place? Please describe.
   • Are there local goals for education in your district/school?
     —What are they?

III. District/school's relationship to DOE
   • How often do you or anyone else at your district/school interact with the SDE in any way?
     —What are the occasions for these interactions?
     —How would you characterize these interactions—attitude, tone, purpose, substance—what exactly have you been doing with the Department?
     —Have your interactions with the SDE changed in any way over the past few years?
   • Vermont has a number of education reforms under way. Which if any of these reforms have affected what takes place in your district/school? (In terms of governance, teaching and learning, working with the community, expanded opportunities for children, integration of services, etc.)
     —Assessment?
     —Common Core of Learning?

—Professional Standards Board?
—Reinventing Vermont Schools
—Carnegie Middle Schools Initiative
—Deregulation
—SDE Restructuring?
—Governance?
—Teaching and learning?
—Act 230

- Has your own teaching been affected by these reforms in any way?
- Have you, as a practitioner, had any input into the shaping of these reforms? Have others that you know of?
  —Do you feel that you could have input and/or be involved in their planning if you wished to?
- Do you see any relationship between these reforms?
- How do all of these reforms fit with your local goals?
- What are the goals of these reforms collectively? [ONLY ask if see a relationship]

IV. Role of district (Ask district staff)
- What is the role of the district and district office in all of these reforms?
- How do you and the district office work with the SDE?
- How much input have you had into the shaping of these reforms?

V. Effects of the state reforms
- How has your district/school been affected by these reforms?
  —What has changed?
  —What is in the process of changing?
  —How have these state efforts affected your district/school's earlier reform efforts—pushed them ahead, slowed or stopped them?
- What key challenges/problems are your district/school facing in implementing these reforms?
  —What could help you to address these problems?
  —Where would you see this help coming from?
- What successes are you most proud of thus far?

VI. Role of the SDE
- What role(s) does the SDE play in Vermont?
  —Has the role of the SDE changed in Vermont over the past 4–5 years? How?
- What could the SDE do that would be most helpful to you?
- What do you as a practitioner think of the SDE overall? What do you think the majority of school people in Vermont think of the SDE?

- If you had the opportunity to give the department advice, what would it be?

In addition to these general questions, I also asked questions about particular aspects of the reforms that the individual had direct experience with. For example, if the informant was a 4th or 8th grade teacher, we tended to discuss the portfolio assessment process at some length. My Kentucky practitioner protocol focused on similar issues but asked about various Kentucky, as opposed to Vermont, reforms. As with the protocol for SDE staff, this protocol should be viewed as a rough guide to the conversations that took place.

Knowledgeable Others

I chose the knowledgeable others whom I interviewed in a couple of ways. First, some were obvious choices due to role. Legislative leaders and members of state boards of education, for example, fell into this category. Second, there were individuals who were recommended to me by other informants as people who were knowledgeable about and active in various pieces of the reform.

Interviews with these individuals varied according to their roles and expertise. They generally focused on aspects of the reform they were involved in, as well as their overall impression of the work of the SDE, changes in the SDE, and changes in education in general that had occurred as a result of the reforms.

DATA ANALYSIS

The vast majority of my interviews were tape recorded, and all that were recorded were transcribed. I took copious notes on those interviews that could not be recorded and those notes were also transcribed.

I analyzed my data through coding, reflections, memos, and shorter papers. I analyzed each case individually in its entirety prior to doing my cross case analysis, although I did keep track of common issues through writing memos (described below).

I started by coding all of my interview data. My codes emerged from the interviews themselves, from the particular state's reforms, and from my analytical framework presented in Chapter 2. Examples of codes in each of these categories are "customer"—which emerged from interview data on Vermont's Total Quality process; "SBDM"—which referred to Kentucky's school-based decision-making reform; and "SDE decision-making"—

which came from my analytical framework. I coded all of the information in my interviews for easy retrieval, even though I did not foresee using all of the codes in this analysis. I ultimately used the subset of codes needed to answer the questions generated by my framework. I used a data analysis package called HyperResearch for the coding and sorting of my data.

I also analyzed the data within each of the codes I used in the following manner. I generally had a large amount of data under each of my codes, due to my large number of informants. I consequently read through all the data under a given code and wrote a brief summary statement of the viewpoint expressed by each informant and the page number(s) where these data were located. These data summaries allowed me to weigh confirming and disconfirming evidence and also to pick out representative quotes relatively quickly. I also analyzed the data within codes to see if the variation in viewpoints expressed was systematically related to some other factor shared by a number of informants—their position in the SDE hierarchy or the type of district they worked in, for example.

I worked to ensure the validity of my analysis by analyzing my data in this way and by triangulating my interview data with the information contained in state documents and gained through the limited observation of SDE activity that I was able to do. I also checked my understandings and preliminary interpretations with various informants at the end of interviews and on occasion asked for feedback on pieces of written work.

In addition to the data analysis described above, I also tape-recorded reflections on my field work, the data I was gathering, and emerging hypotheses while I was in the field. These reflections were transcribed and coded as appropriate. They sometimes became the subject of longer memos.

I wrote memos to myself on a host of topics throughout my research and data analysis. Memoing is an informal method of recording reactions, fleshing out emerging analysis, and tracking ideas. I have a total of 33 memos. Their topics range from my selection strategy for districts and schools and thoughts for my concluding chapters to work plans and reactions to presentations I gave on this work.

Finally, I wrote shorter papers and presented them at conferences to further portions of my analysis. One of these papers presented the argument that I later developed into my analytical framework (Lusi, 1994). The other presented my analysis of the SDE portion of my Kentucky data (Lusi, 1993).

Notes

Chapter One

1. What defines "the beginning" of these reforms is open to some interpretation. I say 1990 because that was the year in which the Kentucky Education Reform Act was passed, and when Vermont's education goals were adopted by the State Board of Education. The discussions that led up to these reform efforts started earlier, at least in the late 1980s.

2. A third challenge that has been raised is that systemic reform will not improve, and may exacerbate, educational inequities. O'Day and Smith address this challenge in "Systemic School Reform and Educational Opportunity" (O'Day & Smith, 1993).

Chapter Two

1. This chapter is adapted from an earlier paper in which I develop the argument for changes that need to take place in the internal and external working relationships of SDEs engaged in systemic school reform (Lusi, 1994), as well as the framework section of a draft paper I presented at a conference on changes in the Kentucky Department of Education (Lusi, 1993).

2. This is because SDEs are what Wilson terms "procedural organizations"— "[organizations in which] managers can observe what their subordinates are doing but not the outcome (if any) that results from those efforts . . ." (Wilson, 1989, p. 163). According to Wilson, "If the manager cannot justify on the grounds of results leaving operators alone to run things as they see fit, the manager will have to convince political superiors that the rules governing government work are being faithfully followed. . . . Management becomes means-oriented in procedural organizations" (p. 164).

3. For a discussion of this type of change in norms in another bureaucratic organization, see Barzelay's (1992) Chapter 4, "Reworking the Culture and Producing Results" (pp. 58–78, especially pp. 60–61).

Chapter Three

1. These statistics were taken from *Rankings of the States* (National Education Association Data Search, 1992) and *Digest of Education Statistics* (National Center for Education Statistics, 1994). Based on these sources, Kentucky ranks 23rd in the nation for total population, 25th in number of instructional staff, and 24th in number of students. The per pupil expenditure figure represents "estimated expenditures for

public elementary and secondary schools per pupil in average daily attendance" (National Education Association Data Search, 1992, p. 59, Table H-11). Per pupil expenditure was even lower before passage of the Kentucky Education Reform Act, which included substantial new funding for schools.

2. The author cites Amended Complaint at 19, Council for Better Educ. v. Collins (No. 85-CI-1759) (filed June 11, 1986 in Franklin Cir. Ct.), and the Kentucky Constitution, Section 183.

3. It should be noted that the level of understanding of the reform package varied among members, with the legislative leadership having the clearest understanding of the reform proposals. The leadership closed off debate when the bill was introduced, which probably further limited the understanding of the larger membership (Thomas James, personal communication, October 26, 1994).

4. The most severe sanction—the "school in crisis" designation—was delayed until the end of the 1994–96 biennium, due to the passage of House Bill 256 in the 1994 legislative session.

5. Exceptions to the SBDM requirement include districts with only one school and schools that are performing above their threshold level whose staff have voted to be exempt from SBDM.

6. The above description of the KERA reform provisions is drawn from Legislative Research Commission, 1991, September. This source also briefly describes all other provisions of KERA.

7. Alternative SBDM council structures are allowed if approved by the State Board of Education. However, only 11 alternative structures had been approved as of February 1993.

8. This section of the case is an edited version of Lusi, 1993, *Systemic School Reform: The Changes Implied for SDEs and How One Department Has Responded.*

9. In the data cited below, a respondent referred to as "a commissioner" is either an associate or deputy commissioner in the KDE. "The Commissioner" refers to Commissioner of Education Thomas Boysen. A respondent referred to as "a program consultant" is either a consultant or a branch manager.

10. The three-part assessment system consists of portfolios, performance events, and transitional tests, which are composed of multiple choice and open-ended questions. (See Epilogue for recent changes in the assessment system.)

11. The baseline standard indicates the performance of each school in the first round of testing. The threshold standard indicates the level of performance each school is supposed to attain over the next biennium.

12. It should be noted that this tripartite personnel system was not Commissioner Boysen's first choice. Boysen has advocated for a separate pay scale for KDE employees, apart from the state's current merit structure, arguing that higher salaries are required to attract top professionals. However, legislative leaders declined Boysen's request for a special session in 1991 to consider an alternative salary system (Schmidt, *Education Week,* May 15, 1991, pp. 18 and 20), and the KDE temporarily abandoned its effort in 1992 because the governor asked most state employees to forego a cost-of-living increase (Editorial Staff, *Education Week,* March 18, 1992, p. 21).

13. Data on the controversy caused by the KDE's personnel systems was taken from interviews with KDE staff and others outside the department.

14. At the time of this interview, the KDE personnel systems were receiving negative press in Frankfort's *The State Journal.*

15. The Division of Curriculum Development was moved to the Office of Assessment and Accountability Services after this interview took place. However, the main thrust of this quote—that KDE staff should be working across divisions and offices—is still accurate.

16. The process described here differs from the official process for *Program Review* generation outlined in *Program Advisory* No. 91-AAAA-001. According to the advisory, *Program Reviews* (originally called *Program Advisories*) are sent to the Commissioner only after they have been approved and recommended by a deputy commissioner. Approval by a deputy takes place after four or five drafts of the document have cleared earlier stages of approval. The Commissioner may then either take the *Review* to the cabinet or sign off immediately. There is also the option of "fast-tracking" *Reviews* in urgent situations. These cases are to be designated by the Commissioner.

I have chosen to describe the *Review* generation process as told to me in interviews, as opposed to as stated in official KDE documents, because other staff members interviewed also talked about *Reviews* going back and forth to the Commissioner, giving credence to the account given above.

17. This fast-tracking procedure was described to me in early 1993. When I had a follow-up conversation with a KDE staffer later that year, I was told that fast-tracking had virtually stopped.

18. For a more detailed description of the strategic planning process, see *KDE Strategic Planning Process for Fiscal Year 1993–94 Action Plans and Biennial Request for 1994 General Assembly* (KDE, 1992, October 23).

19. I visited three schools in each district—an elementary, middle, and high school. In the "troubled district," I actually visited four schools due to the wishes of district staff. I interviewed the principal and at least three teachers in each school, in addition to the superintendent and at least one other district-level staff person in each district. It should be noted that some districts only had one elementary, middle, or high school to choose from. In addition, given the exigencies of school schedules, it is probably fair to say that principals chose teachers on the basis of their availability to talk, as well as their involvement with the reforms.

20. All of the information on KERA-related change that follows is based on self-reports. Such reports are problematic because they may or may not reflect the degree of change that would actually be observed. These reports do, however, give us an indication of whether or not practitioners are trying to change in accordance with KERA, and also give us factual information such as whether or not schools are participating in school-based decision-making.

21. Some examples of the concerns expressed: One teacher, who had been quite extensively trained in the state's portfolio assessment, said that the scoring was still too subjective for the portfolios to constitute a fair assessment. Another teacher expressed concern about the time math portfolio exercises took, saying they prevented him from covering all of the content students needed to do well on the SAT or ACT exams.

22. This particular school had been plagued by attendance and discipline prob-

lems, as well as a divided administration. A new administration was put in place for the 1991–92 academic year (the year prior to my visit), and spent its first year establishing order in the school.

23. Since Kentucky's is an outcomes-based reform, a word should be said about the most recent assessment results. According to a report issued by the KDE in February 1995, over 95% of Kentucky schools scored higher on their 1992–94 statewide tests than on 1992 tests, although 32% did not reach their improvement goals established by the state (KDE, 1995, February, p. 5). A six-person Technical Review Panel formed by OEA, however, released a report in June 1995 stating that "KIRIS is seriously flawed and needs to be substantially revised." Major findings include: Evidence from other assessments fails to show any reflection of the large gains observed on KIRIS; repeated use of ad hoc judgmental procedures for linking assessment in 1992, 1993, and 1994 result in an accumulation of equating errors that make year-to-year comparisons of KIRIS results of questionable validity; and, due to rater inconsistency and so forth, portfolio assessment was deemed currently inappropriate for use in the KIRIS accountability system (Office of Education Accountability, 1995, June, pp. 1–6).

24. Cohen, Ball, and others also found a range of changes in practice in response to instructional reforms in California (Cohen & Ball, 1990).

25. For more information on the early implementation of and range of change resulting from the primary school and SBDM reforms, see Raths, Katz, and Fanning, 1992, and David, 1992. For more information on the implementation of Kentucky reforms in general, see David, 1993.

26. See Fullan on the importance of vision-building to the implementation process (Fullan, 1991, pp. 81–83). Odden says that teacher effort and commitment are critical for change, but adds that "commitment can emerge at the end of the implementation process rather than at the beginning" (Odden, 1991, p. 324).

27. A school's threshold improvement goal is based on its accountability baseline index, developed by combining students' scores on the various assessments along with the school's non-cognitive data. The accountability baseline index is some number between 1 and 100. A school's threshold improvement goal for each biennium is calculated with the formula $(100 - \text{Index})/10 + \text{Index}$. A score of 100 means that all students have reached proficiency in the state's assessments (KDE, 1993, February, p. 14).

28. The *Final Report* of Kentucky's Task Force on High School Restructuring recommended that the State Board for Elementary and Secondary Education rewrite some existing regulations, including those pertaining to time and teacher certification. The Task Force recommendations would allow for more flexible use of time in schools and for teaching in interdisciplinary and multi-age groupings (Task Force on High School Restructuring, 1993, June, p. 27).

29. It should be noted that when Commissioner Boysen heard of this example, he said that the Regional Service Centers should absolutely not have reviewed these plans. This extra step should not have been in the process. This example shows, however, that the KDE, as a whole, has not sufficiently shifted away from regulation of process.

30. The option to use five instructional days for professional development was

subsequently extended through the 1995–96 school year by Senate Bill 162, enacted during the 1994 Regular Session.

31. There has been at least one notable exception to the KDE's piecemeal approach to professional development in the form of the Integrated Professional Development series, designed to integrate the KERA strands. An integrated series was developed for the preschool, primary, middle, and high school levels, and five people from each region were trained in each integrated series. These people were trained for one week in the summer and two weekends during the 1992–93 academic year to present a five-day integrated program. These trainers did work with some schools during that academic year, but the effort has not continued. This work might have continued, in the opinion of one person involved in the series, had the Director of Professional Development in the KDE not changed.

32. That school-based decision-making schools take time to evolve is one of the conclusions reached in Hill and Bonan's (1991) *Decentralization and Accountability in Public Education*. According to the authors: "After an initial period of floundering, in which many school staffs concern themselves with labor-management and budget issues, schools that are free to solve their own problems will develop specific and well-defined missions, climates, and methods of instruction" (Hill & Bonan, 1991, p. vi).

33. This line of argument parallels Bardach and Kagan's (1982) argument that regulatory unreasonableness can be experienced as government-imposed injustice, and when experienced in this way could lead to alienation from the activities of government as a whole (Bardach & Kagan, 1982, pp. 28–29).

34. There is at least some evidence that segmentalism has persisted in the reform effort since the time of this research. A 5-year study of 21 schools in 4 rural Kentucky school districts found that "After five years, KERA implementation is primarily strand by strand, rather than integrated as envisioned by those who designed the law" (Appalachia Educational Laboratory, February 1996, p. 1).

35. This is extending Meyer and Rowan's (1991) argument somewhat, as they argue only that societal myths influence formal organizational structure. It seems reasonable to posit, however, that if society holds these myths or shared understandings of what an organization should look like, it probably also holds some shared understandings of how an organization should do its work.

36. I was first introduced to this idea of using a lens or framework to judge proposed action against broader goals in the state of Vermont. The Vermont Department of Education worked with the State Board of Education to adopt a lens for examining any proposed regulation prior to passage to ensure that it worked toward the state's larger goals. This lens is further discussed in the following chapter on Vermont.

Chapter Four

1. The statistics in this section were drawn from *Vermont Education Directory* (VDE Information Systems Unit, 1991–92), *Rankings of the States* (National Education Association Data Search, 1992), and *Digest of Education Statistics* (National Center for Education Statistics, 1992). Based on these sources, Vermont ranks 49th in the nation

for total population, 48th in number of instructional staff, and 50th in number of students.

2. A key difference between Vermont and Kentucky is that although there are publicly established time lines for the Vermont reforms, none of these time lines is set forth in legislation.

3. The institutionalization of Vermont's reforms is now being tested. Richard Mills left Vermont in September 1995 to become the Commissioner of Education in New York State. Marc Hull became Vermont's new commissioner on October 7, 1996.

4. In the data cited below, a respondent referred to as "a manager" is either an internal or external manager in the department or the Deputy Commissioner. "The Commissioner" refers to Commissioner of Education Richard Mills. A respondent referred to as a "team member" is anyone who is not in the top levels of management.

5. While PSA did become more flexible in interpretation, the State Board of Education concluded that the process could not be substantially redesigned until all schools had met the current standards. As of the fall of 1995, only a very few schools still needed to pass the existing PSA requirements, and the process was winding down.

6. For a further description of the development and piloting of Vermont's assessment system see VDE, 1990–91a and VDE, 1990–91b. For interim evaluations of the state's assessment efforts, see Koretz, McCaffrey, Klein, Bell, & Stecher, 1992, and Koretz, Stecher, & Deibert, 1992). For more recent updates on the status of the program, see Koretz, Klein, McCaffrey, & Stecher, 1993, December; Koretz, Stecher, Klein, & McCaffrey, 1994, Fall; Stecher & Mitchell, 1995, May; and VDE, 1993, January.

7. For example, an internal VDE document entitled "What Do External and Internal Managers Do?" describes how the department's Teaching and Learning Team, created as part of the restructuring, will differ from what preceded it: "Team will work to develop resource systems and networks and provide less direct technical assistance" (VDE, 1992, July 28 Draft).

8. Salary and working conditions in the department have been on ongoing problem. (See Augenblick, Van de Water, & Associates, 1986, pp. VI-13–VI-15.)

9. The National Alliance is a project of the National Center on Education and the Economy, based in Rochester, NY. The purpose of the Alliance is to bring together a number of sites engaged in education reform so that people from those sites can learn from one another. Vermont withdrew from the National Alliance in 1995 and started its own Vermont Alliance.

10. The above information on the VDE's TQM training was taken from interviews and "State Departments of Education: Restructuring and Total Quality Management" (National Alliance for Restructuring Education, n.d.).

11. There is evidence that the VDE's data have improved since the time of this research: The VDE did not even have a state-wide list of 4th and 8th grade writing and math teachers when its assessment system started. A mailing list and eventually a database were developed including the names of those who had attended training sessions, served on committees, and participated in scoring sessions. In addition, the department created a school report card in 1995 and has started to develop a database on school change efforts as part of the newly created Vermont Alliance.

12. There are numerous internal documents that provide further information on the VDE's restructuring and demonstrate how the design of the new structure evolved. These include: "Restructuring the Department of Education: Presentation to Commissioner Mills" (VDE, 1991, November 4); a memo to department staff from Mills re: Restructuring the Department of Education (Mills, 1991, November 26 Memo); "Department of Education Restructuring Home Team Proposal" (VDE, 1992, March 9); a memo to department staff from the Transition Team re: Why Change? (VDE Transition Team, 1992, June 4); a draft description of what external and internal managers do and the responsibilities and construction of each Home Team (VDE, 1992, July 28 Draft); and a description of Work Groups/Focus Teams (VDE, n.d.-a).

13. At the time of this research, there were pay differentials in the VDE due to civil service rules that would not allow a reduction in the pay of former managers, even if they were no longer managers in the new department.

14. I actually visited a fourth district in Vermont, to add a larger district to my sample. My findings in this district, however, did not vary significantly from those in the other districts. Consequently, I have used the data from this district as supplemental information, rather than developing a fourth category for it in my sample.

15. As explained in Note 19 of Chapter 3, I visited three schools in each district and interviewed the principal and at least three teachers in each school, as well as the superintendent and at least one other district-level staff person. There were a couple of exceptions to this strategy in Vermont. In one or two schools, I interviewed less than three teachers due to scheduling difficulties, and in one district the superintendent was the only district-level administrator. As in Kentucky, some Vermont districts only had one of each type of school to choose from, and teachers' schedules, as well as their involvement in the reforms, were factors in assigning teachers for me to interview.

16. As explained in Note 20 of Chapter 3, the reader should bear in mind that all of the information on school change that follows is based on self-reports.

17. The state's Act 230, aimed at mainstreaming the vast majority of special education students, was also frequently mentioned, sometimes as a reform bringing about major change, and sometimes as an effort that basically reinforced what the district had already done. Since Act 230 falls outside of the scope of this study, I will not address it further here.

18. A RAND Corporation survey of 80 Vermont schools participating in portfolio assessment found that portfolio use was expanding beyond what was required by the state. Principals in approximately half of the sample schools reported that portfolios were being used in their schools in some form beyond the required grade levels and subject areas (Koretz, Stecher, Klein, & McCaffrey, 1994, March 8).

19. Practitioner concern over the lack of reliability was fueled by the release of an interim report on scoring reliability done by the RAND Corporation (Koretz et al., 1992).

20. Writing portfolios were moved to the 5th grade subsequent to this research to relieve the burden on 4th grade teachers.

21. A former VDE team member reported, however, that over time experienced scorers learned to score a portfolio in 20 minutes.

22. This statement requires some qualification. There was evidence of attempts at restructuring in all of the *supervisory unions* visited. However, in the supervisory union labeled the "troubled district," the restructuring efforts were taking part in a school that, while part of the union, is actually in another district that is not troubled.

23. Despite establishing this direction for the district, district leadership still has concerns over the reliability of the assessment system. According to the superintendent: "[The RAND report] certainly caused . . . some problems for us . . . having embraced a systemic change around [portfolios], to then have the RAND report come out and really look at the reliability and the validity, obviously, it raises questions in the mind of faculty. . . . Although I think everyone agrees that probably the greatest change portion of [portfolios] is the way [they've] affected instructional practice. I think we've got a long way to go in terms of the assessing piece and how we use that data."

24. Again, these generalizations are drawn from one particular district. I visited a school in another district of the supervisory union where practitioners were quite enthusiastic about the state's reforms and were working to adopt some of them.

25. The State Board of Education adopted a slightly modified version of this proposal on March 16, 1993. For more recent information on Vermont's approach to waivers and deregulation more generally, see VDE, 1995, September 27.

26. Timar and Kirp found this same irony in their study of Texas education reforms in the 1980s (Timar & Kirp, 1988, p. 80).

27. In fact, reliability and teacher consensus did improve over time, particularly in math. (See the epilogue for further information on reliability.) A former team member of the VDE explained that consensus improved dramatically as teacher investment increased. She explained that teachers initially thought of reliability as for the state, rather than for the kids. Teachers soon realized, however, that common standards required reliability and consequently became more invested in consensus.

28. This quote is a composite of a group interview of a teaching team. I have not differentiated between speakers because they were all speaking from the same point of view.

29. A school in the early adopter district was cited as out of compliance with PSA in part because of having no scope and sequence for bicycle safety.

Chapter Five

1. I say "partially responsible" because it would also be possible for the legislature, state board, or even an outside group to take the lead in forging such an agreement.

2. This point relates to Fullan's (1991) argument that it is important for practitioners to perceive a need for the proposed reform (p. 69).

3. Another recent study of a state-level reform initiative also found that local context caused state reforms to play out differently from school to school. Wilson and Rossman (1993) write: "Fostering experimentation and innovation at the local level has long been a concern of state policymakers. Much of the success of any new initiative, however, rests in understanding variation in local capacity and will. Our research clearly shows the influence of local capacity, of organizational constraints and

resources, and of the culture of the local school and district on the implementation of state initiatives" (p. 199).

4. This argument relates to Bardach and Kagan's argument that the distribution of "good and bad apples" among firms has implications for appropriate enforcement strategies (Bardach & Kagan, 1982, p. 65). As the reader will see, however, I am further dividing the good apples into two types.

5. This statement assumes that the traditional model of state–local relationships between SDEs and schools continues to exist. If these relationships were decentralized, by making networks of schools responsible for accountability, for example, the need for SDE staff to know each school might disappear. (See, for example, Education Commission of the States, 1994, January 3, Draft; Clune, 1993.)

6. This issue of how to treat special needs students in state assessment processes is not specific to Vermont. A teacher in Kentucky also expressed her frustration at not being able to read the directions of the state assessments to her special needs students, who could not read well.

I also do not want to imply that the solution to the problem of how to treat special needs students is obvious. Clearly, one danger of the state's allowing these students to be assessed differently is that it could give schools incentives to label marginal students as "special needs" in order to exempt them from the assessment process.

7. There are many other potential joint learning strategies. For example, SDEs could develop partnerships with universities, other professional development providers, or professional organizations. I give just one example to illustrate the larger category of joint learning strategies.

8. Rodney L. Reed, Senior Policy Analyst, Education Department of Victoria, Melbourne, Australia, introduced the term "critical friend" to the staff of the Coalition of Essential Schools on which I served.

Epilogue

1. In preparation for writing this epilogue, I reviewed a number of materials. On Kentucky, these materials included summaries of all education-related articles appearing in the *Lexington Herald-Leader* from 1993 to mid-1995, and *Education Week* articles on Kentucky from this same time period. Both of these sets of materials were provided to me most generously by Thomas James. In addition, I have reviewed summaries and in some cases full reports produced by the Office of Education Accountability and the Prichard Committee for Academic Excellence. I am grateful to Joanne Thompson for producing the summaries.

Regarding Vermont, I reviewed notes on a follow-up interview I did with Richard Mills in 1995, as well as comments on my Vermont chapter given to me in 1996 by a former team member of the VDE. In addition, I reviewed data on staff surveys done in the VDE as well as reports on issues and changes in Vermont's assessment system.

2. 21.6% of all schools were "Successful in Year 2," meaning that their 1992–94 scores were below their thresholds but their 1993–94 scores met or exceeded their

goals. 27.5% of all schools were "Improving" and 4.4 pecent of schools were "In Decline" (KDE, February 1995, p. 5).

3. Early research on the effects of rewards raises a number of questions: "[Researchers] found no evidence that the rewards actually functioned as incentives; indeed, in some cases controversy over use of the money appears to have torn schools apart. The evidence also suggests that, in some schools that weren't rewarded, the goals of the statewide reform effort may have been undermined, not reinforced" (Miller, 1996).

4. The percentage of positive scores for 1995 is very close to that of 1992 in the category of "Organization Style and Culture." The percentages were 50.7 and 52, respectively (VDE, 1995, p. 5).

5. In the 4th grade, the "estimated mean percent correct" for Vermont students was 58%, while it was 51.9% for the NAEP sample. In the 8th grade, Vermont students achieved 63%, while the NAEP sample achieved 57.4% (Vermont Assessment Program, 1993–94, pp. 5, 11).

References

Appalachia Educational Laboratory. (1996, February). Five years of education reform in rural Kentucky. *Notes from the Field: Education Reform in Rural Kentucky, 5*(1).

Associated Press. (1995, September 8). State board approves 5% pay raise for Boysen. *Lexington Herald-Leader*, p. C1.

Augenblick, Van de Water, & Associates. (1986). *Balancing competing demands: An assessment of the Vermont Department of Education: A report to the Vermont legislative council.* Denver, CO: Authors.

Bardach, E., & Kagan, R. A. (1982). *Going by the book: The problem of regulatory unreasonableness.* Philadelphia: Temple University Press.

Barzelay, M., with the collaboration of B. J. Armajani. (1992). *Breaking through bureaucracy: A new vision for managing in government.* Berkeley: University of California Press.

Behn, R. (1988, Fall). Management by groping along. *Journal of Policy Analysis and Management, 7*(4), 643–667.

Berman, P., & McLaughlin, M. W. (1978). *Federal programs supporting educational change: Vol. VII. Implementing and sustaining innovations.* Santa Monica, CA: RAND Corporation.

Boysen, T. C. (1991). *Kentucky Department of Education: National catalyst for educational transformation: Mission, beliefs, parameters, goals, strategies.* Frankfort, KY: Kentucky Department of Education.

Boysen, T. C. (1992, December). *Organization design for the new Kentucky Department of Education.* Frankfort, KY: Kentucky Department of Education.

Boysen, T. C., Thompson, J. W., & Matthews, B. A. (n.d.). *Planning and approval process for the five additional professional development days.* Frankfort, KY: Kentucky Department of Education.

Burns, T., & Stalker, G. M. (1961). *The management of innovation.* London: Tavistock Publications, Ltd. (distributed in the U.S. by Barnes & Noble).

Campbell, R. F., & Sroufe, G. E. (1967). The emerging role of state departments of education. In R. F. Campbell, G. E. Sroufe, & D. H. Layton (Eds.), *Strengthening state departments of education* (pp. 76–92). Chicago: Midwestern Administration Center, The University of Chicago.

Campbell, R. F., Sroufe, G. E., & Layton, D. H. (Ed.). (1967). *Strengthening state departments of education.* Chicago: Midwestern Administration Center, The University of Chicago.

Clune, W. H. (1993). The best path to systemic educational policy: Standard/centralized or differentiated/decentralized. *Educational Evaluation and Policy Analysis, 15*(3), 233–254.

Clune, W. H., with White, P., & Patterson, J. (1989). *The implementation and effects of high school graduation requirements: First steps toward curricular reform.* New Brunswick, NJ: Center for Policy Research in Education.

Cohen, D. K. (1988). Teaching practice: Plus que ça change . . . In P. W. Jackson (Ed.), *Contributing to educational change: Perspectives on research and practice* (pp. 27–84). Berkeley, CA: McCutchan Publishing Corporation.

Cohen, D. K., & Ball, D. L. (1990). Relations between policy and practice. *Educational Evaluation and Policy Analysis, 12,* 331–338.

Cohen, D. K., McLaughlin, M. W., & Talbert, J. (1993). *Teaching for understanding: Challenges for policy and practice.* San Francisco: Jossey Bass.

Cohen, D. K., & Spillane, J. P. (1992). Policy and practice: The relations between governance and instruction. In G. Grant (Ed.), *The Review of Research in Education* (pp. 3–49). Washington, DC: American Educational Research Association.

Consortium for Policy Research in Education. (1992). *Ten lessons about regulation and schooling.* New Brunswick, NJ: Consortium for Policy Research in Education.

Council of Chief State School Officers. (1983). *Educational governance in the states: A status report on state boards of education, chief state school officers, and state education agencies.* Washington, DC: U.S. Department of Education.

Council of Chief State School Officers. (1995). *Status report: State systemic education improvements.* Washington, DC: U.S. Department of Education.

Cuban, L. (1990). Reforming again, again, and again. *Educational Researcher, 19*(1), 3–13.

Curriculum Committee Task Force on Education Reform. (n.d.). *Statement of principles.* Frankfort: Kentucky Department of Education.

Darling-Hammond, L. (1994, August). National standards and assessments. *American Journal of Education, 102*(4), 478–510.

David, J. L. (1992). School-based decision making: Observations on progress. In *Primary School, School-Based Decision Making, Family Resource/Youth Services Centers: First year reports to the Prichard Committee.* Lexington, KY: Prichard Committee for Academic Excellence.

David, J. L. (1993). *Redesigning an education system: Early observations from Kentucky.* Washington, DC: National Governors' Association.

David, J. L. (1994). *Transforming state education agencies to support education reform.* Washington, DC: National Governors' Association.

Dove, R. G., Jr. (1991). *Acorns in a mountain pool: The role of litigation, law, and lawyers in Kentucky education reform.* Lexington, KY: Prichard Committee for Academic Excellence.

Downs, A. (1967). *Inside bureaucracy.* Santa Monica, CA: RAND Corporation.

Editorial Staff. (1992, March 18). Kentucky education officials have temporarily abandoned their effort to create a higher-paid personnel system distinct from those of other state agencies. *Education Week, 11*(26), 21.

Education Commission of the States. (1994, January 3, Draft). *Achieving flexibility in an educational system.* Denver, CO: Education Commission of the States.

Elmore, R. F. (1990). Introduction: On changing the structure of public schools. In R. F. Elmore (Ed.), *Restructuring schools: The next generation of educational reform* (pp. 1–28). San Francisco: Jossey-Bass.

Elmore, R. F., & Fuhrman, S. H. (1993, September). *Opportunity to learn and the state role in education.* New Brunswick, NJ: Consortium for Policy Research in Education.

Elmore, R. F., & McLaughlin, M. W. (1988). *Steady work: Policy, practice, and the reform of American education.* Santa Monica, CA: RAND Corporation.

Firestone, W. A., Fuhrman, S. H., & Kirst, M. W. (1989). *The progress of reform: An appraisal of state education initiatives.* New Brunswick, NJ: Consortium for Policy Research in Education.

Friedman, B. D. (1971). *State government and education: Management in the state education agency.* Chicago: Public Administration Service.

Fuhrman, S. H. (1993). The politics of coherence. In S. H. Fuhrman (Ed.), *Designing coherent policy: Improving the system* (pp. 1–34). San Francisco: Jossey-Bass.

Fuhrman, S. H., Clune, W. H., & Elmore, R. F. (1988). Research on education reform: Lessons on the implementation of policy. *Teachers College Record, 90*(2), 237–257.

Fuhrman, S. H., & Elmore, R. F. (1995, March). *Ruling out rules: The evolution of deregulation in state education policy.* New Brunswick, NJ: Consortium for Policy Research in Education.

Fuhrman, S. H., & Fry, P. (1989). *Diversity amidst standardization: State differential treatment of districts.* New Brunswick, NJ: Center for Policy Research in Education.

Fullan, M. G. (1991). *The new meaning of educational change.* New York: Teachers College Press.

Fullan, M. G. (1994). Coordinating top-down and bottom-up strategies for education reform. In R. F. Elmore & S. H. Fuhrman (Eds.), *The governance of curriculum: 1994 yearbook of the Association for Supervision and Curriculum Development* (pp. 186–202). Alexandria, VA: Association for Supervision and Curriculum Development.

Fullan, M. G., & Miles, M. B. (1992). Getting reform right: What works and what doesn't. *Phi Delta Kappan* (June), 745–752.

Gideonse, H. D. (1980). Improving the federal administration of education programs. *Educational Evaluation and Policy Analysis, 2*(1), pp. 61–70.

Gouldner, A. W. (1980). About the functions of bureaucratic rules. In J. A. Litterer (Ed.), *Organizations: Structure and behavior* (3rd ed.) (pp. 250–260). New York: Wiley.

Gross, S. (1991). *Vermont common core of learning update.* Montpelier: Vermont Department of Education.

Hambleton, R. K., Jaeger, R. M., Koretz, D., Linn, R. L., Millman, J., & Phillips, S. E. (1995, June). *Review of the management quality of the Kentucky Instructional Results Information System, 1991–1994, final report.* Frankfort: Office of Educational Accountability, Kentucky General Assembly.

Harp, L. (1995, February 22). In a surprise, schools chief in Kentucky resigns. *Education Week, 14*(22), 1, 11.

Harp, L. (1995, March 8). Fervor spreads to overhaul state agencies. *Education Week, 14*(24), 1, 13.

Hill, P. T., & Bonan, J. (1991). *Decentralization and accountability in public education* (No. R-4066-MCF/IET). Santa Monica, CA: RAND Corporation.

Kanter, R. M. (1983). *The change masters: Innovation for productivity in the American corporation.* New York: Simon and Schuster.

Kanter, R. M. (1988). When a thousand flowers bloom: Structural, collective, and social conditions for innovation in organizations. *Research in Organizational Behavior, 10,* 169–211.

Kentucky Department of Education. (1992, Draft). *School transformation plan guidebook.* Frankfort: Author.

Kentucky Department of Education. (1992, October 23). *KDE strategic planning process for fiscal year 1993–94 action plans and biennial request for 1994 General Assembly.* Frankfort: Author.

Kentucky Department of Education. (1993, February). *Kentucky teacher.* Frankfort: Author.

Kentucky Department of Education. (1993, October 14). *Program Review.* Frankfort: Author.

Kentucky Department of Education. (1995, February). *Celebrate the progress! 1992–1994 Kentucky accountability results summary news packet.* Frankfort: Author.

Kentucky Department of Education & Kentucky Education Professional Standards Board. (1992). *Outcome-based teacher preparation, assessment, and licensure: A proposal to the United States Department of Education Fund for the Improvement and Reform of Schools and Teaching: Schools and Teachers Program.* Frankfort: Kentucky Department of Education.

Kentucky Education Association and Appalachia Educational Laboratory. (1993, March). *Finding time for school reform: Obstacles and answers.* Charleston, WV: Appalachia Educational Laboratory.

Kingdon, J. W. (1984). *Agendas, alternatives, and public policies.* Boston: Little, Brown.

Koretz, D., Klein, S., McCaffrey, D., & Stecher, B. (1993, December). *Interim report: The reliability of Vermont portfolio scores in the 1992–93 school year.* Santa Monica, CA: RAND Reprints.

Koretz, D., McCaffrey, D., Klein, S., Bell, R., & Stecher, B. (1992). *The reliability of scores from the 1992 Vermont portfolio assessment program, interim report.* Santa Monica, CA: RAND Institute on Education and Training, National Center for Research on Evaluation, Standards, and Student Testing.

Koretz, D., Stecher, B., & Deibert, E. (1992). *The Vermont portfolio assessment program: Interim report on implementation and impact, 1991–92 school year.* Santa Monica, CA: RAND National Center for Research on Evaluation, Standards, and Student Testing.

Koretz, D., Stecher, B., Klein, S., & McCaffrey, D. (1994, Fall). The Vermont portfolio assessment program: Findings and implications. *Educational measurement issues and practice,* 5–16.

Legislative Research Commission. (1984). *Education bills passed 1984 General Assembly.* Frankfort, KY: Author.

Legislative Research Commission. (1991, September). *The Kentucky education reform act of 1990: A citizen's handbook.* Frankfort, KY: Author.

LeMahieu, P. G., & Lesley, B. A. (1994). State education agencies: Partners in reform. In J. L. David (Ed.), *Transforming state education agencies to support education reform.* Washington, DC: National Governors' Association.

Lindsay, D. (1995, March 8). N.C. poised to slash size, power of state education agency. *Education Week, 14*(24), p. 12.

Lipsky, M. (1980). *Street-level bureaucracy: Dilemmas of the individual in public services.* New York: Russell Sage Foundation.

Lusi, S. F. (1993). *Systemic school reform: The changes implied for SDEs and how one department has responded.* Paper presented at the annual meeting of the American Educational Research Association, Atlanta.

Lusi, S. F. (1994). Systemic school reform: The challenges faced by state departments of education. In R. F. Elmore & S. H. Fuhrman (Eds.), *The governance of curriculum* (pp. 109–130). Alexandria, VA: Association for Supervision and Curriculum Development.

McDonnell, L. M., & Elmore, R. F. (1987). Getting the job done: Alternative policy instruments. *Educational Evaluation and Policy Analysis, 9*(2), 133–152.

McLaughlin, M. W. (1991). The Rand change agent study: Ten years later. In A. R. Odden (Ed.), *Education policy implementation* (pp. 143–156). Albany: State University of New York Press.

McNamara, B. (1995, June 24). Memo to "Education Leaders" regarding "Invitation to attend the organizational meeting for the Vermont Alliance." Montpelier: Vermont Department of Education.

Madsen, J. (1994). *Educational reform at the state level: The politics and problems of implementation.* Washington, DC: Falmer Press.

May, L. (1993, August 27). Untitled. *Lexington Herald-Leader*, p. B1.

May, L. (1994, September 10). Boysen's reform efforts earn him good marks in annual review. *Lexington Herald-Leader*, p. B1.

May, L. (1995, February 18). State should provide reliability of tests, review says. *Lexington Herald-Leader*, p. A7.

Merton, R. K. (1980). Bureaucratic structure and personality. In J. A. Litterer (Ed.), *Organizations: Structure and behavior* (3rd ed.) (pp. 229–236). New York: Wiley.

Meyer, J. W., & Rowan, B. (1991). Institutionalized organizations: Formal structure as myth and ceremony. In W. W. Powell & P. J. DiMaggio (Eds.), *The new institutionalism in organizational analysis* (pp. 41–62). Chicago: University of Chicago Press.

Miller, E. (1996, January/February). Early reports from Kentucky on cash rewards for "successful" schools reveal many problems. *The Harvard Education Letter, 12*(1), 1–3.

Mills, R. P. (1991, November 26 memo). *Restructuring the Department of Education.* Montpelier: Vermont Department of Education.

Nathanson, S. (1993). *Restructuring and accountability strategies: New York State's School Quality Review Initiative in context.* Unpublished paper, Brown University.

National Alliance for Restructuring Education. (n.d.). *State departments of education: Restructuring and total quality management.* Washington, DC: Author.

National Center for Education Statistics. (1994). *Digest of education statistics 1992* (No. NCES 92-097). United States Department of Education, Office of Educational Research and Improvement, Washington, DC.

National Commission on Excellence in Education. (1983). *A nation at risk: The imperative for educational reform.* Washington, DC: U.S. Department of Education.

National Education Association Data Search. (1992). *Rankings of the states.* Washington, DC: National Education Association Research Division.

O'Day, J. A., & Smith, M. S. (1993). Systemic reform and educational opportunity. In S. H. Fuhrman (Ed.), *Coherent policy: Improving the system* (pp. 250–312). San Francisco: Jossey-Bass.

Odden, A. R. (1991). New patterns of education policy implementation and challenges for the 1990s. In A. R. Odden (Ed.), *Education policy implementation* (pp. 297–327). Albany: State University of New York Press.

Office of Education Accountability. (1995, December). *Annual report.* Frankfort: Office of Education Accountability, Kentucky General Assembly.

Olson, L. (1994, October 5). "Dramatic" rise in Ky. test scores linked to reforms. *Education Week, 14*(5), 13, 15.

Patton, M. Q. (1990). *Qualitative evaluation and research methods* (2nd ed.). Newbury Park, CA: Sage.

Perrow, C. (1986). *Complex organizations: A critical essay* (3rd ed.). New York: McGraw-Hill.

Perry, E., Moore, K., & Walker, D. (1993). *Internal memo to Rick Mills re: Strategic planning/putting the pieces together.* Montpelier: Vermont Department of Education.

Peters, T. J., & Waterman, R. H., Jr. (1982). *In search of excellence: Lessons from America's best-run companies.* New York: Warner.

Prichard Committee for Academic Excellence. (1994 Special Legislative Edition). Developments from the 1994 General Assembly. *Perspectives*, pp. 1–3.

Raths, J., Katz, L., & Fanning, J. (1992). The status of the primary school reform in Kentucky and its implications. In *Primary school, school-based decision making, family resource/youth services Centers: First year reports to the Prichard Committee.* Lexington, KY: Prichard Committee for Academic Excellence.

Rose v. Council for Better Education, Inc., 790 S.W. 2d 186 (1989).

Schaver, M. (1995, June 28). State accepts 10 of 12 suggestions for KERA test. *Louisville Courier Journal*, pp. B1, B4.

Schmidt, P. (1991, May 15). Workers anxiously await overhaul of education agency. *Education Week, 10*(34), 18, 20.

Scott, W. R. (1992a). Conceptions of environments. In *Organizations: Rational, natural, and open systems* (3rd ed.) (pp. 125–149). Englewood Cliffs, NJ: Prentice Hall.

Scott, W. R. (1992b). Organizations as open systems. In *Organizations: Rational, Natural, and open systems* (3rd ed.) (pp. 76–94). Englewood Cliffs, NJ: Prentice Hall.

Senge, P. M. (1990). *The fifth discipline: The art and practice of the learning organization.* New York: Doubleday Currency.

Sizer, T. R. (1984). *Horace's compromise: The dilemma of the American high school.* Boston: Houghton Mifflin.

Sizer, T. R., McDonald, J. P., & Rogers, B. (1992–93). Standards and school reform: Asking the basic questions. *Stanford law and policy review, 4*, 27–35.

Smith, M. S., & O'Day, J. (1990). Systemic school reform. In *Politics of Education Association Yearbook 1990* (pp. 233–267). New York: Taylor & Francis.

Sroufe, G. E. (1967). Selected characteristics of state departments of education. In R. F. Campbell, G. E. Sroufe, & D. H. Layton (Eds.), *Strengthening state departments of education* (pp. 18–28). Chicago: Midwestern Administration Center, The University of Chicago.

State of Vermont Board of Education. (1992, January 21). *Policy statement on deregulation.* Montpelier: Vermont Department of Education.

State of Vermont Board of Education. (1992, June 16). *Public school approval.* Montpelier: Vermont Department of Education.

State of Vermont Board of Education. (1993, March 16). *Policy on deregulation for performance.* Montpelier: Vermont Department of Education.

Stecher, B. M., & Mitchell, K. J. (1995). *Portfolio-driven reform: Vermont teachers' understanding of mathematical problem solving and related changes in classroom practice.* Santa Monica, CA: RAND Corporation.

Steffy, B. E. (1990–91). Matrix management for a state department of education. *National forum of applied educational research journal, 4*(1), 6–12.

Steffy, B. E. (1992). Assault on the bureaucracy: Restructuring the Kentucky Department of Education. *International Journal of Educational Reform, 1*(1), 16–31.

Task Force on High School Restructuring. (1993, June). *Final report.* Frankfort: Kentucky Department of Education.

Timar, T. B., & Kirp, D. L. (1988). *Managing educational excellence.* New York: Falmer Press.

Vermont Assessment Program. (1993–94). *Assessment results: Writing and mathematics, 1993–1994.* Montpelier: Author.

Vermont Department of Education. (1990, September 14). *A guide for the establishment of Local Standards Boards.* Montpelier: Author.

Vermont Department of Education. (1990–91a). *"This is my best": Vermont's writing assessment program.* Montpelier: Author.

Vermont Department of Education. (1990–91b). *Looking beyond "the answer": Vermont's mathematics portfolio assessment program.* Montpelier: Author.

Vermont Department of Education. (1991a). *A brief history of education reform in Vermont* (Appendix one of a grant proposal submitted to the National Science Foundation in 1991). Montpelier: Author.

Vermont Department of Education. (1991b). *Revised standards for approving Vermont's public schools.* Montpelier: Author.

Vermont Department of Education. (1991, September). *A green mountain challenge: Very high skills for every student; no exceptions, no excuses.* Montpelier: Author.

Vermont Department of Education. (1991, October). *A conceptual framework for reinventing Vermont schools.* Montpelier: Author.

Vermont Department of Education. (1991, November 4). *Restructuring the department of education: Presentation to Commissioner Mills.* Montpelier: Author.

Vermont Department of Education. (1992, March 9). *Department of education restructuring home team proposal.* Montpelier: Author.

Vermont Department of Education. (1992, June 18). *Department of education restructuring: Home and focus team proposal.* Montpelier: Author.

Vermont Department of Education. (1992, July 28 Draft). *What do external and internal managers do?* Montpelier: Author.

Vermont Department of Education. (1992–93). *A green mountain challenge: Very high skills for every student: No exceptions, no excuses.* Montpelier: Author.

Vermont Department of Education. (1993, January). *Vermont assessment program, 1992–93.* Montpelier: Author.

Vermont Department of Education. (1993, January 12). *Deregulation for performance, Draft for state board review.* Montpelier: Author.

Vermont Department of Education. (1995). *1995 staff survey highlights.* Montpelier: Author.

Vermont Department of Education. (1995, June 20). *The green mountain challenge: High skills for every student: No exceptions, no excuses.* Montpelier: Author.

Vermont Department of Education. (1995, September 27). *Education flexibility plan.* Montpelier: Author.

Vermont Department of Education. (n.d.-a). *Work groups/focus teams.* Montpelier: Author.

Vermont Department of Education. (n.d.-b.). *The Vermont common core of learning: Education for the 21st century, Draft.* Montpelier: Author.

Vermont Department of Education. (n.d.-c.). *Vermont's portfolio-based assessment network: Information and professional development.* Montpelier: Author.

Vermont Department of Education Information Systems Unit. (1991–92). *Vermont education directory.* Montpelier: Vermont Department of Education.

Vermont Department of Education Transition Team. (1992, June 4). *Memo to department staff re: Why change?* Montpelier: Vermont Department of Education.

Viadero, D. (1995, April 5). Even as popularity soars, portfolios encounter roadblocks. *Education Week, 14*(28), 8–9.

Weick, K. E. (1976). Educational organizations as loosely coupled systems. *Administrative Science Quarterly, 21,* 1–19.

Wilson, B., & Rossman, G. (1993). *Mandating academic excellence: High school responses to curriculum reform.* New York: Teachers College Press.

Wilson, J. Q. (1989). *Bureaucracy: What government agencies do and why they do it.* New York: Basic Books.

Index

Accountability
  Kentucky Education Reform Act
    (KERA) and, 28, 29–30, 56–57,
    76–77, 80, 154, 177, 178
  and systemic school reform, 9
Anderson, John, 181
Appalachia Educational Laboratory, 72,
  197 n. 34
Armajani, B. J., 170, 171, 173
Assessment systems. *See* Performance-
  based assessment
Augenblick, John, 26, 198 n. 8

Ball, D. L., 11, 196 n. 24
Bardach, E., 197 n. 33, 201 n. 4
Barzelay, M., 170, 171, 173, 193 n. 3
Behn, R., 18
Bell, R., 198 n. 6
Berman, P., 5, 11
Bonan, J., 197 n. 32
Boysen, Thomas C., 30, 31, 32, 42–43,
  51, 66, 75–77, 155–156, 158, 159,
  175–176
Burns, T., 18, 19, 20, 74

California, mathematics framework in,
  11
Campbell, R. F., 21, 168
Capacity-building
  barriers to, 9
  changes in, with complex school re-
    form, 15, 21–22
  local. *See* Local capacity-building
  organizational. *See* Organizational
    capacity-building
Closed systems
  Kentucky Department of Education
    as, 73–75
  Vermont Department of Education
    as, 145–148

Clune, W. H., 1, 5, 8, 201 n. 5
Cody, Wilmer S., 30
Cohen, D. K., 5, 7, 8–9, 11, 167, 196
  n. 24
Collaborative external connections,
  22–23
  need for, 173–174
  in Vermont, 99–101, 113–115, 124,
    133–139, 181
Complex school reform
  broad lessons of, 167–174
  changes in substantive work and, 14
  collaborative external connections
    and, 22–23, 173–174
  contextual factors in, 153–157
  and expected changes in state depart-
    ments of education, 13–23
  in Kentucky, 2, 3, 24–83
  local capacity and, 21–22
  local implementation of, 11
  organizational capacity and, 15
  organizational flexibility and, 15–20
  problems of, 10–12, 160–167
  systemic reform versus, 3
  in Vermont, 2, 3, 84–151
Consortium for Policy Research in Education, 165–166
Contextual factors, in school reform,
  153–157
Coping organizations (Wilson), 10–11
Council for Better Education (Kentucky), 24–26
Council of Chief State School Officers,
  2, 16, 167
Cuban, L., 5
Culture
  expected changes in, 19–20
  in Kentucky, 47–49, 51, 71–73
  in Vermont, 109–113
Cunningham, Lavern, 26

About the Author

Susan Follett Lusi is Director of Policy for the Annenberg Institute for School Reform and Visiting Assistant Professor at the Taubman Center for Public Policy, both at Brown University. She received her Ph.D. in Public Policy from Harvard University in 1994. She is interested in the interface between policy, practice, and school reform and is currently focusing on rethinking traditional notions of accountability. She has worked with state departments of education in a number of consulting and assistance capacities and worked for the Coalition of Essential Schools form 1986–89. Raising two happy and healthy small children is one of Susan's highest priorities.